Businesses

–Based PC

Rick Benzel

NOTICES

CYMA™	CYMA Systems, Inc.
File Express™	Expressware Corp.
IBM™	International Business Machines
Lotus™	Lotus Development Corp.
Med-Flex by ISC™	National Healthcare Support Corp.
MediSoft Patient Accounting®	The Computer Place, Inc.
Microsoft™	Microsoft Corp.
Microsoft Windows™	
OneClaim™	Santiago Data Systems, Inc.
SmartOffice™	E-Z Data, Inc.
The Medical Manager™	Personalized Programming, Inc.
Timeslips™	TIMESLIPS Corp.

All other product names are trademarks of their respective manufacturers.

FIRST EDITION
THIRD PRINTING

© 1993 by **Windcrest**, an imprint of McGraw-Hill, Inc.
The name "Windcrest" is a registered trademark of McGraw-Hill, Inc.

Library of Congress Cataloging-in-Publication Data

Benzel, Rick.
    Health service businesses on your home-based PC / Rick Benzel.
      p. cm.
    ISBN 0-8306-4303-6   ISBN 0-8306-4302-8 (pbk.)
    1. Medical transcription. 2. Medical fees. 3. Home-based
businesses. 4. Medicine—Data processing. 5. Collection of
accounts. I. Title.
R728.5.B46 1993
651'.961—dc20   92-41241
                                                        CIP

Editorial team: Lori Flaherty, Supervising Editor
                Joann Woy, Indexer
Production team: Katherine G. Brown, Director
                Rhonda Baker, Coding
                Tina Sourbeir, Coding
                Susan Hansford, Coding
                Lisa M. Mellott, Layout
                Marty Ehrlinger, Computer Illustrator
                Tara Ernst, Proofreading
Design team: Jaclyn J. Boone, Designer
                Brian Allison, Associate Designer
Cover design: Lori E. Schlosser

4327
EPC1

To my family—Terry, Rebecca, and Sarah.

Dedication

The Entrepreneurial PC Series brings the hottest new work-at-home options and essential information and advice to the new breed of PC-based home business owners—information they can use.

Other books in the series

The Entrepreneurial PC, David, (4483)

The Information Broker's Handbook, Rugge/Glossbrenner, (4104)

Information for Sale: How to Start and Operate Your Own Data Research Service, Everett/Crowe, (3057)

Bookkeeping on Your Home-Based PC, Stern, (4328)

Contents

**5 Ten steps to
    starting your business 165**

Preface

If you are reading this book, then you have an interest in one of the fastest growing sectors of our economy: health services. The health service professions in this country are already employing thousands of people in every community, and, even better, they are growing quickly in numbers as one portion of our population ages and another portion, the baby boomers, create their own boomlet in the next generation. As in many professions, growth creates opportunity, and today, much of that opportunity is in home-based small businesses. This book examines three solid health service businesses that you can operate with your home-based PC.

I probably don't need to convince you of the benefits of working from your home. Working from home allows you greater freedom, flexibility, and control of your time. It provides you with an opportunity to be your own boss and reap your own rewards. And working from home can change your entire point of view on the meaning of life. I know, because it has changed mine.

After a 15-year career in publishing, and working for several companies in Boston and Los Angeles, I recently made a transition into my own home business as a writer, editor, and literary agent. While some part of my decision was forced upon me like thousand of others who have become caught in the web of corporate mergers and layoffs, I was also quite thrilled at finally having a chance to make it on my own. I had worked with Paul and Sarah Edwards, authors of many books on home businesses, and throughout my five years of knowing them, I had always dreamed of being able to live out the words I was editing in their manuscripts. Now I had my chance.

When the opportunity to write this book developed, I jumped on it. Although I was not familiar with the health services area, the writer in me said, "No problem . . . piece of cake, just a little research and the job is done." Well, let me mention that the research was not as minimal as I had thought. The home-based business field turned to out to be quite complex, even confusing, yet definitely fascinating.

I mention this fact for two reasons. First, for those of you who have any background in medicine or in the health services, I want to tip my hat to you because I now realize the level of skill and knowledge you bring to your work. If you have worked with ICD-9 and CPT codes, and regularly chew on acronyms like HCFA and RBRVS, then you have my respect. Second, for those of you who, like me, have no experience in the health area, I assure you, you can learn everything you need to know. It will take a bit of time, and perhaps reading this book more than once, but you will undoubtedly agree that these health service professions are exciting and learnable.

I have tried to portray in each chapter home-based PC businesses as fully and as accurately as possible. To this end, I hope you will especially enjoy the profiles and statements of people whom I interviewed in the course of my research. I spoke with dozens of entrepreneurs in each field, with the directors of the national associations and organizations involved with each profession, with several software company executives, and technicians about medical and business software, and with a few special associations in Washington, such as the Health Insurance Institute of America. The profiles contain what may be the most valuable information in this book—the true-life stories of the people who shared with me (and you) many details about their work backgrounds, their personal goals, and even a few secrets of how they make their business successful. I thank them for their openness and honesty, and hope that you will appreciate the indirect role they may end up playing in your life.

Last, let me point out that the health field undergoes many changes on a frequent basis. The technology changes, the federal and state government rules and regulations about Medicare and Medicaid change, the insurance companies that underwrite our health insurance policies change, and even doctors and hospitals change as well. In short, while I believe this book to be as accurate and up-to-date as possible, you might learn slightly different information, rules, and regulations by the time this book reaches your hand or when you get into business.

Perhaps you already have an extensive medical background, having worked in a physician's office or hospital. Perhaps you are currently a student in a health field and are looking for information to help you determine your future once your classes are over. Or perhaps you picked up this book up without knowing anything about the health area but you are attracted either to the field of health services in general or to a good business opportunity you've heard about. Whichever of these scenarios might be your situation, this book will open up new vistas in your entrepreneurial explorations that can help you find a satisfying career and a good income.

Acknowledgments

As is the case with nearly every book published, many people behind the scenes contributed to the project in some form. I would like to thank especially the following people for their assistance, guidance, and encouragement.

First, I thank my loving wife, Terry, and my daughters, Rebecca and Sarah, for their patience and understanding while I wrote this book. My family also thanks Margarita Guandique for her support and assistance. I also thank my mother and father, who provided much encouragement and even assistance in research, and my personal friends Mark and Denise Weston, Steve Adler, Tony Camas, and Daniel Moulin for their encouragement. I next express my gratitude to Paul and Sarah Edwards, who in many ways have been my mentors in showing me the path to working from home.

In working on this project, I utilized many resources, particularly the knowledge and experience of many people in these businesses. I thank Greg Duvall, Phil MacDonald, Brad Sweigart, and Bill Orr at Hi-Tech Management Systems, who graciously provided a lot of time and much information about the medical billing industry; Gary Knox, who shared his research with me about billing software; Jeff Ward, of Medisoft, who fielded many phone calls to answer questions; Merry Schiff, who provided much information and commentary; Joe Kopacz and Melanie Karaffa at PMIC, who provided me with many valuable reference materials; Norma Border, who took time from her busy schedule as Director of NACAP to talk and review a chapter; Harvey Matoren of Health Claims of Jacksonville, Inc.; Nancy and Tom Koehler of In Home Medical Claims; and Mary Ellen Fitzgibbons of Fitzgibbons & Associates, all of whom spent many hours in interviews and reading the medical claims assistance chapter; Pat Forbis of the AAMT, for her invaluable assistance on medical transcription; Cole Thompson of At-Home Professions, for an opportunity to review their courses; Donna Avila-Weil, who checked the medical transcription chapter in great detail and provided many excellent suggestions; and Gary Opalewski and Lanier Voice Products, who provided photos and information about medical transcription equipment.

I especially thank Cliff Hartfield, Linda Noel, Irene Card, Vickie Fite, Rikki Horn, Joan Walston, Lynne Rutherford, Carolyn Yeager, Jay Lerner, Rhonda Habit, Barbara Burnett, and the many others whom I interviewed on this path.

1 The booming healthcare business

The healthcare professions are booming. Whether you are seeking to enter a new career or branching out from a health-related field, now is a great time to consider a business in healthcare. Today, and for many decades into the future, healthcare is a growing, thriving, recession-proof, profitable business. Consider the demographics of America's aging population and their growing needs for medical attention, along with the new baby boom (albeit smaller than the one before) and a number of other factors, and you have an irrefutable fact: the healthcare professions abound with opportunity. Healthcare has already become the second largest occupational sector in the United States. According to the *1991 Statistical Abstracts of the U.S. Department of Commerce*, slightly more than 9 million Americans were employed in the health field in 1988, and projections for growth through the year 2000 are extremely high.

The upshot of this trend is a boon for those people interested in operating a home or small business. With insurance companies, hospitals, labs, doctors' offices, and many ancillary health businesses looking to save money and lower their costs, many opportunities exist for the home-based operator and small business entrepreneur. Smaller businesses can operate more efficiently, cut expenses, and be more productive, and are an important key to halting or at least slowing the expensive 10 percent plus annual growth rate in healthcare expenditures. New technology and new ways of working are also changing the face of health careers, all of which home-based and small business entrepreneurs can profit from.

Astounding facts & figures

Consider these statistics, which demonstrate the enormity of our healthcare industry and its opportunities:

❑ In 1991, the American national health expenditure was slightly more than $738 billion, which includes personal healthcare expenses for hospitalization and physician care, dental services, home healthcare, drugs and medications, vision products, nursing home care, as well as program administration, research, and construction of facilities. This amount is up 11 percent since 1990, when we spent $666 billion, of which, $585 billion was spent on personal healthcare. In 1989, it was only $600 billion. The 1991 amount is equal to an astonishing $23,000 per second spent on medical care, more than $2 billion per day. Figure 1-1 shows a typical breakdown by service of how our health dollars are spent.

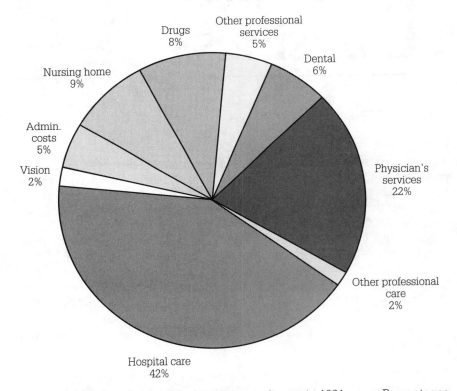

1-1 *Breakdown of personal healthcare expenditures in 1991. NOTE: Percentages do not total 100% because of rounding.* Health Care Financing Administration.

❑ Out of the $738 billion spent in 1991, Medicare accounts for $114 billion, covering 36.6 million people, and Medicaid—a combined federal and state government program—spent an additional $77 billion to cover more than 28 million people (there is some overlap with people covered by both

Medicare and Medicaid). In addition, private insurance companies doled out nearly $209 billion.

❑ According to the National Center for Health Statistics, in 1989 there were more than 1.32 billion physician contacts between doctors and patients, representing an average of 5.4 contacts per person.

❑ There were 5384 community hospitals in the United States in 1990 with nearly a million hospital beds; and an average 66 percent occupancy rate. The average cost per day is more than $686 with the average length of stay being 7.2 days.

❑ The number of doctors in the United States is mushrooming. According to figures from the Healthcare Financing Administration, it is estimated that by the year 2000 there will be approximately 656,000 doctors , 161,000 dentists, and 40,000 osteopaths practicing in the United States, nearly double the number in 1970.

As you can see, the healthcare industry is on a roller coaster ride upwards, with no major downturns expected. Actually, a number of trends make future healthcare growth a certainty, and business people would be wise to notice these major factors:

American demographic facts   The American population continues to expand. Whereas we were 190 million in 1960, we are now more than 250 million and growing. More important, the distribution of the American population is such that a large proportion of it is in need of regular healthcare services. For example, in *each year* of this decade, nearly 4 million babies will likely be born. More than 20 million children will be below age five, more than 4 million people will turn 45, and more than 2 million people will become 65. As you might imagine, such figures are indicative of a growing level of healthcare use among specific populations, as new mothers and babies, toddlers, middle-aged forty-somethings, and seniors are those who most frequently utilize healthcare services.

Another demographic fact is that life expectancy in the United States has been on the rise for decades. In the last decade alone, men averaged 71.5 years in 1988, up from 70 years in 1980, and women averaged 78.3 years, up from 77.4 in 1980. Advances in fighting the three leading causes of death in the United States (heart disease, cancer, and stroke) are one reason for this, as new lifesaving technology and pharmaceuticals help people survive formerly fatal diseases. Many more advances are likely to be discovered and implemented in the future as well, another sign that the healthcare field is burgeoning.

The increase in health insurance coverages   Health insurance statistics support these demographic facts, as more people use health insurance policies from commercial insurance companies, employer-funded plans, and government sources. Whereas in 1985 204 million Americans had public or private health insurance, more than 220 million Americans were covered in 1991. Similarly, private insurance companies paid out $117 billion in claims benefits in 1985 versus $212 billion in 1990, the latest figures available according to the Health Insurance Association of America. Medicare and Medicaid payments grew from $107 billion in 1985 to $191 billion in 1991.

Health-consciousness fever   Over the past two decades, the American population has been growing more conscious of the value of health and fitness. Advances in science, as well as the vanities of the baby boom generation, have made staying young and fit both desirable and possible. More people are recognizing that life extension depends on their own efforts to eat properly, exercise, sleep well, and reduce stress.

The ramifications of this increasing interest in health are actually twofold. Although many people are staying in better shape and practicing preventive medicine, many of them are nevertheless getting more frequent checkups as they age or whenever a health or dental problem occurs. This translates into more dollars spent in the healthcare industry in direct costs, insurance premiums, and insurance benefits.

Testing craze   According to the *Complete Guide to Medical Tests* by H. Winter Griffith, MD., medical tests have become extremely important—if not a requirement—in nearly every healthcare situation for two reasons. First, tests help doctors make an accurate diagnosis. Whether it's sending a patient out for a simple $25 blood or urine test or for a $1500 coronary angiography, most doctors have come to rely on medical technology to rule out hypotheses or to validate a diagnosis. Second, medical malpractice insurance costs for doctors have risen sky high, to the point that hardly any doctor puts forth a diagnosis without the use of testing to back up his or her opinion. Doctors with two years of experience and doctors with twenty years of experience both recognize that testing protects them against the vagaries of distrustful patients, nuisance suits, and perhaps an occasional wrong decision. Tests become part of a permanent record for each patient, thus proving that the doctor has made every attempt to ascertain the underlying problem and to treat it accordingly.

Testing is so prolific that there are now more than 1500 types of tests—more than 900 analyses on blood alone—and 100 or more new tests are invented each year. Dr. Griffith estimates that nearly 10 billion tests are ordered every year, costing between $100 billion and $150 billion annually—that's nearly 1 out of every 3 of our healthcare dollars!

Government and commercial insurance regulations   Another factor that points to continued growth in healthcare usage and expenditures is, ironically, the increase in medical regulations and rules from federal and state governments and commercial insurance companies. While Medicare and Medicaid laws, for example, require various types of testing, second opinions, and recordkeeping procedures to try to limit their skyrocketing costs, the overall effect is that millions of people in these programs have access to greater healthcare than what they might have had otherwise. Commercial insurance companies now also require extensive testing procedures and detailed records, all of which probably explains the previously mentioned statistic that Americans had 1.32 billion contacts with their doctors in 1989.

Many regulations are aimed at curbing abuse and fraud. *Time* magazine reported in November 1991 that fraud might account for $73 billion of the annual U.S. healthcare expenditures, and that the American Medical Association estimates defensive medicine and over-testing account for an additional $21 billion in unnecessary charges.

No matter how you look at these trends and figures, you will have a hard time not finding some niche to fill in the healthcare field if you have an inclination to get involved. Healthcare is only going to get larger, with more and more services needed by a growing number of Americans, as well as increasing numbers of practitioners. The savvy entrepreneur knows that for each doctor in the profession and for each consumer, a corresponding array of service personnel are needed, and therein lies your opportunity!

While there are many careers in the medical professions, this book focuses on three businesses that can be run as home-based or small businesses, most likely on a full-time basis but also part-time. Each business offers a reasonably moderate to high-income potential and all indications are that each business will remain a solid opportunity over the course of the next decade and beyond.

Overview of three healthcare businesses

Medical billing services submit or process claims on behalf of doctors, chiropractors, therapists, dentists, and other medical care providers to commercial insurance companies and government agencies such as Medicare and Medicaid. Given that more than 220 million Americans are covered by private or public health insurance and every patient contact with a doctor, laboratory, clinic, or hospital generates at least one bill, you will not find it surprising to learn that an estimated 6 billion or more insurance claims are filed each year. Medicare alone receives more than 500 million claims per year.

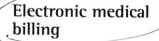

Electronic medical billing

In the past, filing claims was a tedious and cumbersome process. Every insurance company had their own rules, regulations, and complex paper forms to use, and the government agencies of Medicare and Medicaid had different procedures. Healthcare providers who agreed to process claims for their patients faced a veritable mountain of paperwork, and many simply gave up on collecting a certain portion of their claims out of frustration or confusion, costing them millions of dollars each year. The situation became even more critical for doctors in September 1990, when the government took the claims burden off of consumers and began requiring that ALL doctors file the claims to Medicare on behalf of their patients in the program.

Over the course of the last decade, however, PCs and new software have brought about a new technology called *electronic claims processing*. With this technology, a medical billing service can manage the entire insurance claims process for doctors that not only keeps track of patient transactions and accounts but also electronically transmits health insurance claims over phone lines to the private insurance companies and representatives of government agencies like Medicare.

Electronic claims processing (ECP) has many advantages, including simplifying the recordkeeping and accounting process used by doctors and medical offices. More important, electronic medical billing software substantially reduces the number of errors made in processing paper claims—estimated as high as 30 percent—and, therefore, speeds up the time it takes for a doctor to receive reimbursement from the insurance carrier, a benefit doctors obviously appreciate.

With the rising cost of labor, insurance companies have recognized the value of electronic claims processing because it saves thousands of dollars in overhead and salaries for claims processors and examiners. Medicare in particular has been a strong force in encouraging all medical providers to switch from paper to electronic claims filing. In fact, Secretary of Health and Human Services Louis W. Sullivan is looking to electronic claims filing and other high technology to shave $8 billion off our health costs each year.

Chapter 2 examines the business of medical billing services in a more detailed explanation of the history of the business and specific information about how the business works, knowledge and background required to run a billing service, and how to get started. You will also learn a few caveats about entering this business, such as the level of detailed knowledge you will need about insurance regulations and government/Medicare rules, as well as the complex medical coding systems you will need to understand. If you have no background in the medical field, or limited experience in sales and marketing, your learning curve will be steep and your frustration level high. Nevertheless, medical billing is an interesting and highly profitable business if you like numbers-oriented and accounting-type businesses, as well as direct contact with doctors and medical office personnel.

Medical claims professional

The flip side of a medical billing service, a claims assistance professional (CAP) is also involved in working with claims and insurance companies, but this business helps consumers—not doctors. Consumers who have a need or desire either to process their own insurance claims or to appeal claims that have been denied by insurance companies can turn to a claims assistant. Because some doctors do not file claims on behalf of their patients (except Medicare claims), many people must file their own claim each time they see their physician, chiropractor, or psychologist. In addition, because insurance companies and Medicare regularly dispute claims, many people are unwittingly dragged into the claims submission process even when their physician did the filing.

A CAP is, therefore, someone who helps confused, forlorn, or just plain busy consumers through the complex maze of the health insurance world. Like a tax preparer who assists individuals in filing their annual taxes to their best advantage, a claims assistance professional tries to maximize the coverage and reimbursement each person can obtain out of their insurance carrier. Claims professionals must, therefore, understand insurance policies, Medicare and Medicaid regulations, and such details of insurance billing procedures as copayments, deductibles, lifetime caps, stop loss limits, and so on. While the business is not heavily computer-oriented, claims assistants must be quite detail-oriented, have good math skills, exceptional negotiation and communication skills, and be able to work well with many types of people. CAPs must also have an action-oriented, fighting personality that believes in perseverance, stick-to-it-iveness, and getting the job done.

Chapter 3 explores a career as a medical claims assistance professional, including what background and skills are needed to get started and how to market and price your services.

The third business covered in this book is medical transcription. In researching this field, hardly a conversation went by in which I was not told about the serious shortage of transcriptionists in the United States, perhaps because medical transcription is a rigorous and technical profession that requires extensive training and often a few years of experience to make it on your own. Medical transcriptionists are not just typists or secretaries. They must have a good command of English grammar, AND know thousands of words of technical medical vocabulary, AND understand the garbled dictations of doctors who eat lunch while they dictate or doctors who hardly speak English because they come from many parts of the world to practice in the United States, AND be able to type 60 to 90 words per minute (or faster). As you can see, these are serious qualifications that are not easy to come by.

Medical transcription service

Because of these rigorous requirements, though, medical transcription is an extremely valuable profession that is becoming more important. From routine patient visits and hospitalizations to complex surgery situations and psychological exams, physicians are generally required by law and ethics to prepare numerous reports for their patient records. In some cases, such as accidents, lawsuits, and denied medical claims, doctors must also prepare documents for insurance companies, police departments, employers, lawyers, and state-funded worker's compensation boards.

The transcriptionist's job is not an easy one. He or she must type up each report accurately, using good English and proper medical terminology. The transcriptionist also must have the report back to the doctor or hospital within the deadline, usually 1 to 3 days. Most transcription today is done using basic word processing software and personal computers.

Chapter 4 examines the world of medical transcription and explains how to obtain training and preparation. Note, however, that unlike the previous two businesses, which most people can get into after a few months or even a half year of preparation, medical transcription requires much more extensive advance planning, education, and long-term commitment, as it can take up to two years or more to develop the skills if you do not have a prior medical background. For many people though, a career in medical transcription could be the ticket to independence, freedom, and financial self-sufficiency, and with the proper planning and educational courses, becoming one is not an insurmountable task.

How to use this book

The next three chapters are the heart of this book and contain the essential information about the three businesses profiled. Each chapter follows a roughly similar format, in that they are divided into two major parts: Background and Getting started. In the first part, basic information about the business is discussed, including what the business does, how it works, the level of knowledge and skills you'll need, and an assessment of the income and earnings potential. The explanations include both the pros and cons.

My goal is to present you with a realistic portrayal of the business so that you can glean both an analytic assessment and an emotional feeling. With both of these inputs, you will more likely develop a balanced view of the business. There is also an informal 15-question checklist you can use to assess your feelings about the business and chances of personal satisfaction and success.

Should you decide that the business is not for you, you can probably skip or skim the second part of the chapter, Getting started. However, if you have any interest in seriously pursuing the business in question, you most definitely should read this second part. Valuable information and tips on hardware and software (as appropriate), are included, how to locate training and resources to develop your skills, ideas for how to market your business and price your service, and a final section on overcoming common start-up problems in the health service business are also covered.

Scattered throughout each of the chapters are various shaded "sidebars," with information based on the many interviews I conducted with people engaged in the business, or extra explanatory notes about a topic of interest in that chapter. While these sidebars are not necessary reading, they often contain valuable information about running the business, marketing, and lessons learned from the battlefield. There is often no greater wisdom than that of someone who trod before you, although each person's experience will vary depending on locale, luck, and personal talent. Nevertheless, most of us take inspiration from others who have made a success of their own ventures.

The final chapter, which contains a memorable method for remembering the 10 steps you need to consider if you are to start a health services business, is DREAM BIG for $ & ☺ ,and you'll see what each letter stands for when you get an important one. A mnemonic device (a memory aid) is used as follows: to that chapter. Many people fail to consider the extremely important issues that are the foundation and elemental truths behind starting any new business venture. I urge you to read this last chapter. The information is gleaned from many experts and my own personal experience in the business world.

I have chosen these three businesses for a variety of reasons. First, none requires a specific academic or medical background prior to preparing for the business, and so each is more or less fully open to any hardworking, dedicated individual who wants to operate his or her own business. You do not need an M.B.A. in health administration, a B.A. in chemistry, or an R.N. to be in any one of them.

Choice of businesses

Nevertheless, it probably helps to have worked in one of these areas. If you have worked in a physician's office or insurance company, if you were a nurse or physician's assistant, or had any other type of experience in the health profession, you clearly will be a leg up on someone who comes into the field with no background. Each profession does require a definite level of knowledge and skills, especially medical transcription.

In every case, the necessary skills are learnable, and most people will have no problem picking them up. You need to assess the amount of time, energy, and money you have to learn the background of a new business. If you have a medical background related to the business at hand, you might find you will need only a few weeks or months before setting up your business. If you come from a totally different field, however, you will need to choose between your priorities: a short-term investment of time and money versus a long-term gain of a new profession.

Second, as mentioned earlier in this chapter, I also chose these businesses because they appear to offer good potential for both personal satisfaction and income. While people are always reluctant to discuss their incomes, everyone interviewed for this book was optimistic and upbeat about what they were earning. Most answered affirmatively when asked if someone working full-time at this profession could earn $30,000 to $60,000.

None of these businesses are, however, a get-rich-quick operation. All require hard work, dedication, and even ambition, and there is still no guarantee. Running your own business is tough. You are the receptionist, marketing manager, sales agent, and professional running the shop. You ARE the business, and you will most likely need to work long hours to build your business up until you are earning a decent income.

Third, these businesses should be around for some time, so your initial investment of time and money will pay dividends for years. Technology can change our world in the flash of an instant, however, and the medical field is particularly prone to advances in technology. Perhaps voice recognition computers will change medical transcription so that doctors will need only to speak out their notes and the computer will automatically produce a perfect document. Perhaps our country under Bill Clinton will adopt a national heathcare plan that abolishes health-insurance claims, and both the medical billing and claims assistance businesses will fall by the wayside. Many changes are possible, but most are more than doubtful at this writing, and so I feel confident recommending these businesses to you.

Last, I believe these are the best businesses to be in. In planning this book, I evaluated other opportunities, and ruled them out because they appeared to require exceptional talent, experience, or skills (like medical practice consulting) or they required major degrees and medical experience. While the end result is that the book includes only three professions, I expect that this is an excellent start for most people with or without medical backgrounds to hop onto a ground floor opportunity in any of these three businesses.

Using your PC in business

The title of this book, *Health Service Businesses on Your Home-Based PC*, suggests that these businesses heavily utilize computers and software. However, let me mention up front that the extent of computer usage in these businesses varies extensively. In descending order of computerization, medical billing is very computer-intensive and requires a fair knowledge of hardware and software. Medical transcription is less computer-intensive and requires only the level of sophistication needed to operate a basic word-processing software package. No other special software is used in medical transcription. Medical claims assistance is hardly computerized at all, because, as you will learn, insurance companies do not accept electronic claims from individuals who are filing claims one at a time. These claims must be handled using the old tried-and-true paper claim forms. In short, the computer skills necessary to be in these industries are not outrageously difficult to learn.

These businesses also include extensive marketing and sales components, and this means you could benefit from using your PC and software to fulfill many general business functions. With word-processing and desktop publishing software, you can design your own brochures, newsletters, and other marketing documents. With database software, you can send out hundreds or thousands of direct-mail fliers using mail merge functions with a list of your potential clients. With contact management software, you can maintain accurate files of your appointments and schedules, and on which clients you've contacted when, what their response was, and so on. And with time management software, you can keep track of your productivity and do automatic invoicing for clients on a per-hour basis, as is sometimes done for all three of these businesses.

Think of it this way: in today's market, if you are not using a computer to your best advantage, your competitor probably is, and that means you are likely losing opportunities and even contracts that could be yours. So while you might not use any specialized software for medical claims assistance work, or for medical transcription, you would be wise to use technology for many other important business functions. I've highlighted a few such programs and suggest how you can use them to support your endeavors later in the book.

Can you mix and match businesses? Most certainly. It is, in fact, quite worthwhile to point to out that several people interviewed in this book practice more than one of these businesses at a time. While your level of skills and business acumen must undoubtedly be higher to do this, it is entirely conceivable that you too might want to offer medical billing and transcription, or billing and claims assistance, or any other combination you can handle.

Mixing and matching businesses

Linda Noel of Linda's Billing Service in Los Angeles does medical billing and medical transcription, for example. As she explained, "I offer a personalized service, which is the key to getting clients. It helps me to be a full-service agency, handling two areas of need for my clients." Linda's company is profiled in chapter 2.

Irene Card, founder of Medical Insurance Claims, Inc. in Kinnelon, New Jersey, also offers two businesses. Her primary business is claims assistance to the public, which she started in 1980 in her spare time. Irene explained how she began her business. "I was a medical consultant helping doctors, and I was seeing people who were too weak, too sick, and too upset to look after their insurance needs. A lot of these people were over 65, and many didn't even know what types of insurance were available." Within two years, Irene had plenty of clients and was operating full-time from an office building. In time though, Irene decided to seek out other ways to bring in revenue, so she expanded her business into medical billing for doctors. She purchased a software package that does electronic billing and began developing a clientele. When her original software company went bankrupt, stranding her with unsupported software, she switched to High-Tech Management Systems, another medical billing software company in Pasadena, California that offered her more stability and support for the software.

Irene now does both sides of the equation: billing for physicians using Hi-Tech's electronic claims software, and claims assistance for individual consumers. She currently has six employees and more than 2000 individual clients coast-to-coast, as well as a number of doctors for the electronic billing side of the business. Irene was even profiled in December 1991 by *Entrepreneur* magazine!

As in any entrepreneurial enterprise, the sky is the limit for the ambitious, hardworking, and serious person. Whatever your goals, if you have an interest in the health professions, you will surely find something enticing for you in this book!

2 Medical claims billing services

Electronic medical billing services are riding the wave of change in the medical industry. Some have called them a paradigm shift, a new way of thinking and doing medical claims, while others have simply called them a gold mine for the savvy entrepreneur.

It was indeed hard to investigate medical billing services without practically starting one myself, given the potential they offer. However, let me temper this enthusiasm with an important caveat I learned during my research. While a medical billing service offers exceptionally good income potential, it requires knowledge, perseverance, and good business skills. Like most new ventures, medical billing is undoubtedly a very good opportunity for some people, but it is not for everyone.

This chapter looks at the basics of this business, the pros and cons of starting one and how to begin, should you decide it is for you. Through the sidebars in this chapter, you'll also learn a little about the complexities of the health insurance business and meet some people who have started medical billing services with a modicum of success and personal satisfaction.

Most people intuitively know what a medical billing business does, having had some experience filing out convoluted claim forms and then negotiating between their doctor and insurance company how much is owed to whom. For the sake of clarity, let's define exactly what medical billing services are and are not.

What is a medical billing service?

The main activity of a medical billing service is to process physician, dentist, and other healthcare provider insurance claims to the nearly 300 private, group, accident, and government insurance companies. One common error is thinking that medical billing services process claims directly for individuals, but that job is for the medical claims assistant processor or professional, which is covered in the next chapter.

Until recently, medical billing was usually done by typing out and mailing claim forms to various insurance carriers. Today, the thrust of the medical billing industry is to offer fast, efficient, and nearly error-free electronic claims processing using computers to log and transmit the claims to the insurance companies over phone lines via communications software and modems. In fact, electronic claims processing has gained sufficiently broad acceptance to have engendered its own unique acronyms. Many people refer to the field as *electronic claims processing* (ECP), *electronic claims submission* (ECS), *electronic media claims* (EMC), *electronic medical claims transfer* (EMT), or more simply, *E*. Throughout this chapter, I use ECP.

ECP has many significant advantages over paper claims processing. Electronic claims save an enormous amount of time and labor, because they eliminate the typing and mailing paper claims to insurance carriers, who in turn must typically sort, check, and key them into a system for recordkeeping and payment. Figure 2-1 contrasts insurance carriers' procedures for handling paper claims versus electronic processing.

As a result of electronic processing, labor and overhead costs are reduced. The Health Care Financing Administration (HCFA), the umbrella agency that administers the federal Medicare program, estimates that electronic processing saves $0.50 per claim. Given that Medicare pays more than 600 million claims per year, that equals a savings more than $300 million. As for physicians, a 1988 American Medical Association (AMA) study estimates that it costs physicians between $6 and $12 in labor and overhead to process a paper claim compared to $3 to $5 for electronic claims. The actual cost to physicians varies greatly depending on administrative expenses, salaries, and other factors, but it's readily apparent that paper claims require more time and effort and cost more.

Perhaps the greatest advantage of electronic claims to providers is the increased speed at which doctors get paid. Claims are filed with insurance carriers in a more timely manner, and contain far fewer mistakes due to systemic editing and error checking as they are processed. Some estimates indicate that nearly 25 to 30 percent of paper claims contain coding errors, because of data entry mistakes made at the physician's office or at the insurance carrier's office. Because claim forms contain dozens of "fields" (units of information such as name, address, policy number, diagnosis, procedures performed, etc.), it is easy to understand how typing errors can occur so frequently.

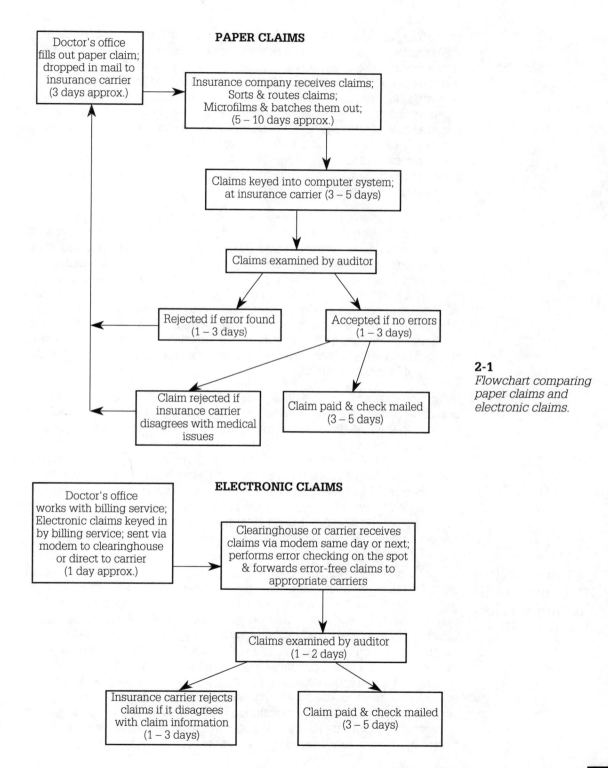

PAPER CLAIMS

Doctor's office fills out paper claim; dropped in mail to insurance carrier (3 days approx.)

Insurance company receives claims; Sorts & routes claims; Microfilms & batches them out; (5 – 10 days approx.)

Claims keyed into computer system; at insurance carrier (3 – 5 days)

Claims examined by auditor

Rejected if error found (1 – 3 days)

Accepted if no errors (1 – 3 days)

Claim rejected if insurance carrier disagrees with medical issues

Claim paid & check mailed (3 – 5 days)

2-1
Flowchart comparing paper claims and electronic claims.

ELECTRONIC CLAIMS

Doctor's office works with billing service; Electronic claims keyed in by billing service; sent via modem to clearinghouse or direct to carrier (1 day approx.)

Clearinghouse or carrier receives claims via modem same day or next; performs error checking on the spot & forwards error-free claims to appropriate carriers

Claims examined by auditor (1 – 2 days)

Insurance carrier rejects claims if it disagrees with claim information (1 – 3 days)

Claim paid & check mailed (3 – 5 days)

In contrast, electronic claims reduce errors in several ways. First, medical billing software typically stores records for each regular patient a doctor has, so the need to rekey basic patient information is minimized. Also, the software usually performs error checks. Some examples of this include verifying that numeric characters are not used in place of alphabetic entries, ensuring the correct number of characters are used, or verifying that all required fields are completed. These and other electronic edits reduce claim error rates to an estimated 3%. Furthermore, when there is an error in an electronic claim, the provider finds out about it quickly because the insurance carrier or the intermediate processing company bounces the claim back almost immediatley.

The ramifications of this improvement in speed and accuracy are *that electronic claims get done more quickly and are paid much faster*. Payment on paper claims can take more than 30 days, even if they are error free. If they require multiple corrections and correspondence, it may be more than 90 days before they are paid. Electronic claims are typically paid in 15 working days, and in some cases 7 working days by commercial carriers. According to *Medical Economics* magazine many healthcare providers can get as much as 80 percent of their gross earnings from Medicare and commercial insurance companies. It is easy to see how an electronic billing service can play a vital role in helping physicians manage businesses by improving cash flow and the use of human resources.

Insurance companies also realize savings from electronic claims processing and more carriers are now moving toward greater support. HCFA, which led the way in the mid 1980s will soon require electronic claims for all Medicare reimbursements, and has been notifying healthcare providers and billing centers since 1990 that electronic claims are given priority processing over paper claims. New legislation in process at the time of this writing will require that electronic Medicare claims be paid within 15 days while paper claims may sit for 27 days before they are paid. There are also rumors in the industry that the federal government is considering a surcharge of $1. or more per claim for physicians who continue to process Medicare claims on paper.

Other services offered by billing services

In addition to electronic claims processing, some billing services also perform other functions for physicians, such as complete accounts-receivables management, or what is sometimes referred to as "reimbursement management." The extent of this extra service may vary, but in general, the billing centers assume responsibility for ensuring that the physician is reimbursed as much as possible from all sources—the patient's primary insurance carrier, any secondary carriers, and the patient. Their goals are to "zero out" the patient's balance as quickly and efficiently as possible, and computerize the accounting and other practice-management records. Other services might include resubmitting rejected claims for payment, filing claims to secondary or tertiary insurers and issuing monthly bills to patients for balances that represent the patient's portion of what is owed.

Some billing centers that provide these extended services manage soft collections (sending out past due notices and reminders). Some also perform various business analysis functions, such as supplying weekly or monthly reports on a variety of data that can help practitioners track and improve operating efficiency and cash flow. A few medical billing software companies, like Hi-Tech Management Systems in Pasadena, California, now provide billing services, which purchase their software, the ability to offer electronic funds transfer (EFT). EFT provides doctors a convenient way to have patients pay their medical bills with an automatic monthly debit from their bank account. Some billing companies also offer to either buy accounts receivables from doctors, or make cash loans against them. We'll examine these functions in greater detail later in this chapter.

To avoid confusion, note that some people make the following distinction in characterizing software for medical billing centers. Software that performs only electronic claims processing is referred to as *medical claims filing* or *billing software*. Software that handles a full range of accounting, patient billing, and business analysis reporting is called practice management software. Additionally, you will find the business referred to as a billing service, a billing center, a claims filing service, or a claims service.

Medical billing is not such a new field to attract all this attention. As industry veteran Bill Saracini, a C.P.A. and President of Intramarket Systems Corporation in Mission, Kansas told me, "This industry is at least 50-plus years old; there's been a cottage industry that's existed ever since there was insurance, from large CPA firms that had a specialization in medical practice management, to women at home who had a few accounts." So why has medical billing leaped into the limelight recently?

Why medical billing services are so hot

Two answers immediately come to mind: the skyrocketing cost of healthcare in America, and the sheer number of claims that Medicare, Medicaid and commercial insurance carriers process each year. It was a case of a problem looking for a solution, and computer technology provided at least part of that solution. A quick review of the history of medical billing will highlight the sequence of events that led to the need for electronic medical billing services.

In the 1950s, a small number of data processing companies targeted the medical field. These companies used large mainframe systems and worked mostly with hospitals and medical practices filing substantial claims volumes to only a few insurance carriers. The 1980s brought several events which caused the billing industry to undergo cataclysmic change.

In the early 80s, a few software companies began developing software for filing claims using microcomputers. This small step was largely focused on getting doctors to automate their offices with computer hardware and software for claims filing and billing. Unfortunately, too many problems plagued the industry to allow it to take off: hardware limitations, software glitches, vendors that went out of business without providing promised support, stonewalling doctors who didn't appreciate the value of computerization, and dependence upon floppy disks or magnetic tape which still had to be mailed to the insurance company.

In addition, the claim format was not standardized and therefore doctors could not send a universal claim form to all insurance companies. A few companies tried to resolve this problem by establishing themselves as clearinghouses where claims of any kind could be edited and processed to each carrier's requirements, but conversion of the industry to a uniform data exchange standard remained distant.

Medicare leads the way to claims sanity

In 1983, HCFA took several steps to push the industry forward. Faced with enormous growth in healthcare costs, enrollments, and claim volumes, the agency considered the future of Medicare and projected exponential growth during the 1980s and beyond. As a result, the HCFA began an aggressive campaign to shift hospitals and physicians to electronically transmitted claims to reduce costs, and eliminate paperwork and huge backlogs. The HCFA also endorsed a schedule of diagnostic codes and procedure codes, thus paving the way for a uniform coding on all electronic claims.

Not surprisingly, HCFA's prediction was right on target. A torrent of Medicare claims flooded the administration within a few years. In 1989, Medicare alone generated 494 million claims, 80 percent of which were from physicians, suppliers, and laboratories. TABLE 2-1 shows the growth of Medicare between 1980–1989 in both the number of enrolled persons and benefit dollars paid.

The HCFA's efforts to launch electronic claims processing paid off. By 1989 36 percent of claims from physicians and laboratories were received electronically. And according to *Medical Economics* magazine, Medicare increased that percentage to nearly 50 percent by 1991. At the time of this writing, Medicare has directed those insurance carriers that process its claims to raise the level to 55 percent with a target to achieve a full 100 percent electronic rate by 1997.

Commercial insurance companies have been much slower to catch on to electronic claims processing. Eleven of the largest companies formed the National Electronic Information Corp. (NEIC) in 1981 to serve as a clearinghouse for processing commercial health insurance claims. It remained greatly underutilized for most of the decade. In the late 1980s, NEIC began to play a larger role and opened the door for more commercial insurers to handle their claims electronically. Nonetheless, many commercial carriers proceeded very cautiously. In 1987, an estimated 3 billion claims were filed annually to all insurers from hospitals, doctors, laboratories, and pharmacies. This estimate rose to 6 billion claims by 1990. However, *Medical Economics*

Table 2-1
Medicare enrollment and benefit payments (1980–1989)

	Hospital and/or medical insurance Part A + B		Hospital insurance Part A		Supplementary medical insurance Part B	
	Number of enrolled persons (millions)	Benefit payments ($billions)	Number of enrolled persons (millions)	Benefit payments ($billions)	Number of enrolled persons (millions)	Benefit payments ($billions)
1980	28.5	33.9	28.1	23.8	27.4	10.1
1981	29.1	41.2	28.6	28.9	27.9	12.3
1982	29.5	49.2	29.1	34.3	28.4	14.8
1983	30.1	55.6	29.6	38.1	28.9	17.5
1984	30.5	60.9	30.0	41.5	29.4	19.5
1985	31.1	69.5	30.6	47.7	29.9	21.8
1986	31.8	74.1	31.2	48.9	30.6	25.2
1987	32.4	79.8	31.9	49.8	31.2	29.9
1988	32.9	85.5	32.4	51.9	31.6	33.7
1989	33.6	94.3	33.1	57.4	32.1	36.9
1990	34.2	108.7	33.7	66.2	32.6	42.5
1991	34.9	113.9	34.4	68.5	33.2	45.5

Source: U.S. Department of Health and Human Services, Health Care Financing Administration, Bureau of Data Management and Strategy.

magazine estimates only 6 to 8 percent of commercial insurance claims were processed electronically in 1991, a mere drop in the bucket of the six billion claims filed annually by that time.

Electronic claims processing was given a gigantic push when HCFA issued a directive that took effect in September 1990 requiring *all* physicians to file healthcare claims on behalf of their Medicare patients. This new policy shifted the burden of filing for payment from the consumer to the doctor. Finding themselves suddenly swamped with claims that needed to be properly filed to be turned into cash, many physicians eagerly sought outside billing experts because they were not prepared to handle them.

Today, few doubt that our national healthcare budget and the volume of claims will continue to soar. As mentioned earlier, our total national healthcare expenditure (NHE) rose to $738 billion in 1991. Physicians' services accounted for nearly $150 billion, three-fourths of which is paid by Medicare and commercial insurance carriers. The remaining 25 percent is paid directly by consumers. In short, medical billing has become a booming business because more people are using the healthcare system more frequently, filing more claims, for more money, to pay more doctors. Although it's a business which has been around for decades, new technology is changing the way medical billing works, making the field open to virtually anyone with some savvy, medical knowledge and computer skills.

This time of opportunity portends both good news and bad for the entrepreneur. The good news is, we have a young industry open to new competitors, smaller players with a chance to move quickly. At the same time, however, a medical billing service entrepreneur must proceed cautiously in this ever-evolving high-technology profession. The bad news is, with constant changes occurring in healthcare, the insurance industry, Medicare, and in medical software, the new entrepreneur essentially faces a moving target in starting business. This means that in order to succeed, you must keep yourself steeped in a changing stream of rules, regulations, and business procedures. Let's now examine in greater detail how a billing service operates and the skills and knowledge you need to get started.

How billing services work

To understand how a billing service works, I have divided the operations of a medical billing service into four subtopics:

❏ Background About the Health Insurance Industry.
❏ The Medical Office and the Paper Claims Process.
❏ The Medical Office and the Electronic Claims Process.
❏ Advanced Practice Management Functions.

Whatever your background or previous experience, I suggest you read or skim each of these sections to be sure you have an accurate view of how the service works before starting your business.

The health insurance industry

Although most of us have some familiarity with the health insurance industry, a billing service must have a clear understanding of how insurance operates and how the companies interact with healthcare practitioners. With more than 1500 different insurance programs in this country, you would be wise to develop as much knowledge as you can about the business.

First, health insurance can be divided into two general categories: private and public. Private health insurance is offered primarily by commercial companies—often called carriers—in the form of individual and group plans. Private insurance also includes Blue Cross and Blue Shield plans and prepayment plans such as Health Maintenance Organizations (HMOs). Public health insurance consists of federal and state government-run programs, including Medicare, Medicaid, Civilian Health and Medical Program of the Uniformed Services (CHAMPUS), Veterans Medical Care, Federal Employees Health Benefits Program (FEHBP), and various other local plans. The following is a brief look at the most important health insurance categories.

Commercial carriers   Commercial carriers are insurance companies that underwrite health and dental policies for individuals and for groups—group policies being the largest subcategory. A 1990 study by the Health Insurance

Association of America estimated that 82 million Americans were covered under group policies and 10 million were insured by individual or family policies.

Group and individual health insurance policies vary greatly—from what types of illnesses and physicians each policy will cover, to how much the individual or family will have to pay in deductibles and coinsurance (sometimes called copayment). The deductible is an amount the individual or family must pay toward healthcare expenses in each calendar or policy year before the insurance company will pay anything. This usually ranges from $100 to $250 for an individual or $500 to $1000 dollars for a family. The coinsurance is an amount the policyholder owes the medical provider for covered services as part of the payment. Most health insurance policies pay for or reimburse only 80% of a physician's charges for outpatient services, office visits, and many procedures. The total coinsurance an individual or family must pay in the course of a year is usually capped at $1000 to $4000. Some policies likewise have an annual or lifetime maximum, limiting the charges the carrier is responsible for.

Commercial health insurance generally comes in three basic types: basic plans, which pay for limited services performed in a hospital, x-rays, lab tests, drugs and medications and outpatient doctor's visits; major medical plans designed to pay large amounts in the event of catastrophic illness or major surgery, but not for minor health problems; and comprehensive medical plans, which offer both basic and major medical coverage. Policies differ greatly. One policy might cover psychiatric benefits up to $1000 per year for outpatient visits, but not reimburse for chiropractic treatment or eye examinations as another policy does.

Most commercial health insurance is offered on a fee-for-care basis, meaning that the insurance company pays for care only as needed. The advantage of fee-for-service policies is that the patient can choose any doctor and the insurance company will pay the claim according to what it has established as a reasonable fee. The insured party is then responsible for the balance of the doctor's bill (copayment), unless the physician accepts the carrier's payment as full payment.

The main problem with fee-for-service plans is that healthcare costs began skyrocketing and both insurance companies and patients were paying higher claims and copayments. As a result, a new type of arrangement in commercial health insurance was developed—*managed care*. Designed to lower costs, these plans are often labeled *preferred provider organizations* (PPOs), because the insurer makes arrangements with independent physicians and pays them according to an agreed fee. Individuals enrolled in the plan are encouraged to use PPO practitioners, and if they use physicians outside the group, they must pay a much higher copayment. The American Managed Care and Review Association indicates 48 million Americans used PPOs in 1990.

Blue Cross and Blue Shield   Originally, Blue Cross was a nonprofit organization designed to provide healthcare services under a prepayment plan in which subscribers paid in advance for the health services they might need during a hospital stay. Likewise, Blue Shield Plans were nonprofit plans established for subscribers to pay in advance for surgery, in-hospital medical treatment, and some outpatient services. Today, Blue Cross and Blue Shield have essentially joined ranks with other insurers to ensure hospital and non-hospital services and compete directly with commercial carriers. Each organization is actually an independent insurance company, loosely affiliated with a national association from which they license the Blue Cross and Blue Shield names. Currently, many reports have surfaced that "the Blues" in about 20 states are experiencing some degree of financial distress due to mismanagement and to a high level of payouts as compared to commercial insurers which typically have been able to be more selective of the people they choose to insure. Many Blue Cross and Blue Shield organizations are also the same insurance companies that process Medicare claims in many states, as are discussed later.

Health maintenance organizations (HMOs)   Originating in the 1930s, HMOs have grown quickly in the past decade because of their cost-cutting measures and efficiency. Essentially, HMOs both insure and provide the care. In an HMO plan, the individual or group employer prepays a monthly fee and usually does not make any additional payment for any amount of care. In some cases, a small copayment of $2–$5 dollars for each office visit may be required. Many of these plans require patients to use only the doctors and facilities associated with the HMO. The advantage of an HMO is that the patient does not get involved with any billing or claim forms. All invoicing for

Table 2-2
Private health insurance claims
payments by type of insurer (billions)

Year	Insurance Companies	Blue Cross-Blue Shield	Self-insured & HMO Plans	Total
1980	37.0	25.5	16.2	76.3
1981	41.6	29.2	18.9	85.9
1982	49.2	32.2	21.6	97.1
1983	51.7	34.4	24.1	104.1
1984	56.0	35.7	26.1	107.5
1985	60.0	37.5	32.5	117.6
1986	64.3	40.6	36.8	128.5
1987	72.5	44.5	56.5	151.7
1988	83.0	48.2	62.8	171.1
1989	89.4	50.7	79.8	185.3
1990	97.7	55.9	96.7	212.4

Source: Health Insurance Association of America, annual survey of health insurance companies.

a doctor's care is handled internally. Other types of HMOs are more like PPOs, and so patients and doctors still need to file claims. HMOs have increased in popularity to the tune of more than 550 of them in operation as of 1990, enrolling about 14 percent of the U.S. population. HMOs are especially popular in California.

TABLE 2-2 contrasts the growth of total claim payments through the 1980s among the three major types of private insurance: commercial, Blue Cross-Blue Shield, and Self-Insured & HMO plans. Figure 2-2 depicts the increases in commercial group and individual insurance payments between 1980 and 1990 for hospital and physician services.

Medicare/Medicaid   The federal government began Medicare in 1966 to assist elderly and disabled citizens (typically on a fixed income) who also face rapidly rising costs in medical and hospital care. Medicare is under the aegis of the Social Security Administration but is run by the Health Care Financing Administration. Today, more than 40 million Americans are covered by Medicare. Medicare coverage is actually divided into two parts:

1. Part A covers hospital, skilled nursing facility, and home healthcare. Part A of Medicare becomes automatically available and virtually free of charge for almost every American over the age of 65 and the permanently disabled. It is financed through payroll taxes for Social Security. Each eligible subscriber pays a deductible for each hospitalization, and then Medicare picks up the tab for 60 days of inpatient hospital care during the

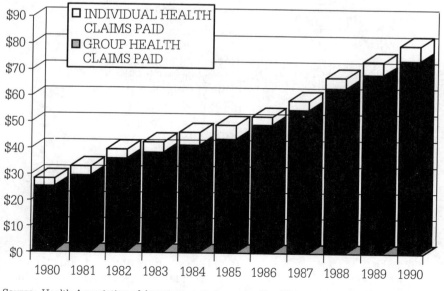

2-2
Growth of commercial insurance claims payments for hospital and medical care in billions of dollars—1980–1990.

Source: Health Association of America, annual survey of health insurance companies.

benefit period. In general, billing centers are not involved with claims for Part A coverages, as hospitals process these claims directly to Medicare intermediaries. These intermediaries in each state are usually insurance carriers or data processing centers.

2. Part B of Medicare also called Supplementary Medical Insurance (SMI), pays for doctor's services performed in a hospital, clinic, doctor's office, or home, as well as laboratory tests and x-rays. Part B of Medicare is voluntary, but most people sign up for it, paying a monthly premium ($31.80 in 1992) which can be deducted from their Social Security payments. Part B insurance covers the subscriber for 80 percent of what Medicare has determined are "allowable" charges according to geographic area and specialty-based fee schedule. The beneficiary is responsible for the annual deductible ($100 in 1992) and a copayment.

Billing services typically handle many Part B claims for providers by processing them to the insurance company in each state or region of a state which has been selected by HCFA to act as the Medicare carrier. TABLE 2-3 lists those carriers by state for 1992.

Table 2-3
Medicare carriers 1992

State	Carrier
Alabama	Blue Cross & Blue Shield of Alabama
Alaska	Aetna Life & Casualty
Arizona	Aetna Life & Casualty
Arkansas	Arkansas Blue Cross & Blue Shield
California—southern	Transamerica/Occidental Life Insurance Co.
northern	Blue Shield of California
Colorado	Blue Shield of Colorado
Connecticut	Traveler's Insurance Co.
Delaware	Pennsylvania Blue Shield
District of Columbia	Pennsylvania Blue Shield
Florida	Blue Shield of Florida, Inc.
Georgia	Aetna Life & Casualty
Hawaii	Aetna Life & Casualty
Idaho	Equicor
Illinois	Blue Cross & Blue Shield of Illinois
Indiana	Associated Insurance Companies, Inc.
Iowa	Blue Shield of Iowa
Kansas—Johnson Wyandotte	Blue Shield of Kansas City
rest of state	Blue Shield of Kansas
Kentucky	Blue Cross & Blue Shield of Kentucky
Louisiana	Blue Cross & Blue Shield of Louisiana
Maine	Blue Shield of Massachusetts/Tri-State

Maryland—Montgomery & PG counties	Pennsylvania Blue Shield
rest of state	Maryland Blue Shield
Massachusetts	Blue Shield of Massachusetts, Inc.
Michigan	Michigan Blue Cross & Blue Shield
Minnesota—11 counties	Traveler's Insurance Co.
rest of state	Blue Shield of Minnesota
Mississippi	Traveler's Insurance Co.
Missouri—western counties	Blue Shield of Kansas City
eastern counties	General American Life Insurance Co.
Montana	Blue Shield of Montana
Nebraska	Blue Cross & Blue Shield of Nebraska
Nevada	Aetna Life & Casualty
New Hampshire	Blue Shield of Massachusetts/Tri-State
New Jersey	Pennsylvania Blue Shield
New Mexico	Aetna Life & Casualty
New York—southern	Empire Blue Cross & Blue Shield
Queens	Group Health, Inc.
western/northern	Blue Shield of Western New York
North Carolina	Equicor, Inc.
North Dakota	Blue Shield of North Dakota
Ohio	Nationwide Mutual Insurance Co.
Oklahoma	Aetna Life & Casualty
Oregon	Aetna Life & Casualty
Pennsylvania	Pennsylvania Blue Shield
Rhode Island	Blue Shield of Rhode Island
South Carolina	Blue Cross & Blue Shield of South Carolina
South Dakota	Blue Shield of North Dakota
Tennessee	Equicor, Inc.
Texas	Blue Cross & Blue Shield of Texas
Utah	Blue Shield of Utah
Vermont	Blue Shield of Massachusetts/Tri-State
Virginia—northern	Pennsylvania Blue Shield
rest of state	Traveler's Insurance Co.
Washington	Washington Physicians' Service
West Virginia	Nationwide Mutual Insurance Co.
Wisconsin	Wisconsin Physicians Service
Wyoming	Equicor, Inc.

Many people supplement their Medicare coverage with additional group insurance, called *MediGap*, which is purchased from commercial insurance carriers. These health insurance policies provide a variety of coverages to pay for either Part A or Part B deductibles, copayments, lifetime maximums, or other gaps where the consumer otherwise would have to spend out-of-pocket money. In 1992, the federal government took steps to control the vast and confusing array of MediGap policies offered, so that in the future, only 11 standardized MediGap policies will be available from any commercial carrier.

Note that Medicare insurance requires doctors (thus billing services) to track an individual's Medicare status, and many exceptions can apply to their coverages. For example, Medicare is the primary coverage for some individuals, while Medicaid is their secondary coverage. These patients are referred to as Medi-Medi crossovers. For others who are 65 or older and still working, their primary health coverage under their employer's insurance plan will pay first, then Medicare will be secondary. Medicare is also a second payer for claims involving work-related injury, automobile and other accidents, and a few other circumstances.

As mentioned earlier, doctors and suppliers of medical services under Medicare must submit charges to Medicare carriers on behalf of their patients, as of September 1990. The consumer may no longer file Medicare claims. Providers now have two options for getting paid. Each year they can choose either to participate in Medicare, thus becoming a PAR physician by "taking assignment," or not participate, called a *non-PAR*. Taking assignment means a patient has agreed to "assign" the benefits to the physician. Medicare then forwards the check directly to the doctor. For this advantage, the provider agrees not to charge more than an "allowed amount" established by Medicare for a given procedure performed in their geographic area. The practitioner must still bill the patient for the remaining 20 percent.

Doctors who do not participate (non-PARs) must also file claims for patients, but they can decide on a case-by-case basis to reject assignment, and they can bill for an amount greater than Medicare allows. The amount for which non-PAR providers can bill is now capped at 115% of the scheduled fee as of 1993 (called the *limiting charge*). It is noteworthy that, while Medicare pays the usual 80%, it is calculated on only 95% of the scheduled fee, so the non-PAR physician loses 5% off the top as well. Furthermore, the check is sent to the patient, and the physician must bill the patient for the full charge to collect the entire amount—assuming more risk.

TABLE 2-4 compares a patient seeing Dr. Smith, a participating provider, with a patient who sees Dr. Jones, a nonparticipating provider who does not take assignment. Assume here that both patients were treated for the exact same problem and their doctors practice in the same geographic area. Remember that the small monetary difference in this example of what the physician receives as a PAR provider can amount to a great deal of money considering the thousands of claims to Medicare each year.

Table 2-4
Example of difference in charges between a participating provider and a nonparticipating provider under Medicare

	Charges	Fee schedule amount	Paid by Medicare	Balance due
Dr. Smith (PAR)	$70.00	$70.00	$56.00	$14.00
Dr. Jones (NON-PAR)	$80.50	$70.00	$53.20	$27.30

Dr. Smith is a PAR provider and is willing to accept the fee schedule amount. His patient owes only $14 because Dr. Smith has agreed to accept $70 as the full amount allowed. Dr. Smith receives 80% of $70 ($56) from Medicare, and must collect $14 from his patient.

Dr. Jones is a non-PAR provider. He is able to charge a different fee, but only up to 115% of the fee schedule amount (this is called the *limiting charge*). Medicare will then pay him only 80% of 95% of the fee schedule amount. In other words, he loses 5% of the fee schedule amount by not being a PAR provider. In this example, Dr. Jones is entitled to 95% of $70 = $66.50 × 80% = $53.20. He must therefore collect $27.30 from his patient. The patient would have saved $13.30 if he had seen a participating provider. Note also that the nonparticipating physician does not receive the check directly from Medicare but must obtain the balance due from the patient.

To further control costs, Medicare is currently phasing in a new fee schedule over the course of three years—1992 to 1995. The new schedule, called *resource based relative value scale* (RBRVS), replaces the old method of determining fees called Usual, Customary, and Reasonable. Under the new method, Medicare determines the fees providers can charge according to the cost of service by an "efficient" physician, modified by certain relative values such as location, specialty, and so on. A billing service offering full practice management will need to understand this new fee schedule and its implications for healthcare providers.

Medicaid Medicaid is administered jointly by federal and state governments. Each state operates its own program according to general guidelines established by federal law and modified by the funding level at which the state wants to extend the program. Medicaid assists those patients whose incomes are below certain levels. Many physicians do not accept Medicaid patients because the reimbursements for billed charges are typically as low as 30–35 percent of a claim, thereby nearly making it a losing proposition to provide care and process the bill.

Medicaid claims are processed differently in each state, sometimes through carriers or computer service companies which handle the claims and operate the programs. Medicaid also very strictly regulates the types of services covered among the hundreds of different diagnostic tests, procedures, and medications. Hospitalizations are likewise very restricted.

CHAMPUS   The Civilian Health and Medical Program of the Uniformed Services (CHAMPUS) is a health care program for dependents of active and retired military personnel, and their families. Under CHAMPUS programs, covered persons can use civilian doctors rather than military personnel for medical care and have a portion of the care paid for by the federal government. At age 65, CHAMPUS beneficiaries are converted to the Medicare program.

Worker's Compensation   Worker's Compensation covers medical expenses and disability benefits when an illness or injury results directly from the work. Organization that employ more than a certain number of individuals are required to carry this insurance from a carrier of their choice. Workers' Comp claims are generally complex; they require second opinion reviews special reports from the doctors, and a number of state regulations which must be adhered to.

Health insurance is a multifaceted field, and one you must clearly understand to be in the medical claims billing business. If you would like to get more up-to-date information and statistics about the health insurance industry, you can write to the Health Insurance Association of America, 1025 Connecticut Avenue, NW, Washington, DC 20036-3998 or call the association at 202-223-7780.

The medical office and paper claims

Many healthcare practitioners still use old methods of recordkeeping and billing on paper claim forms, traditional accounting ledgers, and journals. The actual use of such systems, described as follows, will vary depending on whether the physician uses computers, *the doctor's relationship to Medicare*, how the practice is run, as well as other factors. Generally though, the procedure for tracking billing and payment via paper forms works as follows:

STEP 1   When a patient first sees the physician (or dentist), a PATIENT REGISTRATION FORM is usually completed which includes the patient's *vital statistics*: name, address, sex, phone number, employer, primary insurance carrier, member number, and so on. The patient will also usually sign a RELEASE & ASSIGNMENT OF BENEFITS FORM which allows the doctor's practice to release information about the diagnosis and treatment to the insurance company so that he or she may bill directly and receive the payment. This form may be part of the registration form or a separate form. Figure 2-3 illustrates a patient registration form.

STEP 2   If necessary, the patient may also fill out a PRE-AUTHORIZATION FORM (also called a Pre-Certification Form) which is used to specify information about a planned procedure or service which requires advance

THE PATIENT REGISTRATION FORM

PLEASE PRINT

PATIENT REGISTRATION

PROFESSIONAL DATA SYSTEMS #302 3/83

DATE		NEW	ADD	CHANGES

PRACTICE	ACCOUNT NUMBER	LAST NAME	FIRST NAME	MI
AFFIX LABEL HERE				

STREET ADDRESS	APT. #	CITY, STATE	ZIP CODE

SEX	BIRTH DATE	SOCIAL SECURITY NUMBER	HOME TELEPHONE NUMBER ( )	BILLING CODES	TYPE

DEPENDENT NAME	BIRTH DATE	REL.	DEPENDENT NAME	BIRTH DATE	REL.
1.			2.		

INSURANCE COMPANY (PRIMARY) | **INSURANCE COMPANY (SECONDARY)**

CODE	NAME		CODE	NAME
INSURANCE COMPANY ADDRESS			INSURANCE COMPANY ADDRESS	
MEMBER OR MEDICARE NUMBER	GROUP NUMBER		MEMBER/POLICY NUMBER	GROUP NUMBER
SUBSCRIBER'S NAME (IF NOT PATIENT)		REL	SUBSCRIBER'S NAME (IF NOT PATIENT)	REL

EMPLOYMENT INFORMATION | **THIRD PARTY BILLING (OR REMARKS)**

EMPLOYER NAME	WORK TELEPHONE ( )	THIRD PARTY NAME
STREET ADDRESS	OCCUPATION	STREET ADDRESS
CITY, STATE	ZIP CODE	CITY, STATE	ZIP CODE

REFERRED BY

NAME		REF. CODE	DR.
	TELEPHONE ( )		

(FOR PRACTICE USE ONLY)   **EMERGENCY NOTIFICATION**

DRIVER'S LICENSE NUMBER	NAME	RELATIONSHIP
TELEPHONE ( )	STREET ADDRESS	CITY, STATE	ZIP CODE

BILLING CODES

					TYPE = ACCOUNT TYPE CODES	
20	BILL PATIENT ONLY	36-46	BILL INSURANCE ONLY (AA)	A INDUSTRIAL	N MEDICARE & PVT	X TWO PVT INS
21	BILL 3RD PARTY	36	BILL PATIENT & INS (AA)	G MEDI MEDI	P NO INSURANCE	Y PVT & MEDI CAL
31	BILL PATIENT & INS (NA)	46	NO STATEMENT - NO INS	I ONE PVT INS	W MEDI-CAL	Z MEDICARE
21-31	BILL 3RD PARTY & INS (NA)					

REL = RELATIONSHIP CODES

3—PATIENT IS MALE SPOUSE   5—PATIENT IS MALE CHILD   7—PATIENT IS MALE OTHER
4—PATIENT IS FEMALE SPOUSE   6—PATIENT IS FEMALE CHILD   8—PATIENT IS FEMALE OTHER

PDS COPY

2-3 *A patient registration form is used to register a new patient and contains important information about the patient's insurance.* Practice Management Information Corporation.

approval by the insurance carrier, Medicare, or Medicaid. If the physician fails to obtain this approval, the claim may be denied payment by the insurance carrier or Medicare. Some insurance companies have 800-numbers for physicians to call during emergencies when immediate authorization is necessary.

STEP 3   The next form, usually called the SUPERBILL, (but also referred to as the fee ticket, visit slip, or encounter form) is used to record the nature of the patient's visit using two sets of coding that most insurance carriers now recognize: diagnosis codes and procedure codes. Since there are thousands of diagnosis codes and procedures codes many doctor's practices design and print their own superbills, listing only those diagnosis and procedure codes most commonly performed in their specialty. The superbill may also contain information for the patient, such as balance owed, next appointment, recall, and payment receipt. Figure 2-4 shows a typical superbill.

STEP 4   After the patient visit, the doctor passes the superbill to the practice's staff person responsible for the insurance payment process and patient billing gets underway. In some cases, the billing person or doctor has the patient pay the fee at the time the service is rendered, and it is then up to the patient to obtain reimbursement from his or her carrier. In the case of Medicare, however, the provider must file the claim on the patient's behalf, and if the physician is PAR, the patient makes either no payment at the time of service or only the 20 percent copayment. In many commercial insurance situations, the provider agrees to take assignment, and therefore, processes the claim for the patient.

STEP 5   If the office is not computerized, the billing staff person refers to the superbill and then types out a paper claim form using the preprinted blank form, called the HCFA 1500 (pronounced *HicFa fifteen hundred*). This is a universal form accepted by many insurance carriers and by Medicare. Prior to the HCFA 1500, every insurance company had their own unique claim form, but over the past decade, this standardized version (shown in FIG. 2-5) has become the accepted paper claim form. The sidebar on the HCFA 1500 explains how this form came about, and the continuing controversy about it.

The HCFA 1500

The story behind the HCFA 1500 form is important to know. It helps you become familiar with some terminology and sheds light on why the healthcare industry has been so slow to implement logical, efficient procedures in the health insurance arena.

Before the HCFA 1500, filing claims was truly a nightmare. Nearly every carrier had its own paper claim form. Keeping track of which form was to be used for which carrier was a major job. Every form had its peculiar requirements of the method for reporting the doctor's diagnosis, procedures performed, fees, and so on. Filing claims was about as fruitful an endeavor as building the Tower of Babel. For this reason, doctors came to expect patients

SUPERBILL

INTERNAL MEDICINE GROUP 4186
4727 Wilshire Boulevard
Los Angeles, CA 90010
(708) 920-0700
LICENSE: P12345
FEIN: 95-4210732

DATE OF SERVICE   ACCOUNT NUMBER

ACCOUNT NAME (LAST, FIRST)

TIME

☐ NEW PATIENT   ☐ ASSIGNED?   DX #1   DX #2   DX #3   DX #4

CODE	DESCRIPTION	E/M	DX	FEE
OFFICE VISITS NEW PATIENT				
90000	Brief	99201		
90010	Limited	99202		
90015	Intermediate	99203		
90017	Extended	99204		
90020	Comprehensive	99205		
OFFICE VISITS ESTABLISHED PATIENT				
90030	Minimal	99211		
90040	Brief	99212		
90050	Limited	99213		
90060	Intermediate	99214		
90070	Extended	99215		
90080	Comprehensive			
CONSULTATIONS INITIAL				
90605	Intermediate	99242		
90610	Extended	99243		
90620	Comprehensive	99244		
PROCEDURES				
10060*	Drain Skin Lesion			
20550*	Injection, Tendon Sheath			
36415*	Routine Venipuncture			
45330	Sigmoidoscopy			
93000	EKG Complete			
93040	Rhythm EKG with Report			
94010	Spirometry Complete			

CODE	DESCRIPTION	DX	FEE
INJECTIONS AND IMMUNIZATIONS			
90702	Immunization; DT		
90703	Immunization; Tetanus Toxoid		
90724	Immunization; Influenza		
90782	Injection, IM/SQ		
90784	Injection, IV		
90788	Injection, Antibiotic		
RADIOLOGY			
71010	X-Ray Exam Chest		
71020	X-Ray Exam Chest		
LABORATORY			
80019	Lab Panel 19+ Tests		
80052	Premarital Profile		
80070	Thyroid Panel		
80072	Arthritis Panel		
80060	Hypertension Panel		
80061	Lipid Profile		
81000	Urinalysis		
82270	Stool for Occult Blood		
82310	Calcium		
82465	Serum Cholesterol		
82565	Blood Creatinine		
82643	Ria for Digoxin		
82951	Glucose Tolerance Test		
83718	Blood Lipoprotein		
84075	Alkaline Phosphatase		

CODE	DESCRIPTION	DX	FEE
LABORATORY (Cont'd)			
84295	Blood Sodium		
84450	SGOT		
84460	SGPT		
84478	Blood Triglycerides		
85014	Hematocrit		
85022	Automated Hemogram		
85031	Manual Hemogram		
85048	White Blood Cell Count		
85580	Blood Platelet Count		
85610	Prothrombin Time		
85651	RBC Sedimentation Rate		
86585	Skin Test, TB		
87060	Culture, Throat or Nose		
SUPPLIES			
99070	Supplies & Materials		
MISCELLANEOUS			
99361	Med Conference, 30 Min		
99362	Med Conference, 60 Min		
99371	Telephone Call, Brief		
99372	Telephone Call, Intermediate		
99000	Specimen Handling		
99080	Special Reports		

UNLISTED PROCEDURE   CODE   DESCRIPTION   FEE

DIAGNOSIS   ICD-9 CM

Abnormal loss weight 783.2	B. neoplasm lg bowel 211.3	Diaphragmatic hernia 553.3	Hypercholesterolemia 272.0	Myeloma multiple 203.0	Pneumonia, org NOS 486
acute bronchitis 466.0	Bronchitis NOS 490	Diverticula colon 562.1	Hyperlipidemia 272.4	MI unsp 410.90	Polycythemia vera 283.4
Acute URI NOS 465.9	Bronchitis obstr chr 491.2	Diverticulitis colon 562.11	Hypertension benign 401.1	MI old 412	Polymyalgia rheum 725
Allergic rhinitis 477.9	Calculus kidney 595.0	Diverticulosis colon 562.10	Hypertension essential 401.0	Nasopharyngitis acute 460	Preop chest xray/EKG V99.99
Alzheimer's disease 331.0	Cardiomyopathies 425.4	Duodenal ulcer unsp 532.9	Hypertension NOS 401.9	Neuralgia, neuritis 792.2	Prostate hyperplasia 600
Anema iron def unsp 280.9	Cataract NOS 366.9	Dyspepsia 536.8	Hyperten heart dis NOS 402.90	Obesity 278.0	Pul heart dis unsp 416.9
Anemia unsp 285.9	Cerebrovasc dis other 437.0	Edema 782.3	Hypopotassemia 276.8	Osteoarthrosis unsp 715.90	Pyrexia unk origin 780.6
Anemia protein def 281.9	Cerebral Thrombosis 434.0	Emphysema other 492.8	Hypothyroidism unsp 244.9	Osteoporosis NOS 733.00	Renal failure 586
Angina pectoris unsp 413.9	Cerebrovasc dis NOS 437.9	Esophagitis 530.1	Impacted cerumen 380.4	Osteoarthrosis gen 715.0	Rheumatoid arthritis 714.0
Anxiety state NOS 300.00	Chest pain NEC 786.59	Gastritis unsp 535.5	Intermed cor syndrome 411.1	Other abn blood chem 790.6	Rhythm disord, other 427.89
Aortic valve disord 424.1	Chest pain NOS 786.50	Gen osteoarthrosis 715.09	Intest obstruction NOS 560.9	Other comp med care 999.9	Senile dementia 290.0
Aortocoronary bypass V45.81	Chr airway obstr NEC 496	Gout NOS 274.9	Intracereb hemorr 431	Other bursitis 727.3	Sx: abd pain, cramps 789.0
Apoplexia 436	Chr isch heart dis NEC 414.8	Gouty arthritis 274.0	Irritable colon 564.1	Other cellulitis unsp 682.9	Sx: nausea & vomiting 787.0
Arrhythmia 427.9	Chr renal failure 585	Heart dis isch NEC 411.8	Isch heart dis unsp chr 414.9	Pain in limb 729.5	Sx: shortness breath 786.09
Arthropathy unsp 716.9	Cirrhosis liver 571.5	Heart fail congestive 428.0	Isch heart dis chronic 414.0	Painful respiration 786.52	Sx: headache face pain 784.0
ASCVD 429.2	Constipation 564.0	Heart failure NOS 428.9	Kidney disord unsp 593.9	Palpitations 785.1	Syncope & collapse 780.2
Asthma w/o status 493.90	Contact dermatitis 692.9	Hematuria benign ess 599.7	Lumbago 724.2	Parkinson disease 332.0	Systemic lupus eryth 710.0
Atherosclerosis gen 440.9	Convulsions, seizures 780.3	Hemiplegia 342.9	Lymphomas NEC 202.8	Peptic ulcer unsp 533.9	Thyrotoxicosis NOS 242.9
Atrial fibrillation 427.31	Cough 786.2	Hemorr GI tract unsp 578.9	Malaise & fatigue 780.7	Periph vasc dis unsp 443.9	Trans cereb isch unsp 435.9
Atrial flutter 427.32	Cystitis unsp 595.9	Hemorr rectum & anus 569.3	Melena blood in stool 587.1	Pernicious anemia 281.0	Unsp septicemia 038.9
backache unsp 724.5	Dehydration 276.5	Hemorrhoids unsp 455.6	Mitral valve disord 424.0	Pharyngitis acute 462	Unsp sinusitis chr 473.9
B hypertensive hrt dis 402.1	Depress disord NEC 311	Herpes zoster 053.9	Mixed hyperlipid 272.2	Phlebitis unsp 451.9	Urinary tract infection 599.0
	Diabetes w/comp NOS 250.00		Myalgia unsp 729.1	Pleurisy unsp 511.9	

UNLISTED DIAGNOSIS   CODE   DESCRIPTION

REMARKS OR INSTRUCTIONS

RELEASE & ASSIGNMENT

I authorize release of any information necessary to process my insurance claim and assign and request payment directly to my physicians.

SIGNED _____   DATE _____

RECALL & RETURN

RETURN ☐ DAYS ☐ WEEKS ☐ MONTHS

NEXT APPOINTMENT

DATE _____ TIME _____ AM / PM

ACCOUNTING INFORMATION

PRIOR BALANCE	
TODAY'S CHARGES	
TOTAL DUE	
AMOUNT PAID	
NEW BALANCE	

©1992 PMIC   REV. 01/92

2-4 *A typical superbill from a doctor's office.* Practice Management Information Corporation.

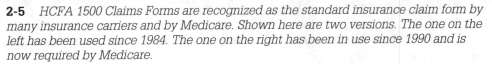

2-5 *HCFA 1500 Claims Forms are recognized as the standard insurance claim form by many insurance carriers and by Medicare. Shown here are two versions. The one on the left has been used since 1984. The one on the right has been in use since 1990 and is now required by Medicare.*

PLEASE
DO NOT
STAPLE
IN THIS
AREA

CARRIER

☐☐ PICA

HEALTH INSURANCE CLAIM FORM

PICA ☐☐

1. MEDICARE	MEDICAID	CHAMPUS	CHAMPVA	GROUP HEALTH PLAN	FECA BLK LUNG	OTHER	1a. INSURED'S I.D. NUMBER	(FOR PROGRAM IN ITEM 1)
☐ (Medicare #)	☐ (Medicaid #)	☐ (Sponsor's SSN)	☐ (VA File #)	☐ (SSN or ID)	☐ (SSN)	☐ (ID)		

2. PATIENT'S NAME (Last Name, First Name, Middle Initial)

3. PATIENT'S BIRTH DATE MM DD YY   SEX   M ☐   F ☐

4. INSURED'S NAME (Last Name, First Name, Middle Initial)

5. PATIENT'S ADDRESS (No., Street)

6. PATIENT RELATIONSHIP TO INSURED
Self ☐ Spouse ☐ Child ☐ Other ☐

7. INSURED'S ADDRESS (No., Street)

CITY   STATE

8. PATIENT STATUS
Single ☐ Married ☐ Other ☐
Employed ☐ Full-Time Student ☐ Part-Time Student ☐

CITY   STATE

ZIP CODE   TELEPHONE (Include Area Code) ( )

ZIP CODE   TELEPHONE (INCLUDE AREA CODE) ( )

9. OTHER INSURED'S NAME (Last Name, First Name, Middle Initial)

10. IS PATIENT'S CONDITION RELATED TO:

11. INSURED'S POLICY GROUP OR FECA NUMBER

a. OTHER INSURED'S POLICY OR GROUP NUMBER

a. EMPLOYMENT? (CURRENT OR PREVIOUS)
☐ YES ☐ NO

a. INSURED'S DATE OF BIRTH MM DD YY   SEX   M ☐   F ☐

b. OTHER INSURED'S DATE OF BIRTH MM DD YY   SEX   M ☐ F ☐

b. AUTO ACCIDENT?   PLACE (State)
☐ YES ☐ NO ☐

b. EMPLOYER'S NAME OR SCHOOL NAME

c. EMPLOYER'S NAME OR SCHOOL NAME

c. OTHER ACCIDENT?
☐ YES ☐ NO

c. INSURANCE PLAN NAME OR PROGRAM NAME

d. INSURANCE PLAN NAME OR PROGRAM NAME

10d. RESERVED FOR LOCAL USE

d. IS THERE ANOTHER HEALTH BENEFIT PLAN?
☐ YES ☐ NO   If yes, return to and complete item 9 a-d.

READ BACK OF FORM BEFORE COMPLETING & SIGNING THIS FORM.
12. PATIENT'S OR AUTHORIZED PERSON'S SIGNATURE I authorize the release of any medical or other information necessary to process this claim. I also request payment of government benefits either to myself or to the party who accepts assignment below.

SIGNED _____ DATE _____

13. INSURED'S OR AUTHORIZED PERSON'S SIGNATURE I authorize payment of medical benefits to the undersigned physician or supplier for services described below.

SIGNED _____

14. DATE OF CURRENT: MM DD YY ◄ ILLNESS (First symptom) OR INJURY (Accident) OR PREGNANCY(LMP)

15. IF PATIENT HAS HAD SAME OR SIMILAR ILLNESS. GIVE FIRST DATE MM DD YY

16. DATES PATIENT UNABLE TO WORK IN CURRENT OCCUPATION MM DD YY FROM TO MM DD YY

17. NAME OF REFERRING PHYSICIAN OR OTHER SOURCE

17a. I.D. NUMBER OF REFERRING PHYSICIAN

18. HOSPITALIZATION DATES RELATED TO CURRENT SERVICES MM DD YY FROM TO MM DD YY

19. RESERVED FOR LOCAL USE

20. OUTSIDE LAB? ☐ YES ☐ NO $ CHARGES

21. DIAGNOSIS OR NATURE OF ILLNESS OR INJURY. (RELATE ITEMS 1,2,3 OR 4 TO ITEM 24E BY LINE)
1. ⌊___ . ___⌋   3. ⌊___ . ___⌋
2. ⌊___ . ___⌋   4. ⌊___ . ___⌋

22. MEDICAID RESUBMISSION CODE   ORIGINAL REF. NO.

23. PRIOR AUTHORIZATION NUMBER

24. A DATE(S) OF SERVICE From MM DD YY	To MM DD YY	B Place of Service	C Type of Service	D PROCEDURES, SERVICES, OR SUPPLIES (Explain Unusual Circumstances) CPT/HCPCS MODIFIER	E DIAGNOSIS CODE	F $ CHARGES	G DAYS OR UNITS	H EPSDT Family Plan	I EMG	J COB	K RESERVED FOR LOCAL USE
1											
2											
3											
4											
5											

25. FEDERAL TAX I.D. NUMBER   SSN EIN ☐ ☐

26. PATIENT'S ACCOUNT NO.

27. ACCEPT ASSIGNMENT? (For govt. claims, see back) ☐ YES ☐ NO

28. TOTAL CHARGE $

29. AMOUNT PAID $

30. BALANCE DUE $

31. SIGNATURE OF PHYSICIAN OR SUPPLIER INCLUDING DEGREES OR CREDENTIALS (I certify that the statements on the reverse apply to this bill and are made a part thereof.)

SIGNED _____ DATE _____

32. NAME AND ADDRESS OF FACILITY WHERE SERVICES WERE RENDERED (If other than home or office)

33. PHYSICIAN'S, SUPPLIER'S BILLING NAME, ADDRESS, ZIP CODE & PHONE #

PIN# _____ GRP# _____

(APPROVED BY AMA COUNCIL ON MEDICAL SERVICE 8/88)

PLEASE PRINT OR TYPE

FORM HCFA-1500 (12-90)
FORM OWCP-1500   FORM RRB-1500
FORM AMA OP050391

PHYSICIAN OR SUPPLIER INFORMATION

PATIENT AND INSURED INFORMATION

2-5 *Continued.*

building the Tower of Babel. For this reason, doctors came to expect patients to bring in and file their own claims.

Then, in the early 1980s the American Medical Association established a task force to develop a uniform physician reporting form acceptable to government agencies and to commercial carriers. The result of their work was the Uniform Health Insurance Claim Form, or HCFA 1500 Form. Originally issued in 1984, it was revised in 1990 to eliminate doctors' written explanations of unusual services or circumstances to support their fee. The new version, called the Red Form (because it is printed in red ink) instead only allows space for doctor to use the standard codes representing the diagnosis and procedure performed. It was also changed to require more information about the patient's secondary insurance carrier, so as to ensure the primary carrier would not pay duplicate benefits.

As of August 1992, all claims to Medicare filed on paper must use the revised HCFA 1500 form. As you might expect, there is now some confusion about using the new and old HCFA 1500 forms. One billing expert I consulted, said that many commercial carriers won't accept the new version, because they find it confusing.

Depending on the doctor's office efficiency, the HCFA form may be typed on the same day as the patient's visit or it may take several days before the billing person completes the claim form for filing. Once completed, it is then mailed to the insurance carrier. Meanwhile, to keep track of the patient's account, the billing person usually writes the charges for the visit in a daily log (often called a pegboard system) and/or a patient ledger card. See FIG. 2-6 for an example of a patient ledger card.

XYZ Medical Practice
1235 Main Street
Anytown, USA

Date	Family Member	Description	Charges	Credits		Current Balance
				Payments	Adjustments	

2-6 *A ledger card is often used by a doctor's office to keep track of each patient's visits, charges, and payments. Obviously, a computerized version of this ledger would be much easier to use.*

STEP 6   The mailed claim form eventually arrives at the insurance carrier's office, where it is opened, screened for completeness, assigned a control number, microfilmed for recordkeeping, and then manually entered into a computer system by a claims examiner. If it is error-free, the physician receives payment for the claim anywhere from 15–60 days, depending on the carrier.

However, if the claim contains errors, such as missing information or a wrong diagnosis or procedure code, it is returned to the physician, and more time passes while the claim is corrected and resubmitted. It is even said that some claims with errors are never returned to the provider, but become "lost" in the system! In fact, at the time of this writing, ABC ran several reports on the potential bankruptcy of Blue Cross carriers in many states, including Florida, where millions of claims were simply shredded into trash because the Blue Cross office could not handle the volume of incoming claims.

In the past, commercial insurance carriers were known to take advantage of the many errors in claim forms to profit from the "float" on the money not paid. In fact, it was common knowledge in the insurance industry that many carriers preferred receiving paper claims where the error rate was very high so that they could pay out more slowly. Each day a provider was not paid was another day of money in the bank for the carriers.

It was also commonly said that claims examiners at insurance carriers were not supposed to check a claim to help correct it, but to reject it if possible. In other words, if an examiner found an error, the claim was immediately rejected and no further error checking took place. The result of this was that if a provider reprocessed a claim that contained an error, but the claim actually had several errors, the claim could pass back and forth between the provider and the insurance carrier several times before finally (if ever) being paid. Therefore, some claims took as long as 60 to 90 days to be paid, and the physician running a practice with thousands of dollars per day in overhead was clearly losing money.

Today, with the cost of labor rising and interest rates falling, some insurance companies are now losing money because of paper claims, but it is probably still true that many of them profit from the delays in processing error-laden paper claims.

STEP 7   When a claim is correct, the insurance carrier or Medicare sends out a document called an Explanation of Benefits (EOB) or an Explanation of Medicare Benefits (EOMB) to either the physician who takes assignment, the patient, or both. The EOB or EOMB shows the amount charged, the amount allowed, and the amount paid for each procedure. Remember that Medicare and most commercial insurance policies pay only 80 percent of the allowed charge for physician services, leaving the patient responsible for a 20 percent coinsurance.

If the physician has accepted assignment, the check is received with the EOB/EOMB. If the physician did not accept assignment, only the patient would receive the EOB with the check, and would then need to forward a payment to the physician.

STEP 8   In an office using traditional accounting methods, any payments are logged onto the patient's ledger and to the daily accounts receivable journal. To keep reminding patients about their due balances and copayments, the physician would also send out monthly statements, often by simply photocopying the ledger cards showing the balance due—a time-consuming task that can take a billing clerk hours or days.

STEP 9   If the patient has secondary insurance, a new paper claim form must also be filed along with a copy of the EOB from the primary insurance carrier showing how much has already been paid. It might then take another 30 days to receive the balance due from a secondary insurer.

The foregoing steps describe the basic billing operation of many medical offices that operate manually. Many practices may be partially computerized and will likely have some kind of medical billing software that maintains accounts receivable books and even prints out on HCFA 1500 forms. However, most of these offices are not doing electronic claims processing using communications software and a modem. Under the best conditions, filing paper claims is still a risky business. With the expense and effort required to fill them out, and the time delay to get reimbursed, combined with the anxiety of dealing with our unpredictable postal service and insurance companies which love to deny claims, you might say that it's like throwing money away. Few people doubt that the days of paper claims are numbered.

The medical office and electronic claims

In an office that utilizes electronic claims processing, the first step mentioned previously is the same, but the process differs dramatically after that. Electronic claims processing removes the claim away from typing paper and eliminates the long time lag between sending in a bill to getting paid. Practice management software also simplifies the accounts receivable recordkeeping part of the job and helps to assure greater efficiency and productivity in the office.

STEP 1   The first step in an electronic office is to set up the software. The setup is perhaps the most time-consuming phase for a billing service, but once it is done it's done, and electronic claims processing takes considerably less time than handling paper forms.

How the setup is done will vary according to the software you are using, but in general, medical billing software involves creating database "records" for each of the patients, doctors, and insurance companies used by the practice, as well as for all the diagnostic and procedure codes and other kinds of information relevant to claims processing (insurance ID numbers, assignment eligibility, and so on). If the software you choose also performs practice management functions (i.e., contains some level of accounts receivable recordkeeping) setup will also include entering account balances for each established patient.

Most medical billing software today works by giving the operator a main menu of basic functions performed by the software. The main menu items then lead to sub-menus for each of the more detailed functions available. In some software, the main menu is a vertical numbered list, from which you would select the number of the desired function. In other software, the main menu is displayed horizontally across the top of the screen, with pull-down submenus that appear as the cursor moves to highlight each main menu option. Figure 2-7 shows a vertically displayed main menu, with examples of submenu choices and FIG. 2-8 shows a horizontally displayed main menu, with submenus that might be available under each main menu function.

Please note that, because the medical software business is quite competitive, and all software packages are considered proprietary, the screen designs you see throughout this chapter are composite simulations to help you visualize how the software works. These screens do not show specific designs or programming from any single software package unless otherwise identified.

Whichever design format your software uses, the setup procedures are usually similar. In most cases, you go to the main menu, select an option such as Set Up or Maintenance, and then you key-in one or more screens of background information for each patient, each doctor in the practice, each insurance company, and so on. For example, if you were entering patients, you would proceed from the main menu through any submenus until you reached a Patient screen that contained the fields to fill in for the first patient. Each field is a discrete piece of information such as name, address, social security number, the primary and secondary insurance company with the insured's ID number and the group number, the employer, and so on. As you can imagine, each patient record contains dozens of fields which comprise a complete record. Figure 2-9 shows a list of the patient fields that are typically required in many software packages.

Similarly, every doctor in the practice will have a record containing his or her address, tax ID number, and many other ID numbers from different insurance companies. Figure 2-10 shows typical screens for filling in patient information and provider information.

Finally, many software programs allow you to key in and store in a data library the most commonly used diagnostic and procedure codes for each provider or practice. Since there are thousands of these codes, inputting 50 or 100 of the most frequently used codes simplifies claims preparation when you are processing actual transactions. Rather than having to type in each code, you need only to place your cursor on a code already entered, hit the tab or

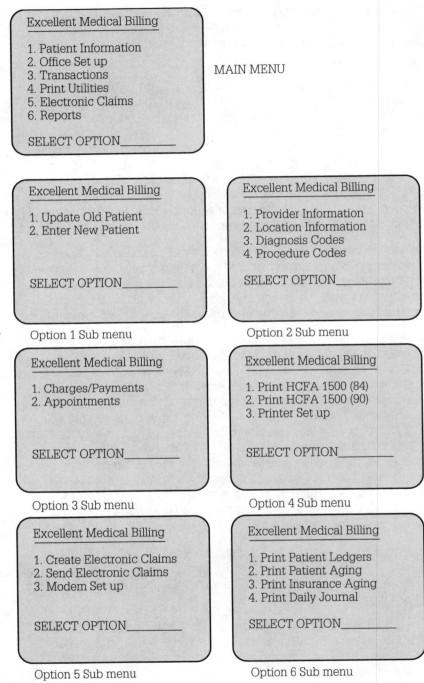

Excellent Medical Billing

1. Patient Information
2. Office Set up
3. Transactions
4. Print Utilities
5. Electronic Claims
6. Reports

SELECT OPTION_____

MAIN MENU

Excellent Medical Billing

1. Update Old Patient
2. Enter New Patient

SELECT OPTION_____

Option 1 Sub menu

Excellent Medical Billing

1. Provider Information
2. Location Information
3. Diagnosis Codes
4. Procedure Codes

SELECT OPTION_____

Option 2 Sub menu

Excellent Medical Billing

1. Charges/Payments
2. Appointments

SELECT OPTION_____

Option 3 Sub menu

Excellent Medical Billing

1. Print HCFA 1500 (84)
2. Print HCFA 1500 (90)
3. Printer Set up

SELECT OPTION_____

Option 4 Sub menu

Excellent Medical Billing

1. Create Electronic Claims
2. Send Electronic Claims
3. Modem Set up

SELECT OPTION_____

Option 5 Sub menu

Excellent Medical Billing

1. Print Patient Ledgers
2. Print Patient Aging
3. Print Insurance Aging
4. Print Daily Journal

SELECT OPTION_____

Option 6 Sub menu

2-7
*Typical vertical
menu-driven
medical billing software.*

TRANSACTIONS	MAINTENANCE	BILLING	REPORTS	UTILITIES
Charges/Payments	Patients	Print Statements	Daily Log	Printer Set up
Batch Payments	Providers	Print Labels	Ledgers	HCFA Forms
	Locations	Electronic Claims	Aging Reports	Modem Set up
	Diagnosis	Paper Claims	Analysis Reports	
	Procedures			

2-8   *Typical horizontal, menu-driven medical billing software program.*

return key, and the code is duplicated on the claim screen (called *pointing and shooting*).

As mentioned earlier, the advantage of today's sophisticated medical claims software is that error checking is usually performed while the typist is keying in information. For example, the software may prevent you from keying in an alphabetic character where only numeric characters are acceptable, or it may beep if you have keyed in only nine digits where ten are expected.

Assuming set up has been done, and the billing service is up and running for electronic processing, let's now contrast the remaining steps of electronic billing to paper claims.

STEP 2   As with paper claims, each patient contact generates a superbill indicating the nature of the visit. The next step involves simply getting the superbill from the physician to the billing service. Some billing services pick up the documents from their clients on a daily or weekly basis, while others obtain them through the mail or via fax machine.

STEP 3   The next step for the billing service is to key in the data for each patient encounter. Nearly all the billing services owners I spoke with estimated that this data entry takes less than one minute per claim. The software only prompts you for the fields necessary to complete a claim because the patient's background record is already in the database. These fields generally include: diagnosis codes, procedure codes, fees, dates of service, location of service, and other data specific to the patient/physician encounter. (Obviously, if the patient is new, the billing service will need to go through the set-up routine for that patient.)The software will usually block entry of incorrect data types or warn about missing information.

Last name
First name
Middle intial
Address 1
Address 2
City
State
Zip Code
Home phone
Work phone
Date of birth
Sex
Patient category (private, insurance,
medicare, medicaid, welfare)
Primary physician's code
Location of service (office = 1, hospital = 2,
branch office = 3, home = 4,etc.)
Referring physician
Facility of services
Date of last service
Date of last payment
Amount of last payment
Date of last statement
Is the condition related to employment? (Y/N)
Is the condition related to an accident? (Y/N)
Date of accident
State in which accident occured
Date of illness/injury/or pregnancy
Date first consulted doctor
Date of similar previous injury
Date of admission to hospital
Date of discharge from hospital
Disability from date
Disability to date
First insurance carrier
Insured person's ID #
Is the insured person related to the patient? (Y/N)
Accepts assignment (Y/N)
Bill the carrier (Y/N)
Patient's signature on file (Y/N)
Pay benefits to patient (Y/N)
Insured person's name (if different from patient)
Medicare coverage
Secondary insurance company
Second insurance related to insured
Accept assignment from second insured (Y/N)
Bill other carrier (Y/N)
Third insurance company/medigap
Medicare other policy prefix
Third insurer/Medicare/supplementary
insurance ID #

Accept assignment from third
 insurer (Y/N)
Bill other carrier (Y/N)
Marital status
Employment status (full-time, part-time,
 retired, no)
Student status (full, part, no)
Prior authorization #
Recall date/time
First diagnosis
Second diagnosis
Third diagnosis
Fourth diagnosis
Primary responsible party (name)
Secondary responsible party
Tertiary responsible party

2-9 *Fields in a typical patient record.*

```
PATIENT RECORD

        Patient Number:  [          ]      Employer:
        Patient Name:                          Address 1:
        Social Security #:                     Address 2:
        Address 1:                             City:
        Address 2:                             Zip:
        City:
        State:                             Primary Insurance:
        Zip:                               Assignment:
        Sex:                               Policy #:
        Marital Status:                    Secondary Insurance:
        Student Status:                    Policy #:
```

2-10
Patient information and provider screens.

```
PROVIDER RECORD

        Physician Number:  [          ]    Tax ID:
        Address 1:                         Medicare PIN:
        Address 2:                         Medicare PIN:
        City:                              Champus PIN:
        State:                             Blue Cross PIN:
        Zip:                               Commercial PIN:
        Phone:
        Social Security #:
```

STEP 4   After the billing service has input all the claims for a single provider or carrier, the operator typically selects the function for "batch" electronic claims filing, allowing an entire group of claims to be sent at once. The software may first prepare a summary report of the claims to be transmited for you to verify before going online. Some software also compresses the data file to increase transmission speed.

STEP 5   The next step is transmission of the claims to the insurance carrier over telephone lines using the communications component of your billing software and a modem.

Most billing services do not transmit claims directly to each insurance carrier, but rather to a central "clearinghouse" that functions as an intermediary between the billing service and the insurers. One reason this is so is that the electronic data formats still differ among insurance companies. Clearinghouses rectify these discrepancies by translating one claims language to another in a matter of seconds. Claims for your local Medicare carrier are translated one way, while claims for Aetna or other commercial carriers are translated in their respective languages.

Billing software is usually configured to work with only one clearinghouse, because it must be programmed (at some expense) to tie-in with the computers at that house. That clearinghouse can translate claims to suit most Medicare carriers in the country, and sometimes for other clearinghouses. The National Electronic Information Corporation (NEIC) is one which functions as a clearinghouse between first-line clearinghouses and over 35 of the largest commercial insurance companies.

A billing service does not have to work through a clearinghouse, but in some cases can transmit claims directly to local carriers such as Blue Cross or regional Medicare carriers. To do this, however, you may need to purchase additional software packages. Depending upon your software, this can prevent the efficiency you aim to offer. Some packages enable you to transmit Medicare claims directly to the HCFA carrier in your area while sending commercial claims to a clearinghouse. This will save money because you will not need to pay a clearinghouse to process your Medicare claims.

Clearinghouses can, however, serve another vital purpose—*online* error checking. The quality and completeness of this checking seems to vary by clearinghouse, but with the combined error checking of most billing software packages and that of most clearinghouses, the error rate on electronic claims is reportedly a minimal 3 percent.

The long-term advantage of clearinghouses is that they effectively save time and money for billing services. Rather than making dozens of transmissions to download claims to every insurance carrier your clients need to bill, you can process all your claims at once, usually with a convenient toll-free 800 number. Likewise, using a single claims software package rather than several simplifies and speeds processing for your clients.

Clearinghouse services are not free, however. Most charge between 50 and 55 cents per claim, sometimes added to an annual registration fee and a per-doctor set-up fee. Also, to ensure billing services know how to use the software, they often require a simple test of submitting twenty or so claims to demonstrate that the billing service operator can code and transmit correctly. The sidebar: The role of clearinghouses contains more information on clearinghouses.

"Clearinghouses are like post offices between cultures," said Karen Weber, Regional Sales Manager for GTE Health Systems in Phoenix, Arizona. "We take letters (claims) mailed in one language, translate them, and deliver them to their proper destination. It's up to the sender to be sure the envelope is the right size, but it's up to us to make sure the data gets there."

What Ms. Weber was referring to is the growing business of clearinghouses handling millions of electronic medical claims zipping around the country over phone lines on their way to insurance companies in every state. With more than 300 carriers nationwide, each with its own format specification for medical claims, clearinghouses serve a vital role in translating codes from one format to another. Without clearinghouses in place, hospitals and doctors would need to maintain dozens of software programs that each work with only one or two insurance companies, and require maintenance for every minor change a carrier makes.

Clearinghouses clearly are useful then, and appear to be getting increasingly popular. As Bob Werder, Chairman of Electronic Tabulating Service (ETS), one of the largest clearinghouses working with billing services says, "The healthcare industry is an industry in gridlock; our country cannot afford to have a healthcare system like we have now. We are part of the solution." He went on to explain how initially, doctors weren't interested in ECP and insurance companies weren't getting enough volume to seriously invest in the process—so neither considered there was much of a future in electronic claims. Then it became too expensive to continue manual claims submission. Today, ETS processes several million claims annually, and their volume is doubling each year. Most of the processing is done directly between their computers and those of the billing services. However, Mr. Werder added that ETS still doesn't have computer connections for about 20 percent of the claims they receive and must then "drop them to paper." This means that ETS prints the claim on a HCFA 1500 form and mails it to the insurance company. Nevertheless, the benefit of the claim having been checked and edited for errors by the ETS system still accrues, and it is more likely to be accurate and thus promptly paid.

ETS appears to be the clearinghouse of choice among billing software vendors and commands the lion's share of the market. Next is GTE Health Systems, which runs EMC Express, a clearinghouse operation purchased from General Electric in 1988 when GE exited that business. Since that time, GTE's business like ETS's, has skyrocketed.

With skyrocketing success comes a price tag. ETS charges a $300 per year registration fee for billing centers plus a $50 set-up fee for each of your clients. (A client is single physician or practice submitting bills under one ID number.) In addition, ETS charges $0.50 per processed claim, $0.25 for rejected claims, and postage at cost for claims forwarded on paper. GTE does not levy an annual fee or set up fees, but charges $0.55 per claim. ETS and GTE are two examples of clearinghouses; there are others, such as NEIC in Secaucus, New Jersey and Teleclaims in Birmingham, Alabama.

It would be worthwhile to consider differences in the quality and cost of service that each clearinghouse can provide you when choosing your software. For example, some clearinghouses receive calls at any time, while others at prescribed times, often late evening. Some clearinghouses immediately confirm your transmission, letting you know how many claims were received and processed. Others provide excellent error checking, including a detailed report identifying the problem in each rejected claim. You should also find out whether the clearinghouse associated with your software choice has links to the insurance companies and Medicare carrier you will need. Last, if you are billing dental claims, you need to make sure your clearinghouse can handle them. As you've undoubtedly observed, you'll need to do some careful planning when selecting your software, since you generally must use the clearinghouse your software vendor has chosen to work with.

There are several reasons why clearinghouses are likely to continue their role into the future. First, America is accustomed to choices. As a result, millions of people live in states other than the state of their insurance company of choice. Employers buy health insurance from a variety of sources too. Second, we are likely light-years away from a centrally computerized national health system, and even regionalization of services will still require intermediaries. Thirdly, the clearinghouses are paving the way of their own future, by offering new services such as electronic pre-authorization approvals, electronic eligibility searches (for physicians needing to find out what the insurance will pay and how much) and electronic funds transfer. As Karen Weber succinctly put it, "The health clearinghouse business today is where banking was fifteen years ago. It can only get better!"

STEP 6   After receiving claims, the clearinghouse notifies the billing service (usually within minutes online), about the claims received and processed to each insurance carrier, and those rejected because of errors. The billing service can then retain a paper copy of this report, called an Audit/Edit Report or Sender Log, for recordkeeping. This feedback is valuable because the billing service can correct rejected claims and resubmit them immediately. If the error relates to the physician's coding or a medical issue, however, it is advisable that the billing service confer with that doctor's office before resubmitting the claim.

Billing services that also perform practice management functions for healthcare providers save their clients time and effort in other ways. Several additional functions that a billing service might provide are:

Whenever a claim is paid to a physician who takes assignment, an EOB is received along with the check. The billing service can continue to manage each patient's account electronically by getting a copy of the EOB from the practice and recording payments. Because payments must be marked against specific items in the bill (called open item accounting), the best billing software enables the billing service to keep track of exactly which procedures were paid for. Any procedure for which payment is denied can therefore be specifically identified and appealed.

Computerization of all charges and payments also allows a billing service to perform accounting functions accurately and efficiently. Through a few simple commands, the software can be instructed to print monthly patient statements for any balances due, along with customized reminders or notes to the patient. However, if the patient has secondary insurance coverage, the billing service must also submit a paper claim to obtain reimbursement. Commercial carriers do not accept electronically submitted claims for secondary coverages because they want a copy of the primary EOB with the original claim to verify what has already been paid. Medicare, which automatically handles Medi-Medi or MediGap secondary payers, is the exception to this.

Billing services using state-of-the art billing software can provide the physician's practice with a variety of monthly reports, such as account aging reports by patient or carrier. Other reports can help a practice understand which procedures account for most of its revenues or from which physicians the most referrals are made (called a Christmas list). Figure 2-11 is a sampling of reports a typical practice management function software package might provide.

A billing center offering complete practice management may also engage more complex billing issues, such as advising the physician about frequently changing diagnostic and procedural codes which in turn determine the amount the physician will be reimbursed. The billing service might also provide consultation on fee schedules, Medicare/Medicaid and commercial insurance regulations, and reimbursement trends.

Working hand-in-hand with a healthcare provider, a good billing center can serve the interests of both the medical practice and the patients. Only insurance companies benefit when claims are not paid on time. Perhaps this fact alone explains why billing services have so quickly been able to capture a growing number of healthcare providers who simply want what's fair—to be promptly paid for their services.

```
                        Aging Report Summary
--------------------------------------------------------------------------
               Past due ->   ->  ->  ->  ->  ->  ->  ->
Type           0 - 30        31-60         61-90         91+
--------------------------------------------------------------------------

Patient Accnt's  2524.00      652.00        829.00        332.00
      %          58%          15%           19%           08%

Insurance        7924.00      879.00        321.00        212.00
      %          85%          09%           03%           02%
--------------------------------------------------------------------------
Totals           10448.00     1531.00       1150.00       544.00
--------------------------------------------------------------------------

Total patient receivables:   $ 4337.00
Total insurance receivables: $ 9336.00
Total receivables:           $13673.00
```

```
                     Summary Aging Report By Ins Co
-----------------------------------------------------------------------------
             Past due -> -> -> -> -> -> -> -> -> ->
      Name   0 - 30      31- 60       61- 90      90+         Totals
-----------------------------------------------------------------------------

01   Medicare    435.00    1359.00      760.00     1232.00      3786.00
02   Medicaid     95.00     327.00      212.00       72.00       706.00
03   U Risk Co.  333.00    2322.00      987.00     4229.00      7871.00
04   YPay, Inc.  945.00     879.00      222.00      809.00      2855.00


Report Totals   1808.00    4887.00     2181.00     6342.00     15218.00
```

2-11 *Sample of reports many practice management software packages can generate each month to show the aged balances of patients and even insurance companies.*

Knowledge & skills needed

Some home businesses are easy to start, while others require a broad range of skills and knowledge. On a scale of one to ten, with ten being the greatest measure of difficulty, medical billing is probably between five and eight for the average person. In researching this book, I met owners who were able to jump right in, with no medical experience or knowledge, and develop their businesses within a few months. I also met people who initially felt uncertain and overwhelmed by the vocabulary, the computer software, or simply the marketing and selling necessary to get clients.

Indeed, many of the business opportunity companies that sell medical billing software and training screen their potential buyers, because they deem it important to work with people who are serious about this business and can uphold the reputation they want their affiliates to have. Understandably, business opportunity companies prefer to work with successful entrepreneurs who will further their interests.

To run a successful medical billing service, you'll need to give attention to three areas of knowledge and skills.

❑ A moderate to high knowledge level in the health claims business, especially medical coding, Medicare/Medicaid, and commercial insurance regulations.
❑ A low to moderate skill level with computer hardware and software.
❑ A moderate to high level of knowledge and skills in business, including marketing, sales, and accounting.

While it is best to have such knowledge and skills at the outset of your new business venture, they can be learned after you start, if necessary. Any one of these areas can be mastered in a few months to a year, but the greater your learning curve the longer it will take to get your business off and running.

Of course, dedication, persistence, and personal outlook have much to do with your ability to traverse the hurdles. If you enter any venture thinking you cannot learn what it takes to succeed, or that you can only handle half the task, you will almost certainly fulfill only that limited vision you have for yourself. You may find that you have to s-t-r-e-t-c-h your thinking and your commitment if you are to succeed.

After reading the following sections, which explain the three areas of knowledge and skill needed for medical billing, try the following informal method of charting your challenge. First, choose a unit of time in which you feel comfortable learning something new; perhaps a month, three months, or six months. Then, for each skill/knowledge area, plot your starting point on a scale of one to ten. For example, if you have a medical background with some computer skills, but no marketing or selling experience, you might give yourself an eight for Medical Knowledge, a four for Computer Knowledge, and a two for Business Knowledge. Then, using those numbers as your starting points, plot your learning curve for each area over the course of time your have allocated for each area. Figure 2-12 shows how the learning curves might differ for a person with a nursing or medical front-office background and a person with sales experience but no medical background.

The purpose of this informal exercise is to help you become aware of your strengths as well as those areas where you will need to concentrate some effort. If you find that you have a low learning curve in only one area, you may be more inclined to move your business plans along quickly. On the other hand, if you find that you have two or three steep curves, it may be better for you to begin preparing yourself in those areas before investing in software or other business paraphernalia. Remember, do this exercise after you have read the following sections presenting a brief preview of each knowledge or skill you need.

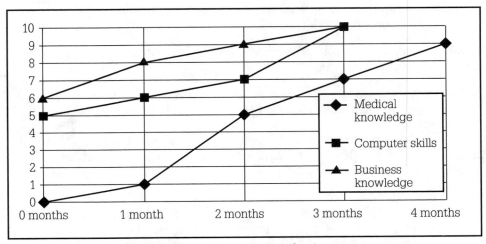

Graph of an entrepreneur with previous experience in business

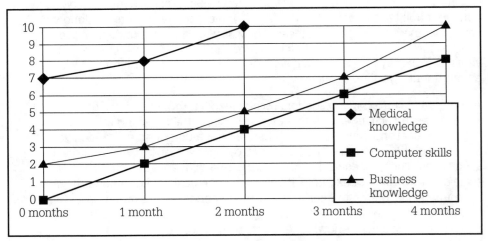

Graph of an entrepreneur with medical background, such as a nurse

2-12 *Plot for calculating your learning curve.*

AREA 1. Medical claims, coding & insurance industry

Earlier in this chapter, I referred to two sets of coding used by insurance carriers and the medical community. These codes are a kind of shorthand for the doctor's diagnosis and services performed. These code systems have come to the foreground of the health insurance industry in recent years due to increased computerization of the business. Understanding them is vital to operating a billing service. Rising healthcare costs and the growing reluctance of insurance carriers to overpay for services or pay for unwarranted procedures has created a greater emphasis on identifying the precise diagnoses and services performed. A brief review of these two code systems, the ICD-9-CM and the CPT/HCPCS follows.

ICD-9-CM diagnosis codes—prior to 1988, healthcare professionals described the reason for their encounter with a patient by writing out longhand the patient's complaints, condition, injury, symptoms and diagnosis. The 1988 Medicare Catastrophic Coverage Act, however, instituted ICD-9-CM coding—already in limited use. ICD-9-CM stands for International Classification of Diseases, 9th Revision, Clinical Modification. ICD-9-CM is now mandatory on all Medicare claims and nearly all commercial insurance claims.

Originally used for statistical recordkeeping and indexing, the ICD-9-CM codes are derived from a coding system developed by the World Health Organization (WHO). The WHO codes are modified for clinical use in the United States as HCFA and the U.S. Public Health Service periodically issue changes and addenda. The ICD-9-CM codes are usually printed in two volumes. The first volume contains the numeric listing from 001.0 through 999.9 (plus some additional "V" codes for vaccinations, some types of exams, treatments, and other issues, as well as a section of "E" codes for causes of external injuries such as traffic and boating accidents); the second volume is an alphabet listing of diseases. Figures 2-13 and 2-14 show page sections from each of these volumes. The ICD-10 will be released in 1995 or 1996.

These codes are used to facilitate automation of the claims process and control payments. Doctors must follow strict requirements when using the ICD-9-CM codes as proof that the services performed (upon which insurance payment is based) are supported by an appropriate and corresponding diagnosis. For example, a physician must use the most specific level of coding possible when the diagnosis is certain. In addition, the coding system does not allow for probable, suspected, questionable, or rule-out diagnoses. Therefore, when a physician does not know the appropriate diagnosis, codes that represent a description of symptoms or a "family history of" classification must be used. There are also rules about which codes must appear first (e.g., primary diagnosis), how many codes may be submitted (up to four), how to code late effects (effects appear before a no-longer-acute cause) as well as how to code for place of service, frequency of service, and level of service provided.

If the diagnosis codes are used incorrectly, the claim can be delayed, denied, or downcoded (i.e., the claims examiner can lower the value of the service because the diagnosis code does not correspond with the procedures listed). The result of these actions is that the provider's reimbursement is delayed or lowered.

As you can imagine, understanding and working with the ICD-9 diagnosis codes requires some knowledge of medical terminology. Although billing services are not responsible for the actual coding of the diagnosis and billing software usually permits you to maintain a library of frequently used codes for each of your clients, the value of your service will be greatly enhanced by

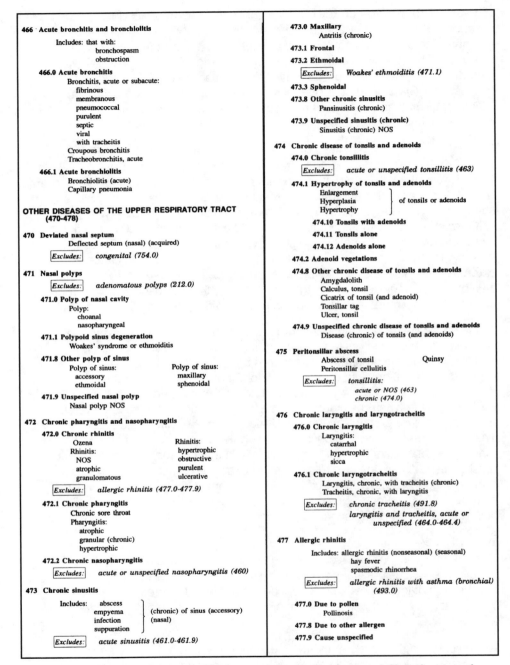

466 · Acute bronchitis and bronchiolitis

    Includes: that with:
           bronchospasm
           obstruction

    466.0 Acute bronchitis
      Bronchitis, acute or subacute:
        fibrinous
        membranous
        pneumococcal
        purulent
        septic
        viral
        with tracheitis
      Croupous bronchitis
      Tracheobronchitis, acute

    466.1 Acute bronchiolitis
      Bronchiolitis (acute)
      Capillary pneumonia

**OTHER DISEASES OF THE UPPER RESPIRATORY TRACT
(470-478)**

470 Deviated nasal septum
    Deflected septum (nasal) (acquired)
    | *Excludes:* | *congenital (754.0)* |

471 Nasal polyps
    | *Excludes:* | *adenomatous polyps (212.0)* |

    471.0 Polyp of nasal cavity
      Polyp:
        choanal
        nasopharyngeal

    471.1 Polypoid sinus degeneration
      Woakes' syndrome or ethmoiditis

    471.8 Other polyp of sinus
      Polyp of sinus: Polyp of sinus:
        accessory   maxillary
        ethmoidal   sphenoidal

    471.9 Unspecified nasal polyp
      Nasal polyp NOS

472 Chronic pharyngitis and nasopharyngitis
    472.0 Chronic rhinitis
      Ozena   Rhinitis:
      Rhinitis: hypertrophic
        NOS   obstructive
        atrophic   purulent
        granulomatous ulcerative
    | *Excludes:* | *allergic rhinitis (477.0-477.9)* |

    472.1 Chronic pharyngitis
      Chronic sore throat
      Pharyngitis:
        atrophic
        granular (chronic)
        hypertrophic

    472.2 Chronic nasopharyngitis
    | *Excludes:* | *acute or unspecified nasopharyngitis (460)* |

473 Chronic sinusitis
    Includes: abscess
             empyema   (chronic) of sinus (accessory)
             infection   (nasal)
             suppuration
    | *Excludes:* | *acute sinusitis (461.0-461.9)* |

473.0 Maxillary
    Antritis (chronic)

473.1 Frontal

473.2 Ethmoidal
    | *Excludes:* | *Woakes' ethmoiditis (471.1)* |

473.3 Sphenoidal

473.8 Other chronic sinusitis
    Pansinusitis (chronic)

473.9 Unspecified sinusitis (chronic)
    Sinusitis (chronic) NOS

474 Chronic disease of tonsils and adenoids
    474.0 Chronic tonsillitis
    | *Excludes:* | *acute or unspecified tonsillitis (463)* |

    474.1 Hypertrophy of tonsils and adenoids
      Enlargement
      Hyperplasia   of tonsils or adenoids
      Hypertrophy

      474.10 Tonsils with adenoids

      474.11 Tonsils alone

      474.12 Adenoids alone

    474.2 Adenoid vegetations

    474.8 Other chronic disease of tonsils and adenoids
      Amygdalolith
      Calculus, tonsil
      Cicatrix of tonsil (and adenoid)
      Tonsillar tag
      Ulcer, tonsil

    474.9 Unspecified chronic disease of tonsils and adenoids
      Disease (chronic) of tonsils (and adenoids)

475 Peritonsillar abscess
    Abscess of tonsil   Quinsy
    Peritonsillar cellulitis
    | *Excludes:* | *tonsillitis:* |
          acute or NOS (463)
          chronic (474.0)

476 Chronic laryngitis and laryngotracheitis
    476.0 Chronic laryngitis
      Laryngitis:
        catarrhal
        hypertrophic
        sicca

    476.1 Chronic laryngotracheitis
      Laryngitis, chronic, with tracheitis (chronic)
      Tracheitis, chronic, with laryngitis
    | *Excludes:* | *chronic tracheitis (491.8)* |
          laryngitis and tracheitis, acute or
          unspecified (464.0-464.4)

477 Allergic rhinitis
    Includes: allergic rhinitis (nonseasonal) (seasonal)
          hay fever
          spasmodic rhinorrhea
    | *Excludes:* | *allergic rhinitis with asthma (bronchial)* |
          (493.0)

    477.0 Due to pollen
      Pollinosis

    477.8 Due to other allergen

    477.9 Cause unspecified

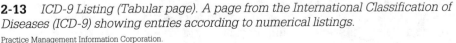

2-13 *ICD-9 Listing (Tabular page). A page from the International Classification of Diseases (ICD-9) showing entries according to numerical listings.*

Practice Management Information Corporation.

Dermatoneuritis of children 985.0
Dermatophiliasis 134.1
Dermatophytide —*see* Dermatophytosis
Dermatophytosis (Epidermophyton) (infection) (microsporum) (tinea) (Trichophyton) 110.9
   beard 110.0
   body 110.5
   deep seated 110.6
   fingernails 110.1
   foot 110.4
   groin 110.3
   hand 110.2
   nail 110.1
   perianal (area) 110.3
   scalp 110.0
   scrotal 110.8
   specified site NEC 110.8
   toenails 110.1
   vulva 110.8
Dermatopolyneuritis 985.0
Dermatorrhexis 756.83
   acquired 701.8
Dermatosclerosis (*see also* Scleroderma) 710.1
   localized 701.0
Dermatosis 709.9
   Andrews' 686.8
   atopic 691.8
   Bowen's (M8081/2)—*see* Neoplasm, skin, in situ
   bullous 694.9
      specified type NEC 694.8
   erythematosquamous 690
   exfoliativa 695.89
   factitial 698.4
   gonococcal 098.89
   herpetiformis 694.0
      juvenile 694.2
      senile 694.5
   hysterical 300.11
   menstrual NEC 709.8
   neutrophilic, acute febrile 695.89
   occupational (*see also* Dermatitis) 692.9
   papulosa nigra 709.8
   pigmentary NEC 709.0
      progressive 709.0
      Schamberg's 709.0
      Siemens–Bloch 757.33
   progressive pigmentary 709.0
   psychogenic 316
   pustular subcorneal 694.1
   Schamberg's (progressive pigmentary) 709.0
   senile NEC 709.3
   Unna's (seborrheic dermatitis) 690
Dermographia 708.3
Dermographism 708.3
Dermoid (cyst) (M9084/0)—*see also* Neoplasm, by site, benign

sore (*see also* Ulcer, skin) 707.9
Desertion (child) (newborn) 995.5
   specified person NEC 995.81
Desmoid (extra–abdominal) (tumor) (M8821/1)—*see also* Neoplasm, connective tissue, uncertain behavior
   abdominal (M8822/1)—*see* Neoplasm, connective tissue, uncertain behavior
Despondency 300.4
Desquamative dermatitis NEC 695.89
Destruction
   articular facet (*see also* Derangement, joint) 718.9
      vertebra 724.9
   bone 733.90
      syphilitic 095.5
   joint (*see also* Derangement, joint) 718.9
      sacroiliac 724.6
   kidney 593.89
   live fetus to facilitate birth NEC 763.8
   ossicles (ear) 385.24
   rectal sphincter 569.49
   septum (nasal) 478.1
   tuberculous NEC (*see also* Tuberculosis) 011.9
   tympanic membrane 384.82
   tympanum 385.89
   vertebral disc—*see* Degeneration, intervertebral disc
Destructiveness (*see also* Disturbance, conduct) 312.9
   adjustment reaction 309.3
Detachment
   cartilage—*see also* Sprain, by site
      knee—*see* Tear, meniscus
   cervix, annular 622.8
      complicating delivery 665.3
   choroid (old) (postinfectional) (simple) (spontaneous) 363.70
      hemorrhagic 363.72
      serous 363.71
   knee, medial meniscus (old) 717.3
      current injury 836.0
   ligament—*see* Sprain, by site
   placenta (premature)—*see* Placenta, separation
   retina (recent) 361.9
      with retinal defect (rhegmatogenous) 361.00
         giant tear 361.03
         multiple 361.02
         partial
            with
               giant tear 361.03
               multiple defects 361.02
               retinal dialysis (juvenile) 361.04
               single defect 361.01
         retinal dialysis (juvenile) 361.04
         single 361.01

2-14 *ICD-9 Listing (Alphabetic). A page from the International Classification of Diseases (ICD-9) showing entries arranged alphabetically.*

Practice Management Information Corporation.

your ability to understand what your clients are doing and help them avoid mistakes. Similarly, billing services that offer complete reimbursement management will need even more to be familiar with ICD-9 coding to competently consult with physicians about coding superbills, running the office efficiently, and maximizing reimbursement. Whenever your billing service can catch a mistake or offer advice that reduces errors or improves the reimbursement rate the value of your services to the physician increases.

Procedure codes   Procedure codes are similar to diagnosis codes, in that they represent the services performed by the healthcare provider. Prior to 1983 there were more than 120 different procedure coding systems in the United States. For each of the insurance companies they dealt with, doctors' office staffs had to be familiar with the codes currently in use. This is one reason why physicians passed responsibility for filing claims on to their patients, until HCFA established the current coding preference in 1983. Most insurance carriers now recognize and use this system. Today the system is quite complex and undergoes change each year. In 1992 a major change affected the way physicians are to code the nature of the patient/doctor contact for Medicare reporting.

The coding system is comprised of three levels. Level I codes are the largest and most utilized. This level is called CPT-4, which stands for Current Procedural Terminology, fourth edition. CPT is a list of more than 7000 codes and descriptions of services performed by all kinds of medical personnel. Updated and published each year by the American Medical Association, CPT tracks all currently accepted medical procedures. Obsolete procedures are dropped, as new procedures and nomenclature are added.

The main body of CPT codes is divided into six sections; each section represents a broad field of medicine, such as shown below. Each of these sections contains hundreds of specific procedures, each with a unique five-digit *numeric* code.

Evaluation and management	99200–99499
Anesthesiology	00100–01999
Surgery	10000–69999
Radiology, nuclear medicine, and diagnostic ultrasound	70000–79999
Pathology and laboratory	80000–89999
Medicine	90000–99199

Remember that most healthcare providers do not use all of these codes, because they typically specialize in one field of medicine. Most physicians commonly work with 100 or more codes on a regular basis and may preprint these on their superbills to make recordkeeping and filing claims more efficient.

While use of many procedural codes is straightforward, several areas cause confusion for doctors and billing specialists alike and are frequently the basis for errors. The Evaluation and Management Codes (E/M) were completely revised in 1992 for use with Medicare, although commercial carriers may continue to accept the old codes, often called *Visit codes*.

The new E/M codes are quite complex, with dozens of codes that apply either to new patients or established patients, office visits, home visits, hospital visits, and codes that apply to medical procedures performed on one side of the body but not the other. There is also a range of two-digit supplemental codes (called modifiers) that physicians must append to some primary codes to indicate special prolonged service, concurrent care (more than one doctor attending), repetitive service for chronic care, and other issues insurance companies evaluate for reimbursement.

All this can make the work of the new billing service quite confusing. Just as with diagnosis codes, the wrong code, or mismatched codes on a claim can cause it to be denied, delayed, or downcoded. James B. Davis, author of *The Reimbursement Manual for the Medical Office: A Comprehensive Guide to Coding, Billing, and Fee Management* (PMIC Publishers) estimates that downcoding costs medical professionals and their patients millions of dollars annually. The sidebar on evaluation and management codes will give you some idea of the complexity of CPT coding.

Table 2-5
Factors influencing E/M codes

Number of diagnoses or management options	Amount and/or complexity of data to be reviewed	Risk of complications and/or morbidity or mortality	Type of decision making
minimal	minimal or none	minimal	*straightforward*
limited	limited	low	*low complexity*
multiple	moderate	moderate	*moderate complexity*
extensive	extensive	high	*high complexity*

The CPT Evaluation & Management Codes (E/M) define the physician/patient contact in terms of the time, depth of diagnosis, and decision making and thinking required for a given visit. Naturally, a five minute visit to diagnose a sore throat and take a throat culture does not cost as much as a 45-minute visit to suture a wound. The technical and intellectual requirements for these two procedures are likewise substantially different.

Evaluation & management codes

The E/M codes were completely revised in 1992 to classify the work of doctors for Medicare billing. It is likely that commercial carriers will also require them in the near future. The new codes replace the old six-level visit codes for reporting service using the nomenclature *brief*, *limited*, *intermediate*, *comprehensive*, and so on, with a more complex hierarchical system divided into categories and subcategories. For example, there are categories such as: office visits, hospital inpatient visits, consultations, emergency department services, critical care services, nursing facility services, rest home services, home services, case management services, preventive care services, and newborn care. These categories are divided into two or more subcategories such as office visits—new patient and office visits—established patient, and hospital inpatient visits—initial visit and hospital inpatient visits—subsequent visit.

These subcategories are further divided into levels of service comprised of seven weighted components that define the content of the service provided. These compenents are as follows:

Key factors (these are given the most weight)
❑ History (4 types: problem focused, expanded problem focused, detailed, comprehensive)
❑ Examination (4 types: problem focused, expanded problem focused, detailed, comprehensive)
❑ Medical Decision Making (4 subcategories: straightforward, low complexity, moderate complexity, high complexity)

Contributory factors
❑ Counseling (discussions with family/patient over diagnosis, prognosis, risks of treatment, importance of compliance with treatment, risk factor reduction, patient/family education)
❑ Coordination of Care (a patient encounter with other providers or agencies)
❑ Nature of Presenting Problem (5 levels: minimal, self-limited or minor, low severity, moderate severity, high severity)

Additional factor
❑ Time (face to face time vs. unit/floor time)

As you can imagine, for a doctor to arrive at a decision combining all these factors to convey the service provided is not a simple issue, and significantly impacts reimbursement. The Medical Decision Making category (see TABLE 2-5) alone requires use of a table to assess the appropriate level of decision you are making to be coded.

Ironically, even though physicians must carefully evaluate their patient contacts to use these codes correctly, insurance carriers have developed their own standards for combining codes, thus, in some cases coding is actually a futile exercise.

As stated previously, the CPT codes comprise just the top level of the procedural coding system used by Medicare and many commercial carriers. Below CPT are two additional sets of codes, all of which are referred to as HCPCS (pronounced HicPics), which stands for HCFA Common Procedure Coding System. The Level II codes, called the National Codes, are used to bill Medicare for many items not listed in the CPT, particularly supplies. CPT has only 28 codes for use in billing supplies as compared with more than 2400 codes in Level II for supplies, materials, injections, and services. These codes also cover durable medical equipment (DME) which is often sold or rented to Medicare patients.

The Level II codes are 5-digit alphanumeric character sets, ranging from A0000 to V5999. Figure 2-15 shows a sample page of HCPCS codes from the 1992 edition. These codes are revised every March, and usually have hundreds of additions, deletions, and changes of which healthcare providers must stay informed through Medicare bulletins and coding books. Below is a list of current Level II codes:

Transportation Services	A0000–A0999
Chiropractic Services	A2000–A2999
Medical & Surgical Supplies	A4000–A4999
Miscellaneous & Experimental	A9000–A9999
Enteral & Parenteral Therapy	B4000–B9999
Dental Procedures	D0000–D9999
Durable Medical Equipment (DME)	E0000–E9999
Rehabilitative Services	H5000–H6000
Drugs Administered Other Than Oral Method	J0000–J8999
Chemotherapy	J9000–J9999
Orthotic Procedures	L0000–L4999
Prosthetic Procedures	L5000–L9999
Medical Services	M0000–M9999
Pathology & Laboratory	P0000–P9999
Temporary Codes	Q0000–Q9999
Diagnostic Radiology	R0000–R5999
Vision Services	V0000–V2799
Hearing Services	V5000–V5900

The lowest level of procedure coding is called *the HCPCS Local Level III*. These codes are also alphanumeric, ranging from W0000 to Z0000. These codes are established by the local Medicare office in each state or region, and therefore, vary greatly. Local codes are used to describe new procedures or procedures deleted from the CPT that a local Medicare office may still acknowledge.

VASCULAR CATHETERS

Ⓒ **A4300**   Implantable vascular access portal/catheter (venous, arterial or peritoneal)

INCONTINENCE APPLIANCES AND CARE SUPPLIES

Ⓢ **A4310**   Insertion tray without drainage bag; and without catheter (accessories only)

Ⓢ **A4311**   with indwelling catheter, foley type, two-way latex with coating (teflon, silicone, silicone elastomer or hydrophilic, etc.)

Ⓢ **A4312**   bag with indwelling catheter, foley type, two-way, all silicone

Ⓢ **A4313**   bag with indwelling catheter, foley type, three-way, for continuous irrigation

Ⓢ **A4314**   Insertion tray with drainage; with indwelling catheter, foley type, two-way latex with coating (teflon, silicone, silicone elastomer or hydrophilic, etc.

Ⓢ **A4315**   with indwelling catheter, foley type, two-way, all silicone

Ⓢ **A4316**   with indwelling catheter, foley type, three-way, for continuous irrigation

Ⓢ **A4320**   Irrigation tray for bladder irrigation with bulb or piston syringe

Ⓢ **A4322**   Irrigation syringe, bulb or piston

Ⓢ **A4323**   Sterile saline irrigation solution, 1000 ml

Ⓢ **A4326**   Male external catheter specialty type, (e.g., inflatable, faceplate, etc;) each

Ⓢ **A4327**   Female external urinary collection device; meatal cup, each

Ⓢ **A4328**   pouch, each

2-15
HCPCS Listing. A page from the HCFA Common Procedure Coding System (HCPCS).
Practice Management Information Corporation.

While this three-tier program of codes makes symbolic representation of exactly what transpired between doctor and patient possible, it is often perplexing to all but the most experienced coders. With hundreds of coding changes each year, it goes without saying, the CPT/HCPCS system is difficult to keep up with. Even professional books intended for teaching doctors how to use the codes admit that many healthcare providers are confused about using the CPT, Level II, and Level III codes. Some books also report that physicians often resort to using a few general codes indicating an "unlisted" procedure and service rather than spend time looking for specific codes from among the thousands. They warn, however, that inaccurate or incomplete coding actually increases a practice's workload and delays proper reimbursement.

Obviously, a billing service operator who knows coding has a significant advantage in the market. While memorizing thousands of codes is not necessary, becoming familiar with many of the most frequently used diagnostic and procedural codes will improve your professional image, and enhance the level of service you can provide. Like reading a foreign language, or sports tables in a newspaper, you may at first feel bewildered by the plethora of codes that must be correctly applied. However, it is very possible for someone without a medical background to learn coding in several weeks to a few months. The Resource List appearing later in this chapter includes a number of books and other sources from which you can learn more about coding.

Medicare/commercial insurance regulations   Learning the labyrinth of Medicare and commercial insurance regulations is the last item in this section I'll discuss as necessary to proper operation of a billing service. The overview at the beginning of this chapter merely scratched the surface of the knowledge base you'll need to run a successful business.

Medicare in particular seems to be an ever-changing operation. As our country's elderly population grows and our federal budget continues to be strained, Medicare policy is increasingly subject to frequent updates about reimbursement procedures and allowable fees. The owner of a billing service must therefore sustain an ongoing knowledge of the insurance claims business. As you run your business, you will frequently need to read Medicare bulletins, attend Medicare and Medicaid conferences, confer with other billing specialists, and keep abreast of trends in the insurance industry. Your knowledge and experience will directly impact the quality of your service, and hence your income potential.

The level of computer knowledge you will need in the medical billing business is actually quite modest. This topic is included for those of you who need to know because many people with nontechnical backgrounds may feel disadvantaged if they do not already have significant computer experience.

AREA 2. Computer hardware and software skills

Fortunately, today's hardware and software technology have progressed to where most people can learn what they need to know in a few short hours, or days at most. If you know how to type, learning most software is worry-free. The days of typing complex command sequences and multistep procedures are essentially gone. Most software performs what you want transparently, freeing you from involvement in its many complex actions. Usually, you only need to use the simple English commands it provides.

The highest hurdle with some software is the manuals which often make using the programs seem much more difficult than it actually is. This is not to suggest that the world has seen the end of poorly designed software. Some programs are indeed badly organized and downright cumbersome to use, so testing them before you buy is advisable. There is nonetheless so much good software available these days with intuitive, straightforward functionality. Many packages provide context sensitive help screens, allowing you to obtain help with the push of a single key at any point in an operation.

In short, it will be helpful to understand the following items by the time you're ready to open for business.

DOS   DOS, which stands for disk operating system, is the background software that runs most business PCs. DOS tells your computer what type of keyboard and monitor you are using, how your printer is hooked up to your PC, and which software programs you are running that allow you to work. DOS also allows you to copy information between media, load and run programs, and perform many other maintenance operations.

While your skill with DOS doesn't need to be terribly sophisticated, you do need to be comfortable working your way around your PC with a few DOS commands. Many medical billing software companies will help you in this area if you need it.

Many excellent DOS books are available in bookstores, including some from this publisher. Most will provide you with enough background information if you have not used a PC before going into medical billing. You can also find tutorial software that teaches you about DOS, such as The Basics of DOS™ Course from MasterTech Computer Products International.

Hardware   Most PC hardware today is ready to use out of the box. Computer stores format your hard disk, install internal fax/modem boards, even load your software. The need to understand hardware is ultimately a question of how much you want to get involved. Some people become "hardware junkies," reading dozens of computer magazines to stay abreast of the latest technology improvements. Other people buy a computer, have the dealer install the programs they want, and never again pay attention to hardware until something breaks, in which case they often hurry back to the dealer for repairs without trying to see if they can fix it themselves.

In the medical billings business, you can be anywhere along this continuum although the more you know, the less time and money you may need to spend. You should at least know how to work with hard disks, dot matrix printers, and modems, because medical billing software for electronic claims requires these hardware items. As with the medical billing software, many of the companies selling software or business packages will help you set your hardware up. In the section on Getting Started, I'll review more specific hardware requirements for medical billing software.

Most medical billing software packages are easy to learn, although it may take a few weeks or months to build proficiency. Software packages are usually menu-driven and your first task will be to become familiar with menu contents and commands so that you will be able to process quickly. Error correction, auto-dialing, and automatic file transfer features improve the speed at which you can learn to use the software and feel comfortable entering data.

Medical billing software

However, it is certainly worthwhile to spend time with your medical billing software before you go into business. In fact, some software companies give you case exercises to practice so you can develop proficiency in keying claims. Before you hang out your shingle, now is the time to learn your software, not after.

Other software   Once you are in the medical billing business, much of your time is devoted to keying and transmitting claims using your medical billing software. Since many of these software programs are fully integrated practice management packages, you'll have little or no need to learn stand-alone accounting or database programs. By thoroughly learning your medical billing software, you will meet most of your business' computer literacy requirements.

You may, however, wish to use other types of business software, such as word processors or database managers that allow you to create merged text documents and print mailing labels for your marketing materials. Desktop publishing software can enable you to design and print your own brochures, advertisements, and direct-mail marketing pieces; presentation software can enable you to prepare charts, graphs, slides, and other printouts when you want to present your business to potential clients. Accounting programs can produce invoices and bills to your clients while time management programs can help you schedule your time and appointments. Contact management programs can keep track of your business leads and tax preparation programs to help you with your taxes. Communications software is useful for network links to services such as CompuServe or Prodigy.

Dozens of programs are in each of these categories, ranging from simple to complex. To save money and learning time, you might also consider integrated software packages that combine several of these functions into one package. Chapter 5 addresses general business software in more detail.

If you are a novice, you can easily learn more quickly by picking up a few computer or home business magazines at newsstands or by browsing through the computer sections at your local bookstore. Hundreds of publications are available today to review, and many critique software packages and the never-ending procession of new products that hit the market. Computer store personnel are also helpful but you'll find the best advice by reading several different magazine reviews and from business associates who may be using the software you want. They can help you understand whether a particular product can fulfill your needs.

If you start to feel overwhelmed with how much you have to learn, just relax and give yourself adequate time to study and practice. Plan on at least an extra month to become familiar with business software before you begin your billing service. Thirty days of practice early on may save you months of anguish and extra work later, when you discover that your software can easily handle in one minute what you have been trying to do in a day!

If you are experienced or expert in a few of these software packages, your learning curve will be much shorter. Nevertheless, with everchanging technology, you too have an uphill battle to stay informed. A major problem faced by experienced people is not the investment of time required to learn a new program, but rather the emotional upheaval associated with changing software. Once you get used to a program, you tend to fall into a comfortable routine—it can be a major psychological challenge to abandon your old favorites for something new.

My view of consumers and the computer industry is reminiscent of the legend of Sisyphus, who was condemned to repeatedly roll a huge stone uphill, only to have it roll down again when it reached the top. However, the difference is that our task is not a punishment, but a learning treat! So enjoy your challenge of learning and using new software and hardware products. It's only going to get better!

AREA3. Business knowledge & skills

As Paul and Sarah Edwards wrote in their excellent book *Getting Business to Come to You*, "You are not in business until you **have** business." Their point is especially true when considering medical billing. You can set up the best home office, purchase the most sophisticated software, and study the ICD-9 and CPT books till there is no more to do, but unless you have paying healthcare clients, you are out of business.

Getting clients and keeping them requires hard work, knowledge, and business acumen. Nearly everyone I interviewed told me plainly that getting clients is the hardest part of this profession. They pointed out many reasons for this, such as the:

- Difficulty of getting busy doctors to listen to your service offering.
- Financial and emotional complexity of persuading doctors to hand over their accounts to you.
- Time it takes for doctors or their staffs to make a decision.
- Potential for error.

All these factors add up to a single truth: you must have or be able to develop excellent business skills, especially in marketing and sales, if you want your company to grow and prosper. Let's examine each of these briefly.

Marketing   You will actually find many definitions of marketing, but for our purposes here, marketing is the general skill of getting people to buy your products or services, rather than someone else's. Marketing is actually a combination of skills and knowledge. Marketing includes several types of activities: cold calling, handing out leaflets, direct mail, advertising, and public relations. The name you choose for your company should also have marketing impact. Each of these requires different talents, but together they shape what people think of your business, and whether they will buy from you instead of your competitor.

As suggested, a medical billing service is a highly marketing-driven business. It is no small task to convince a doctor, accustomed to paper claims for years, to switch to this new technology. Getting a busy physician's attention long enough to listen to your sales pitch can be about as easy as roping a cow. Imagine yourself walking into a doctor's crowded office with a waiting room full of sick people and leaning your head over the counter to ask the office manager, "Excuse me, is the doctor free?"

It helps to have any of several marketing talents available to you as you begin in the medical billing business—maybe a flair for graphic design or a way with words. With these skills, you can develop attractive and persuasive brochures and direct mail pieces. Or perhaps you're gifted with a charming personality and an easy conversational style that will enable you to approach the most abrasive receptionist and quickly smooth over relations. With such skill, cold calling is perhaps a marketing strategy you will want to pursue often.

Understanding marketing and developing the skills to do it well is not difficult. Start by examining yourself. I believe that everyone has some natural marketing talent that simply needs to be uncovered, if they haven't done so already. Afterword, consider your previous work experience, and see what marketing skills you've already developed. Ask yourself, "Have I done direct mail? Have I written catalogue copy or product specifications? Called on clients, patients, or doctors and put them at ease during a first meeting?" You may discover that you already have many of the skills necessary to accomplish some of the marketing goals for your new company.

However, if you feel uncomfortable about your ability to do marketing, I highly recommend that you take a marketing course at your local community college, or read some good books on "guerrilla" marketing techniques that explain the basics for the low-budget, home-business entrepreneur. Wherever your studies take you, you will want to learn about "marketing mix," a way of combining the four major marketing methods available to you. (The four methods are advertising, public relations, direct sales, and sales promotions.) There's also the more specific direct mail campaigns, areas of copywriting, market segmentation, niche marketing, and a host of other topics you'll want to catch up on. Remember too that there are many people who can help you with certain aspects of marketing, if you are willing to pay for those services. These include copywriters, designers, printers, and direct mail consultants to name a few.

Sales   Marketing is useless without sales. You could have a brochure when you call on that front office manager, or make your pitch to the doctor, but unless you close a deal you're still out of business.

Unfortunately, many people without sales experience imagine torture and embarrassment when they hear the word sales. They hate the thought of doing sales, and they shudder to think that they may someday "force" someone to buy something from them. Indeed, to many people, sales means pressure tactics, deceit, and manipulation. Well, none of these describe a good salesperson. A more positive way to think of sales is that it is the natural conclusion to a good marketing plan.

Successful selling does require skills. The foremost skill is communications. Knowing how and when to speak so the other person will hear you, and listening carefully are critical. One of the first rules of sales is being prepared to address the (overt or latent) question, "What's in it for me?" Your customers know what's in it for you; they need to know how you can help them. This means being able to describe to your potential clients how you can serve their interests. Fortunately, in medical billing, you have some very good answers. You can:

❏ Improve the healthcare provider's cash flow.
❏ Get quicker reimbursements.
❏ Reduce confusion over claims.

You can probably do all the preceding for less than it now costs the provider.

Next on the list of sales skills is what I call *thoughtful* persistence. This means being persistent enough to know when you're into a worthwhile negotiation, yet astute enough to know when you are probably wasting your time. Many people who "dislike sales" actually dislike the idea of having to ask someone (perhaps repeatedly) to buy their service or product. Thoughtful persistence is needed though, because few people buy right away and you have spent time and money on your marketing campaign. You cannot afford to let a simple, off-the-cuff "No" stop you from recouping your investment.

A third crucial skill in sales is negotiation. Negotiation is both skill and art. You need to know when and how much to compromise as well as compliment, when and how to yield your ground as much as when to hold firm. Often, people without sales experience dislike it because they believe they must throw themselves at the customer's feet in order to get the business. On the contrary, good negotiation conveys that you respect your ability and expect others to pay you for it and treat you appropriately. Ask yourself when you last met a doctor who worked for free. If you are like most people, this humorous prodding simply illustrates for you how important confident negotiation is to your business success.

Charting your challenge

The foregoing sections have laid out three areas for you to assess in terms of your current knowledge base and skills. Reflect upon the depth of your experience and background in each of these areas: medical coding and insurance regulations, computer competence, and general business skill. If you haven't already, you may now want to chart your learning curve as explained previously.

If you are going into business with a partner, don't forget to examine their skills too. It often happens that one person has one set of skills, while the other has a solid background in another. The sidebar on DAPA Medical Billing Services illustrates a couple whose complementary skills turned their new venture into a budding success.

Daniel F. Lehmann and Patricia Bartello, DAPA Support Services, Annadale, VA The saying "two heads are better than one" is an apt assessment of the complementary business partnership of Daniel Lehmann and Patricia Bartello.

Business profile

Dan entered medical billing after 25 years in management and manufacturing, working in high-tech automotive and robotics. He also taught college business courses for a few years, but like so many people who grow tired of working for others, Dan yearned for his own business enterprise. His wife, Pat had a strong medical background with a master's degree in educational psychology. She worked in hospital collections and operated a successful medical transcription business. When they decided to follow their dream, they carefully examined many types of opportunities. They spent months looking into franchises, and eventually decided to buy a medical billing business opportunity package from Hi Tech Management Systems in Pasadena, California.

Dan and Pat agree that it takes a combination of skills to be in this business. Dan contributed good business communications and planning skills. He prepared a business plan for their operation when they started and updates it monthly to track their progress in relation to their goals. Dan also contributed computer experience—enough to avoid becoming confused, with so many other things to learn. As for Pat, she felt that her knowledge of medical terminology and ability to market to doctors were crucial to their success. As Pat told me, "Doctors are very suspicious, and so you have to come across credibly. When you first call on them, they may throw out some jargon just to test you, and if you respond accurately, you've got their ear. But they don't like to change."

Because of their combined skills, Dan and Pat decided to offer not only electronic claims processing, but an entire package of reimbursement management services. As of this writing, they had enough clients to keep them both working 40 hours a week (which forced Dan to abandon remodeling their house) and they plan to hire help shortly as business expands.

"The important thing as a service agency is to respond quickly and accurately," Dan added. "You've got to prove yourself if you have a first-time contract. The doctor is looking to you to unload the burden of doing the claims. What he or she wants is to get by with less office personnel and less hardware and software. You can definitely survive if you do your service well."

The growing home business movement today demonstrates that many people are extremely motivated to learn whatever they must to make their businesses succeed. This section was simply intended to give you a running start on the new path you may wish to pursue.

Again, keep in mind that you can find courses at just about any local community college or extension program for studying the three areas just discussed. Many colleges offer programs in medical billing, marketing and sales. The Resource List appearing later in this chapter also offers a selection of books that you might find helpful.

Income & earning potential

There have been many claims about the claims business, and earning potential is the one area to evaluate carefully if you are seriously considering this field. The difficulty with assessing earning potential lies in the fact that few people are willing to tell how much they really earn. Some of those I interviewed had only recently begun their businesses and could only speculate about the future. Many said that this was not a business in which you could expect to get rich quickly. Nevertheless, everyone I spoke with was optimistic (if not downright buoyant) about their choice. The main reason they gave is that the income potential and profit margin are quite good—if you run your business the right way.

How much you can earn depends upon how you price your services and the number of clients you have. Basically, there are four ways to price your services, all of which offer excellent earnings.

Per-claim-fee basis   In the per-claim-fee method, you would charge the healthcare provider a set fee for each claim you process, regardless of whether the claim is paid by the insurance carrier. (An exception to this is if you make a typographical error and a claim is denied you would not be paid.) This per-claim fee varies greatly around the country, but among the businesses I canvassed, the average fee was $4 per claim, with some charging as little as $2.

We'll use the $4 figure to work through an example of calculated earnings. Let's assume that the billing center uses a clearinghouse that charges a $300 annual fee, plus a $50 annual setup fee per physician, and $0.50 per claim. We will exclude from this calculation the clearinghouse's $0.25 and $0.29 per claim rejection and mailing charges for carriers which do not accept electronic claims. We'll also assume that the billing service has only two clients for its first two months of operation, and then adds a new client every couple of months, for a total of five physicians in the first year of operation. Each physician has roughly 15 claims per day for 20 billable days per month. This equates to 300 claims per month @ $4 per claim. The result is $1200 per month per physician. TABLE 2-6 shows how your income and expense chart would look if you had an operation like this.

From this table (based on a conservative estimate) you can see that a billing service could generate $47,000 in revenue with just five doctors each supplying 300 claims per month. Note, however that this figure excludes marketing costs, which could easily amount to $2000 for brochures, letters, postage, and other items. On the other hand, it also excludes the additional fee you can charge for setting up the account for each physician. In fact, many billing services set a fee of $2 per patient for the initial file setup. So, if a doctor has 250–500 active patients, this would generate an additional $500 to $1000. In our hypothetical example, the billing center could increase its net income to as much as $52,000.

A variation on the per-claim fee is the sliding scale fee schedule. One billing service owner I interviewed charges his clients on the basis of weekly claim volumes, as shown below:

Claims per week	Charge per claim
1–99	$6.00
100–199	$5.00
200–299	$4.50
300–399	$4.00
400–499	$3.50
500 or more	$3.00

Table 2-6
Income and expense projections for a typical billing service charging on a fee basis

Month	1st	2nd	3rd	4th	5th	6th	7th	8th	9th	10th	11th	12th	Total
# of clients	2	2	3	3	3	4	4	4	5	5	5	5	
# of claims @ $4.00 per claim	600	600	900	900	900	1200	1200	1200	1500	1500	1500	1500	$13,500
Gross income	$2400	$2400	$3600	$3600	$3600	$4800	$4800	$4800	$6000	$6000	$6000	$6000	$54,000
Expenses @ $0.50 per claim + $50.00 per client registr. fees	$300 plus $100 new reg. fee	$300	$450 plus $50 new reg. fee	$450	$450	$600 plus $50 new reg. fee	$600	$600	$750 plus $50 new reg. fee	$750	$750	$750	
Total expenses	$400	$300	$500	$450	$450	$650	$600	$600	$800	$750	$750	$750	$7,000
Net income (gross less total expenses)	$2000	$2100	$3100	$3150	$3150	$4150	$4200	$4200	$5200	$5250	$5250	$5250	$47,00

Notes

1. Excludes income from additional fees such as setup charges or patient billing.
2. Excludes expenses for marketing software and other overhead.

The owner chose this method because he had several clients who wanted his services, but processed a relatively small number of claims per week. Because they appreciated his services, they were willing to pay a higher fee per claim to compensate him for the lower volume.

Practice management, however, is the highway to earning much larger fees. The going rate to send out monthly statements to patients is $2 per statement plus postage. If a physician has 200 clients who need to receive monthly statements or reminders, you could add (in our previous example) another $400 per physician per month to your revenue stream. That would mean 5 doctors would yield an added $18,000 to the $47,000 already calculated. This illustration shows clearly how the level of service you offer can significantly increase your income potential.

Hourly basis   Charging clients an hourly rate is a common way of determining fees in many professions, but it is one of the least-used methods in electronic billing. Charging an hourly rate can help you maximize your profit for clients that have only a few claims at a time. The sidebar on Linda's Billing Service exemplifies one such owner who charges by the hour since she has several clients who process only a small number of claims per week. Charging by the hour, in quarter-hour increments, enables Linda to account for the time she spends preparing and transmitting files, and doing patient billing and follow-up phone calls.

Linda Noel, Linda's Billing Service, Los Angeles, CA   Linda Noel was managing a psychiatric clinic in West Los Angeles when she and her husband decided to start their family. Not wanting to give up her career, she made the only logical choice: a home business utilizing her medical experience. She not only got the support of her former employers, but they spread the word and new clients soon joined.

Today, Linda has nine clients, enough to keep her working a comfortable 30 hours per week, leaving her time to tend to the family. For simplicity, she chose to work only with single physician practices, and bills most of them $15 to $21 per hour. For a few, she adds a small percentage fee for collections if the billables are hard to collect. "In my practice," Linda told me, "I do everything from billing to accounts receivables; I function just as someone who works in their office would, including occasionally scheduling appointments. I do transcription and billing, both electronic and paper."

Linda doesn't feel that you absolutely need a medical background, but having worked in a physician's office was helpful to her. Changing Medicare regulations, she says, is one issue to keep up with, and therefore recommends taking the courses offered by Medicare carriers to keep up with the rules.

Business profile

Linda was not lacking in computer competence and runs a professional shop. She proudly announced that she had just bought a new 486 personal computer with a 200-Mb hard drive and a new software package, The Medical Manager, from Specialized Systems, Inc., a reseller in Van Nuys, California. She also has a 9600-baud modem to transmit electronic claims, a fax machine to receive superbills from some clients, and a multi-line phone with call waiting.

"Running a personalized service is key to getting and keeping clients," Linda says. "You've got to have doctors who like you and are willing to refer you to others."

The hourly fee you establish will probably depend on your geographic location, competition, and whether physicians think of you as a professional. If your client is a physician who has had an in-house billing person before, there may be tendency to compare your hourly fee to what they pay their in-house staff. Unless you distinguish your service offering from that staff person, you may not get as much money as you want or need. Whenever you can, you should try to set your rate as high as possible up front, because changing an hourly fee is very difficult to do. While employees may get annual raises, outside services such as yours usually cannot increase their rates every 12 months, so you should consider this when setting your rates. Average hourly fees run from $20–$35.

Your annual income using an hourly fee basis ultimately depends on how many hours you work. If you can work 20–30 hours per week at $25 per hour, your income will range between $25,000 and $37,500.

Percentage basis   The third method of pricing your service is to charge your client a percent of every dollar you bring in, whether it is through electronic claims for insurance reimbursements or patient billing once a month for coinsurance or no-insurance payments. I was told that going rates for percentage billing are between 8 percent and 12 percent of all collectibles. In doing a percentage fee, you and your client need to have a clear understanding of what you get paid for. For example, if you are responsible for obtaining the 80% insurance collectible on a patient's visit, you will probably not get paid on a client who pays the 20% copayment in cash since you did not bill it.

As you might imagine, it can be far more difficult to get a provider to agree to pay you 8 percent or more of the practice's total collectibles than it is to get a few dollars per claim. But the incentive of the percentage method is that you are offering your client an opportunity to improve the "collection efficiency" of the practice. Take a physician who bills $1 million per year, pays 1.5 staff to do billing in-house at a combined salary of $35,000 but is only able to collect at 75 percent efficiency ($750,000) because of poor follow-up, errors, and lax clients. Now contrast that situation with a physician who hires you at 8 percent of collections, and you are able to increase efficiency to 85 percent ($850,000) by following through on all claims and regularly sending out past-due notices. Which physician comes out ahead? Look at TABLE 2-7 for the answer.

Table 2-7
Collection efficiency for two physicians

	Physician A	Physician B
Billables	$1,000,000	$1,000,000
Collection efficiency	75%	85%
collections	$750,000	$850,000
Cost of collections	($35,000)	($68,000)
Net Income	$715,000	$782,000

The percentage method works best if you offer your customers full practice management services. Obviously, this means taking on more responsibility and giving more time to each account because the physician is counting on you to make sure that collectibles are paid. Errors and mistakes can cost you a sizable portion of your income when you work on the percentage basis.

Calculating your annual income may be harder using the percentage method as compared with the others. Using the per-claim method, you will likely be able to project claim volumes per physician, and so assess your income. Likewise you can estimate the number of hours you may work each week for a client. However, with the percentage method, you have little control over how much insurance companies will reimburse, how many bad claims you may get stuck with, and have no way of knowing whether your client treats patients who generally incur costly treatments. If you are planning to charge on a percentage basis, you'll need to sit with each client and have an honest talk about his or her practice before you commit to this method.

Mixed method   The last method of charging for your services is the mixed method. As the name implies, you can mix any of the three methods above. If you have one client with many Medicare and Medicaid patients, you will want to charge on a per-claim basis or hourly basis (since the percentage basis may work against you) because Medicare reimburses at low fees. With another client you might try the percentage basis if you believe you have a good chance at improving the provider's collection efficiency.

Whichever method you choose, balance your income projections with a reasonably accurate estimate of your expenses. Projecting income can be quite difficult for a new business in the first year of operation. Revise your projections each month so that you will be prepared to handle any needed adjustments in your plans.

Finally, whatever projections you hear from others, take with a grain of salt. According to Gary Knox of AQC Resources in San Jose, California, a self-styled consumer advocate who has been tracking the medical billing business for several years, you may have reason to be skeptical about various estimates and projections on the number of claims you can process from a single physician each month. It all depends on your area and the type of customers you can get. Mr. Knox conducted a brief survey of physicians in the San Francisco area and found claim volumes to Medicare, MediCal (the California Medicaid agency) and CHAMPUS to be lower than the 300 per month in my earlier example. Ultimately, you will need to assess your income requirements, expenses, and projections according to the area in which you live and your own goals.

Deciding if this business is for you

The first part of this chapter presented much necessary background to medical billing services: what they do, how they do it, what you need to know, and how much you might earn. Armed with this brief sketch of information, you might be at a point where you would like to decide if this is the business for you. The following checklist will, hopefully, help with your decision or prompt you to think about any conclusions you might have drawn. Take a moment now to go through this 15-question checklist before completing this chapter.

Checklist for deciding if this business is for you

✔ Does the business of medical insurance and computer coding appeal to me?

✔ Do I have the drive to grasp complex medical terminology and coding matters?

✔ Can I work comfortably with doctors, nurses, and their front office medical personnel?

✔ Do I have a modicum of competence in computers or the ability to learn new software packages?

✔ Do I enjoy detailed work, such as keying medical records information?

✔ Can I sell my services face to face and close a deal?

✔ Do I have the drive and persistence to close five or ten deals?

✔ Do I understand direct mail marketing and other forms of marketing?

✔ Do I negotiate well?

✔ Do I want to assume the financial responsibility for ensuring my clients get paid?

✔ Do I have two to three months to get my business started?

✔ Do I have the $500 to $15,000 to purchase medical/dental billing software or a business opportunity package?

✔ Do I have the talents, skills, knowledge, and abilities that can help me in this business?

✔ Does my partner bring the complementary skills to this business that we'll need?

✔ Do I have a suitable location from which I can conduct this business?

If you have answered yes to most of these questions or if you have some doubts but want to proceed, the next section provides you with some brief guidelines for getting started in your business. The section is organized in a sequence of steps you may wish to take: choosing software, choosing hardware training resources, tips for pricing your serivce, guidelines for business marketing, and overcoming common startup problems.

Choosing software

Many medical billing software companies are competing for your business. If you read business magazines such as *Home Office Computing*, for example, you'll notice nearly a dozen companies advertising medical billing software. In fact, hundreds of software companies are involved in writing and/or selling medical practice management programs. Some of them originally began as medical software companies that wrote proprietary software to be sold directly to physicians. Now many offer a version of the same software to outside billing services as a "business opportunity package." Other companies, called *value-added resellers* (VARs), bundle the software with training, documentation, and other extras like phone support and sell it to physicians or billing services. Some companies were founded by individuals with experience in running billing centers, who then went on to help others start similar businesses for a fee.

There is a wide range of choices for billing software, and no single package is right for everybody. Every billing service has its own requirements, and every software package its unique design advantages and disadvantages. If that weren't enough, software is an ever-changing product, with new bells and whistles being added each year. Were I to critique a package today and find it lacking a particular feature, I would not be surprised to learn that by the time this book came to market, that feature and others would have been added. Thus, it is impossible to guide you with specific software recommendations or to companies you should work with. Nevertheless, given that you've paid for this book, let me offer the following four general guidelines to help with your decision.

1. Indeed there are differences in medical billing software. Most products are designed to make the medical billing process more efficient, but the degree to which products I reviewed achieved this purpose varies widely enough that I urge you to explore and evaluate more than one product. Judge for yourself which software package you feel most comfortable with, and think is easiest to use before you spend your money.

2. Most companies are willing to send you a free demo copy of their software. Some may require a minimal deposit that is reimbursed if you send the demo back. Other companies may send you to see their product at a current customer's office. Whichever way you choose, do it. Don't buy

software sight unseen. If a company tells you they have no way for you to see a demo of their product, don't buy from them.

3. Make sure your selection allows you to do the following:

❑ True billing service capability. Because you'll run a billing center, you'll want to be sure your software allows you to track many different physicians (or practices) and their patients, and that this function is efficient. Some software is designed for a single practice (which may have more than one doctor), but this is not the same as software designed for a billing service. Check to see if you will need to load the software into separate disk directories for each of the physicians you service. Does it enable you to easily track patients according to the doctor or practice they belong to?

❑ Claims-only software or practice-management software. Some software allows you to submit electronic claims, but doesn't allow you to do accounting reports, patient billing, and other functions. Buy whichever package you need for the type of business you intend to be in.

❑ Open item accounting (matching a payment to a specific charge). Because Medicare and other carriers post reimbursements to specific charges, you must be able to mirror that process if you intend to provide complete practice management. Thus, if you need to appeal a denied or downcoded claim, you will be able to state specifically which charge is in dispute.

❑ Multiple fee schedule. While many people think it is forbidden, doctors are entitled to have multiple fee schedules. For a given service, they may charge patients with Medicare one fee, while patients who pay cash or use credit cards pay another. Having software that allows you to maintain different fee schedules for a given practitioner enables you to post payments more easily as well as to make account adjustments. (An adjustment is the sum a doctor writes off when patients don't pay their balances so that the account can be closed with credits equalling debits.)

❑ Pop-up windows for procedure and diagnostic codes. Rather than keying the many different diagnostic and procedural codes for each claim you process, you'll want to save time with software that allows you to store the most commonly used codes in each physician's practice.

❑ Program menus. There are good menus and bad menus; be sure that the menus you test at all levels make sense to you. Also, consider the number of keystrokes required each time you need to record a claim. As software improves, you may find some programs that allow you to use a mouse to point and click on your menus choices too. A mouse can double the speed for some people.

❑ Direct submission or clearinghouse. Consider whether the software will allow you to submit claims directly to Medicare and go through a clearinghouse for commercial claims? If so, will this really save you any money? If the software links to a clearinghouse, does the clearinghouse have linkages to major insurance carriers in your area? Some software packages go through clearinghouses in other parts of the country which do not have agreements with insurance carriers in every state, so you can be left stranded with virtually useless software.

4. Balance timing and opportunity costs. If you are anxious to be in business, you probably want to buy your software and get moving. However, if you have time, take a few weeks to explore. Whatever your situation, you need to balance your time, your momentum, and your pocketbook. Like buying computer hardware, the longer you wait, the better the product you'll find for the price, but the more opportunity you may have passed up.

Appendix A is an alphabetical list of companies that responded to my queries for information. I was perplexed by some companies that did not respond to my requests for demonstration copies or information after repeated attempts to contact them. I have listed only those companies whom I knew about that sent me information. I have sought to repeat here, as accurately as possible, information I received, so any errors in explaining any features of programs are accidental.

On this list are some companies that sell their own proprietary software, while others are VARs marketing another company's software. Both types of companies are often selling a "business opportunity," i.e., training, books, support, software updates, and marketing assistance along with the software. Product/service prices range from $2000 to $10,000 except for a few companies selling "software only" packages for $1000 or less. The sidebar, Should I Buy a Business Opportunity should clarify concerns that may arise about such offerings.

Business opportunities, also known as *seller assisted marketing plans* are nothing more than people selling their expertise to help others start a business. Unlike franchising, you are seldom obligated to pay recurring fees, or a percentage of revenues. You're not required to use the company name and adhere to strict rules about how you run your business. With a business opportunity, all you are doing is paying someone to sell you the ways and means to operate what, for them, has been a good business.

There are two operative terms here that you need to think long and hard about. The first is *expertise*. You must ask yourself some questions about the seller's expertise in this business. How long has the seller been in business? Is the seller actually involved in the same business (or just the business of selling you the business)? How much does the seller really know about this business? The second term is *opportunity*. You really need to assess who gets the greater opportunity, you or the seller? Is there really a market for the business or is selling the "business opportunity" to unsuspecting people the only real prospect?

Medical billing software companies

Should I buy a business opportunity?

We have all heard horror stories of people who have invested in something that immediately has gone down the tubes, and many of us correlate such tragedies with shady business opportunity vendors who take advantage of unsuspecting souls. Nonetheless, many business opportunities are completely legitimate ventures, and you must be savvy enough to buy the right one for you and make it work.

Because the business opportunity market has exploded over the past decade, more states are now regulating how sellers and buyers must act. In July 1992, *Entrepreneur* magazine reported that 24 states now regulate business opportunities and seller-assisted marketing plans that require an initial investment of more than $500. A business opportunity vendor selling in any of these states must register no matter where it is headquartered. Most of these regulations require the business to register itself with the state's Attorney General's Office. Often, each prospective customer must be given in advance an offering prospectus listing the company executives, and stating specifically what is included in the price of the business opportunity. In many states, the buyer is often given a grace period, such as three days, during which the buyer can rescind the contract and obtain a refund of his purchase price. The seller is often barred from making representations about how much income you may earn, and some states require the seller to report how many prior purchasers of the plan have made more than the initial investment.

The value of a business opportunity company in medical billing should be found in training and the clout of being able to say you are a part of their "family" of billing services. Affiliation with a larger, credible company can boost your ability to convince a doctor that you have the resources to handle his or her finances. Do be sure to check out as many references as possible through Dunn & Bradstreet, previous buyers, current operators, chambers of commerce, better business bureaus, and the like.

On starting out

Be prepared for a slight delay in filing electronic claims when you first start. If you are working through a clearinghouse, or even direct with a Medicare carrier, you will need to complete several agreement forms, one of which can only be done once when you sign your first client. The doctor must also sign an agreement with the clearinghouse as well. All this can take a few weeks to complete. The clearinghouse or Medicare carrier (or both) will probably ask you to process 20 claims as a competency test. This adds more time. Meanwhile, if you are already taking claims from your provider you will likely have to submit them on paper HCFA 1500 forms for the first few weeks. You'll want to make sure your clients understand it may take six weeks or more before they begin to see the effects of electronic claims processing.

Choosing hardware

You should choose your hardware after first selecting the software you intend to use. Many people have bought computers only to later realize that it does not have enough power to do what they want.

Nearly all of the medical billing and practice management software listed in the Appendix A runs optimally on a 286, 386, or 486 personal computer with a minimum of 640K RAM or more. You can use a PC XT style machine, but your software will run much more slowly. Most of the software companies recommend a hard disk of at least 40 megabytes. Given the low cost of hard drive memory, you would benefit greatly by investing in at least an 80Mb or 200Mb hard drive. You will almost certainly be running other work applications on your computer in addition to the medical billing software, you will likely need more RAM and a larger hard drive memory for files and programs. Some other software such as desktop publishing or database programs require at least a 386 machine with 2Mb or 4Mb of RAM and a 80Mb hard drive. Finally, you will need to be running DOS 3.1 or greater.

If you are just purchasing new hardware, or are upgrading the hardware you own, I recommend thinking of your long-term goals and requirements. Prices are dropping quickly on 486 machines. You may be able to get away with a $1000–$1500 investment to equip yourself with an enormously powerful computer that truly makes your tasks fun and easy. I also recommend the following:

Monitor A color monitor (VGA or SVGA) eases strain on your eyes and helps you work more productively. Colors are often used to distinguish menus and screen entry fields. You might wish to consider purchasing an oversize monitor (larger than the standard 14" monitor). Studies have shown that people are more productive when using the larger screen area.

Fax machine You may have some clients who fax you their superbills. You can choose to have either an internal fax/modem in your PC or an external fax machine. I find that an external fax machine is an advantage. If you only have an internal fax/modem, you'll also need a scanner to input documents not stored in your computer, before you fax them.

Modem Most software and clearinghouses support 1200, 2400, and 4800 baud modems. For faster speeds, consider a 9600 baud modem. One nice feature about an internal modem is that it does not take up desk space. Merry Shiff of Health Software Systems prefers external modems because the indicator lights are helpful in pinpointing problems in your linkup with a clearinghouse if they arise.

Backup devices You will need to keep backups of your files and records for several months, perhaps years. You can do this on floppy disks or you may wish to invest in a backup device which stores data on tape cartridge.

Printer If you are doing patient invoices, the most common form used is a six-part paper patient billing form. It takes a powerful dot-matrix printer to strike through six copies. Most software companies recommend a wide carriage (132-column) printer. A laser printer is not necessary, but will come in handy for your other business printing needs. Considering that a laser printer will cost you between $500 and $1500, it is one item you may put off for budget considerations. You can use a typesetter, desktop publishing service, or copy shop that rents laser printers by the hour to do your other printing.

Office furniture   Processing claims and setting up patient files is tedious work. To prevent neck and back strain, joint problems in your wrists and fingers, and other ailments, quip yourself with an ergonomically designed chair and work area.

Phone lines   Once you're in business, you need to have a business phone that is distinct from your family phone. This is perhaps one of the best investments you can make. A business line will get you a listing in the yellow pages (though you will pay for this). There is little more unprofessional than having your six-year old answer the call from your most important client, or having to tell a caller that the noise in the background is your 18-month-old child who is in the middle of a tantrum. You might consider also having a third line installed for your fax machine. While a dedicated line for the fax machine is not a requirement, think of your alternatives. You will either have to use your family phone for the fax machine so that your business line is always open for voice calls, or you use your business line for both voice and fax. Both choices have disadvantages, but you should make your choices as your budget requires.

Other items   If you will be doing direct mail (discussed in greater detail later in the chapter) you may want to invest in a dedicated label printer. These are usually narrow gauge printers that handle a long line of stick-on mailing labels. This alleviates the drudgery of removing the paper from your printer and changing your pin-feeds to make labels for envelopes.

Resources and training

Preparing yourself to run a medical billing service is perhaps the most valuable step you can take before starting your business. As I indicated throughout the chapter, this is a true profession, so trying to join in the opportunity without adequate training or knowledge will slow you down immensely. The sidebar Business Profile on Cliff Hartfield explains how education can help you get off the ground and increase your chances of success, especially when you have no medical background. Several avenues to educating yourself are worth exploring, depending on your prior knowledge and experience.

Business profile

Cliff Hartfield, Compu-Med Claims Systems, Carson, CA.   The way Cliff Hartfield tells it, you couldn't get a better endorsement for education and training as the way to ensure you start your business on the right foot. Cliff had absolutely no medical background, being a law enforcement retiree in June 1991. His wife, a former airline flight attendant, one night decided to take a medical billing course at a local community college, and Cliff went along for the ride. When the course ended, he was hooked, in part due to guest speaker Greg Duvall, founder of Hi Tech Management Systems, who gave a stunning presentation about electronic billing.

Cliff and his wife then proceeded to take many more courses at community colleges in the Los Angeles area. They studied diagnostic coding, procedural coding, insurance industry trends, claims filing, reimbursement, medical terminology and more. Finally, they took another step and purchased more training and software from Medical Reimbursement Specialists in Chino, California. Medical Reimbursement Specialists is a business opportunity company, run by Joyce Tolliver, which sells off-the-shelf software called Medisoft; Cliff felt that the training by Tolliver was invaluable in getting him up to speed.

Unfortunately, by the time they were ready to roll, with a business license and a firm grip on their software, it was already Thanksgiving, Christmas was around the corner, and there was no business in sight—everyone was preoccupied with the holidays! During March and April of 1992 Cliff worked to get his marketing materials together. "I thought it would take only a short time to get these things organized and written out," he recalls "but it was incredibly time-consuming. I spoke with four doctors to get feedback on the brochures and the viability of the business as well. I consulted with a local printer too."

Cliff's preparation paid off. At the time of our interview, Cliff had several clients representing different types of medical practices. With his background in sales as a wedding photographer in his early years and a love of making a deal, Cliff has taken over running the business. He adds, "I'm 53 and am more or less satisfied, but I am still marketing. You can't stop; like any business, the person who is willing to get the most is the one who gets the job. Marketing, sales, discipline to work from home, and persistence—these are the skills you need to stay in business."

So, if you think you haven't taken enough training, take a lesson from Cliff— there's no such thing as too much learning.

Many community colleges and extension schools offer courses or workshops in medical billing and coding. These are widely offered for front office staff personnel who work for physicians and need training. If you enjoy the classroom atmosphere and pace, this type of training may be for you.

Books on coding and various aspects of billing for doctors are available from many different sources. You might begin by locating a medical bookstore in your city, where you can purchase coding manuals and other reference materials. The ICD-9 is also available from the United States Government Printing Office, and the CPT coding book can be purchased from the American Medical Association. To obtain this book or the AMA catalog, call 800-621-8335. You can also obtain both books from several private companies which republish them under license in easy-to-use formats. Practice

COUNSELING OFFICE

Management Information Corporation (PMIC), for example, offers the CPT 1993 edition in one spiral bound volume for practically the same price as the two-volume soft bound set that you can buy from the AMA. PMIC publishes an array of medical coding books, including the following titles:

Reimbursement Manual for the Medical Office: A Comprehensive Guide to Coding, Billing, and Fee Management
CPT & HCPCS Coding Made Easy!: A Comprehensive Guide to CPT and HCPCS Coding for Health Care Professionals
ICD-9 Coding Made Easy! A Comprehensive Coding Guide for Health Care Professionals
Collections Made Easy!: A Comprehensive Guide For Medical and Dental Professionals
Health Insurance Carrier Directory

PMIC also publishes competitively priced annual editions of the CPT codes and the ICD-9 codes in tabbed, thumb- indexed editions. You can reach PMIC at 1-800-MEDSHOP ext. 432 where Mr. Joe Kopacz can help you with your book needs. There is also a discount of 10 percent to readers of this book.

One other source of information on medical billing software comes from Gary Knox (AQC Resources, a consulting company in San Jose, CA) who has been studying medical software and business opportunity companies for several years. Knox publishes an extensive guide to most of these companies wherein he tries to stay up to date about software prices, the packages offered, and the personalities involved. He can be reached at 1757 West San Carlos Street, Suite 111, San Jose, California, 95128. You can also call him at 408-295-4102. At the time of this writing, Mr. Knox had also begun publishing a monthly newsletter, *Medical Claims Processing*, that he will make available for an annual fee.

Training and skill improvement

You might also want to expand your entrepreneurial skills through courses in marketing, sales, publicity, and business planning. Again, many extension schools and local colleges offer inexpensive, high-quality courses and one- or two-day workshops on a myriad of business topics.

The business book market is, not surprisingly, one of the fastest growing book publishing areas. This is good news for you because dozens of publishers are putting out hundreds of books on how to start home businesses, develop marketing skills, learn sales, run your business, consult, and many other topics of interest to the general business audience. Any bookstore near you will undoubtedly carry an extensive selection of good business books. My favorite titles include three books from Paul and Sarah Edwards: *Working From Home, Making It on Your Own,* and *Getting Business to Come to You.* The latter book was coauthored with Laura Clampitt Douglas (all published by Jeremy P. Tarcher/Putnam). Also read these marketing and sales books by Jay Conrad Levinson: *Guerrilla*

Marketing, *Guerrilla Marketing Attack*, and *Guerilla Selling* (all published by Houghton Mifflin). I also recommend the sales motivational books by Og Mandino. Finally, read through *Marketing Without a Budget* by Craig Rice (Bob Adams) and *How to Get Clients* by Jeff Slutsky (Warner).

Magazines such as *Home Office Computing* and *Entrepreneur*, and newspapers such as the *Wall Street Journal*, the *New York Times*, and *U.S.A. Today* often carry inspirational profiles of successful business people. Though other businesses may be very different from medical billing, you may pick up a sales or marketing technique from another field that could work for you too.

Contact your department of commerce or local chamber of commerce for any booklets and advice they publish about starting a business. SCORE (Service Corps of Retired Executives) and other associations of business people and networking organizations can also be helpful. You will be surprised by how many people are willing to provide you with their expertise and knowledge just for the asking. Start by making a small chart of people you know, and ask each one if they have any friends in the medical field whom you could chat with to get advice and information about your new venture. Many of the people I interviewed spoke first with their own doctors, for example.

Whatever you do, make time each week for learning more about medical billing and doing business as a home-based entrepreneur. Chapter 5 addresses the issues of working from home in more detail.

Choosing your pricing strategy is always a difficult task. If you price too low, you will not maximize your earnings. If you price too high, you may drive away potential clients, or lose them quickly to lower priced competitors. Because this is a service business, your prices need to reflect the level of service you are delivering. Will you process 50, 100, or 150 claims per week for a given physician? Will you also do regular patient billing. Send out late notices, and key in payments to complete accounts receivable? Will you be providing the physician with monthly reports such as aged balances, insurance balances, and practice activity reports?

Tips for pricing

In short, you cannot price your services until you know your clients. It is advisable not to put any representation of your fees in your advertising or direct mail brochures. Your goal should be to find out more about the practice so that you can return to the doctor with a proposal stating your fees. Only by knowing your client's situation and the services you will provide can you decide how much to charge.

On the other hand, you must have some pricing baselines in order to calculate your proposal. You need to know at least if you are aiming for $3.00 per claim or $4 per claim, $1.50 per patient bill or $2.50. You'll need other criteria to decide if you should charge on a percentage basis or a per claim basis. Some guidelines for all these decisions follow:

Location   Location is always a consideration. Living costs in major metropolitan areas are higher than in small cities and town in most parts of the country. You need to get some sense of the fee structure in your community. In some places, you might be able to charge $4 to $6 per claim. However, in most locations, you'll be limited to about $3. If you are pricing only on a per-claim basis, negotiate the highest rate you can because it is very difficult to increase your rates once you have convinced a client that you can save him or her money by using your service. If you go back in six months to ask for a higher fee, you risk losing your customer(s).

Calculate claims per month   Like any business, doctors have good days and bad days, so trying to figure out how many claims a doctor files in one day or one week is just too difficult. Use a month as a good measure of how much business the client may give you. Set your fee structure on a higher per-claim basis if you will be receiving fewer claims, and a slightly lower per-claim basis for more claims. This will give your client physicians the sense that you discount your fees for the greater volume he or she will give you. You could also offer a sliding fee schedule for each month as indicated earlier in the chapter.

Compare per-claim with percentage   To compare these you need to have a frank discussion with your customers to know how many claims are filed each month and the dollar value of billables generated. Many doctors will not want to divulge personal financial information, but if you are able to speak knowledgeably about increasing the collection efficiency of the practice by $50,000 or $100,000, you may get some answers that would allow you to calculate your best method of pricing. If you choose a percentage basis, you should also quote a slightly higher rate than you are willing to take, so that you have room to negotiate.

Be reasonable   Don't think that doctors make so much money that they are perfectly happy to share it with you for helping them. You will not be able to charge per claim PLUS a percentage PLUS various fees for each and every activity report or monthly statement. You want to be seen as a cost savings, not a cost burden. The best thing is to keep your fee structure simple, so that it seems fair, reasonable, cost effective. Even if you decide upon a mixed pricing schedule, such as $3 per claim plus a percentage of all patient billables, make it easy to understand.

Remember that each practice you service doesn't need to know how many other clients you have, or whether you are raking in money. Your objective is to provide each practice with cost-effective billing and/or practice management. Do everything you can to keep each client you get, and treat each as if he or she were your only one!

Marketing guidelines

When I first began exploring the medical services business, nearly every person I interviewed told me, "Getting clients is the hardest part of this business." Although this chapter and many other sources tell you that medical billing is a great business opportunity, you will have difficulty getting customers unless you market your business well.

One reason for doctors' reluctance is that medical billing is typically thought of as an aftereffect of the more important healthcare role. "Okay, we've treated the patient, let's just process this claim and get our money. If we have to, we'll just call the insurance company to straighten it out" went the thinking. Another reason is that many doctors' offices have already explored automating their systems, and have been burned because they bought expensive systems which they underutilized, treating them like glorified typewriters. Some physicians may ask "Why should I spend more money if I've got a billing person and a computer to do all this?" The answer is that today, insurance carriers and Medicare are serious about cutting costs and monitoring reimbursements. The healthcare industry, and small practices in particular, can no longer afford to avoid high technology such as electronic transfers and claims processing in place of billions of pieces of paper.

Nonetheless, you may still face an uphill battle to convince physicians to hire a billing service to manage their accounts, let alone hire *your* billing service as opposed to someone else's. This means that you must do marketing and sales. Following are a few general ideas for conducting your campaign.

New businesses in a new industry can't simply sit back with an ad in the Yellow Pages and wait for customers to come to them. You must engage in several marketing activities, such as direct mail, networking, sales calling, promotions, publicity, and workshops to let people know you are out there and can help them.

Let people know you are in business

Marketing campaigns cost money, but you can't expect to compete or attract attention without high quality brochures, business cards, stationery, and a company logo. I'm not suggesting that you must buy the services of the finest professional designers and printers in your area, but simply that you not be penny wise and pound foolish. Your marketing materials announce that you are a professional businessperson. If your printer tells you that a higher quality business card stock will cost you an extra $30 per thousand, it may well make the difference of one person keeping your card a few months and calling you instead of throwing your cheap card away the day it was received.

Spend money and time to make money

Spending time on your marketing materials is important too. Don't rush through the wording of your introduction letter or brochure. Once you've written a draft, let it sit a few days, and then review your writing to see if you might find a better way to convey your message. Get feedback from your spouse, business partner, friends, and a few doctors. You may love what you have written, but don't be defensive if someone else thinks that your wording is too weak or grammatically incorrect. You may even want to consider having your material read by a professional proofreader or copyeditor.

Keep direct mail simple

Direct mail was the marketing technique of choice for nearly every medical billing person I interviewed. Because your objective is to reach as many doctors as possible to announce your business, direct mail is one of the most efficient and least threatening ways of letting a physician know that you are available.

You can make your own direct mail lists by visiting medical buildings and writing down the names listed on the office registry, or you can buy mailing lists from any of several commercial mailing list houses around the country. The yellow pages will have a list of these, usually under the heading Mailing Lists. Call your local Medicare carrier (or have an elderly relative do it for you) and get their free list of Medicare providers in your area.

When you design direct mail pieces, remember that a busy doctor has little time to read two pages of small print announcing who you are, what you do, and how much you cost. Keep your letters of introduction brief and to the point. It also helps to include some questions in the letter, such as "How many claims per month are you processing?", "How many active patients do you have?", and "Do you know your collections efficiency?" That way, when you speak with the physician, you may be able to get some information to help you figure out how to land the account. Along with your letter include, if possible, a business reply card. If the physician does not have time to call or prefers to do business by mail, he or she can mail in the card requesting more information. On the response card have several check-off boxes that give the reader a few good choices that also help you, such as those shown in FIG. 2-17.

THANK YOU FOR YOUR PROMPT ATTENTION

_____ I would like to know more; please contact me.

_____ I am not interested now, but I may be in the future. Please send me
     more information.

Name: Dr. _____

Phone # : _____

Please call me around _____, which is the best time to
  reach me.

2-17 _Sample business reply card._

Of course, a letter with a reply card is an expensive mailing, so you may wish to start with a simple postcard mailer announcing your opening, with a phone number to call for inquiries. Make it eye-catching and memorable—such as one I received a while ago from a company wishing to sell me banking services, which I found to be one of the most innovative cards I've seen in a long time. The card was the size of a large tourist postcard, and on the front was a beautiful picture of the Eiffel Tower in Paris. On the back was the clever message, "You could have saved enough money to be in Paris right now if you had done your banking with us . . ."

Another popular direct mail piece is the three-fold information brochure. The three fold brochure is often an 8½-x–11 sheet of paper, printed on both sides, and folded into thirds. When planning the brochure, be sure your copy reads sequentially according to the way your brochure is folded. This gives you plenty of room to write about the merits of electronic claims processing, your credentials and business history, and how you can help simplify the physician's life.

One rule of direct mail is that quantity counts more than quality. It is better to spend your money buying a list of 500 names and using a somewhat cheaper brochure than having an extraordinary brochure go out to only 100 names. In addition, the common rule of thumb is that first-class postage attracts more respect than third-class junk mail. You can get bulk mail discounts from the post office for mailings of more than 200 pieces; call 1-800-238-3150 for a free IBM compatible program from the United States Postal Service, which provides information on rates and contains spreadsheets that compare postal discounts. For more information on direct mail, consult *Direct Mail Copy That Sells* by Herschell Gordon Lewis (Prentice Hall) and *The Complete Direct Mail List Handbook*, by Ed Burnett (Prentice Hall).

Focus on service and benefits

In all your marketing materials, focus on the service or benefits you can provide, not on your credentials or on details about the technology of electronics claims. Try to answer the physician's question, "What's in it for me?" If you are offering electronic claims only, let the practice know that you can simplify the reimbursement process, reduce paperwork, accelerate the rate at which they are reimbursed, and increase their collection efficiency. If you are offering full practice management services, add to this list that you can free up permanent staff for more important duties, and maximize office efficiency with management reports and analyses. Figure 2-18 shows what a postcard mailer focusing on service might look like. A postcard mailer helps attract attention to your business and could be a useful preliminary marketing tool before you send out longer, more expensive letters of introduction.

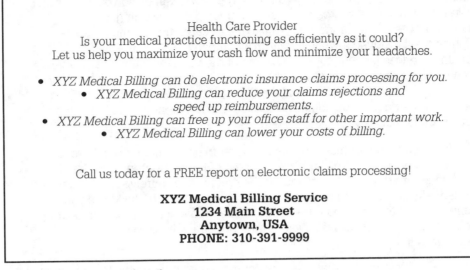

Health Care Provider
Is your medical practice functioning as efficiently as it could?
Let us help you maximize your cash flow and minimize your headaches.

- *XYZ Medical Billing can do electronic insurance claims processing for you.*
  - *XYZ Medical Billing can reduce your claims rejections and speed up reimbursements.*
- *XYZ Medical Billing can free up your office staff for other important work.*
  - *XYZ Medical Billing can lower your costs of billing.*

Call us today for a FREE report on electronic claims processing!

XYZ Medical Billing Service
1234 Main Street
Anytown, USA
PHONE: 310-391-9999

2-18   *Sample postcard mailer.*

Cold calling

Whenever you can, send printed materials in advance of making cold-calls or make use of your network to warm up potential clients to your message. Cold calling is very time-consuming, and usually disruptive to a busy physician's office. Many businesspeople don't like cold calling and therefore don't present themselves very well. Keep in mind, physicians have many sales representatives calling on them every day from pharmaceutical companies, equipment manufacturers, office supply people, temporary agencies, and so on. Your business is important to you, but to a busy front office person, you are just another salesperson. Be prepared for many rejections, but try to leave your name and card whenever you can. Also, remember your opportunity could arise unexpectedly when a staff billing person quits, or a physician may simply get tired of training a new person every two months.

Get to the decision maker

Medical practices vary greatly in terms of who is actually in a position to give you their business. In some practices, the doctor is the only one who can make a decision, but in others, it may be the physician's spouse, or an office manager, or a staff billing person. You need to find out who might be involved in making the decision to do billing offsite, and then convince that person that you can benefit the office in many ways. You may also find that a staff person feels threatened by the possibility of eliminating his or her job. However, many billing service operators I interviewed said that staff people often feel relieved when billing is removed from their job duties because it consumes so much of their time. In most cases, there are plenty of other things for them to do around the office.

Whomever the decision maker is, your goal is to find that person and get a face-to-face interview for at least 20 minutes to 40 minutes during which you can present your services and benefits. Get that person to like you, and more importantly, trust you. Trust is perhaps one of the most essential elements in your relationship with a medical practice that is handing you its financial survival.

When you present, take a folder or binder of nicely prepared materials with you, such as charts and graphs about the electronic reimbursement process. Then ask for details about numbers of patients, claims, billables, and so on that allow you to prepare a proposal to present in a followup meeting within a week. Negotiate for closure that day, or within one more day of your proposal presentation, so that you don't get bogged down in comparisons with other companies or "let me think about it" put-offs.

One additional note: be sure you are dealing with someone who is honest and reputable. The sidebar on Fraudulent Claims points out some useful information for the overly trusting medical billing entrepreneur.

Because a billing service is very closely connected to the entire process of insurance reimbursement, it is worthwhile to address a brief note on your responsibility for wrongful or fraudulently filed claims. In general, a billing service obtains all diagnostic and procedural codes from the physician and is, therefore, not responsible for errors of commission or omission unless the error is specifically traced back to their entry of a code. If you have made a small mistake, it is likely that your claim will be denied as an error because the procedural and diagnostic codes might not coincide. If you make a serious mistake, however, there are Medicare penalties of up to $2000.

On the other hand, you may be unwittingly drawn into a situation where a doctor is practicing fraudulent claim filing or is perhaps stretching the limits of the law in violation of federal laws and insurance regulations. In short, crime does exist in the medical profession, and you would be irresponsible not to pay attention to what your clients give you.

In December 1991, *The New York Times* reported that federal auditors were cracking down on physicians who file fraudulent or inflated bills. One method being used by hospitals and doctors is to bill insurers separately for two or more services that are performed on the same patient at the same time but that are supposed to be reported as one procedure. For instance, a doctor may report several procedures for a hysterectomy separately, rather than submitting a single fee. This is considered "fragmenting" the bill, which is forbidden and can cost taxpayers an additional several thousand dollars. According to *The New York Times*, hospitals, too, are pushing the limits by using such creative billing techniques, especially for x-rays and lab tests. One federal investigation found improper "unbundling" of procedures in 20 percent of the bills submitted by 8000 doctors in Pennsylvania who were

Fraudulent claims

filing Medicare claims for surgery. In another study of three cities between 1985 and 1989, Gerald Anderson, director of the Johns Hopkins Center for Finance and Management, in Baltimore, estimated that as many as one-third of Medicare claims contain overbilling by physicians.

There are also instances where physicians cheats themselves out of money they rightly deserve, because they have not coded properly. A good billing center that has learned the regulations of "appropriate" billing can help a client earn an additional $40,000 or more a year. In a doctor's newsletter published by St. Anthony Publishing in Virginia, gynecologists and obstetricians are told that they can charge $120 more for draining a certain type of cyst by coding one way rather than another.

In the long run, it would be wise to have a clear agreement with your client physicians, preferably in writing, that you assume no responsibility for billing errors outside of data entry mistakes. As Linda Noel of Linda's Billing Service said about changing bills or working in suspicious circumstances, "I don't do anything without permission from the doctor. Some of my clients, in the past, have wanted to do things that I didn't think were legal, so I got rid of them, because I won't work with someone like that, because I don't want to get blamed or sued."

Overcoming start-up problems

It isn't surprising that every business has some common start-up problems that can prevent you from succeeding if you don't resolve them within six months. Following is a brief review of those problems that seem to plague medical billing businesses. Perhaps by reading about them now, before you are in business, you can take steps to avoid them lest they happen to you.

Computer glitches

Don't wait until you are in business to discover computer hardware or software problems. Make sure you know what you are doing before a doctor is relying on you to process claims.

Low direct-mail campaign response

Many people have high expectations when they send out direct mail, but typically a 1 to 3 percent response rate is about all you can expect. That means if you send out 500 cards, don't expect more than 15 call-backs. However, if your response rate is less, consider redesigning your brochure or letter. Get someone to help you, and test it before another mailing by showing it to at least six people for reactions.

Slow build-up of clientele

Many of the billing services I spoke with told me that getting their first client took a few months, but after signing one doctor, they quickly signed another couple and then more over time. You should definitely have enough savings to keep going at least three to six months.

You might find resistance to your services for a variety of reasons. If so, assess if you have tried a large enough variety of doctors; are you doing everything you can to secure the trust of your customers?

Another point of resistance is doctors who say they already have computers in-house. If you hear that, ask "Are you doing electronic billing, including Medicare and commercial carriers?" Also ask whether the prospective client has a high turnover rate among staff, so that he or she is frequently training people and losing time on processing?" Both of these questions, are frequent recommendations by medical practice management consultants, and can help weaken an argument that billing remain in-house.

As you can see, you need to be prepared to answer these persistent issues that physicians read and hear about every day from many kinds of medical consultants. Convincing a physician to use your outside service is possible if you focus on the four Cs:

❑ **C**omplexity—Because insurance reimbursement regulations and coding change so frequently, why burden a staff person with keeping up on this never-ending struggle when *you* are an expert in it? You can stay abreast of changes and reduce mistakes.

❑ **C**ost—It almost always costs more to have a salaried worker do billing rather than you.

❑ **C**onsistency—You can provide round-the-clock coverage in a more consistent manner than a staff that is subject to constant turnover, or who may be preoccupied with dozens of other duties. Daniel Lehmann of DAPA Support Services expresses it this way, "You have to know the correct codings. A lot of doctors' offices do the coding, but many claims are rejected because of inaccurate coding and you just get them back in your lap."

❑ **C**ompetition—In today's competitive world, even the medical profession is feeling the need to provide better service to their customers. Note what James B. Davis writes in the Reimbursement Manual for the Medical Office (PMIC):

"Filing claims on behalf of your patients makes good sense. They appreciate your effort to help them pay for services or get reimbursed from their insurance carrier. By helping patients in this manner, you prove that you recognize them as people as well as patients, and that we care enough to assist them. [Also] . . . if the medical professionals in private practice expect to compete successfully with managed care operations, they must increase their level of service to include filing insurance claims for their patients."

If you take the four Cs and put them together with the four Ps of marketing (price, product, place, and promotion), you get the four PCs, a good mnemonic device to remember the basic guidelines to your business.

If you have this problem, it may be because you have not done enough homework to calculate your pricing schedule more favorably. If this is the case, you need to find some new clients immediately whom you can charge a higher rate, so that little by little you can achieve your profitability objectives. As an alternative, you may attempt to sign up your current clients for additional services at higher fees.

Client turnover

It is advisable to sign clients on with you for at least a yearly contract. This will minimize client turnover and give you twelve months to prove yourself. Even if you make a mistake, you have time to correct it, apologize, and do something special for the client to say that you value his or her business.

Building your business for the future

Many people purchase the software package and/or business opportunity and then do nothing with it. For these people apparently, spending money on the purchase of a new business venture was easy, but getting the business off the ground was not.

As in romance, there is a thrill in the chase, but if you spend the time and money to get into the business, you should be prepared to live with your business for a few years. One common mistake made by entrepreneurs is thinking and acting for the short term.

Electronic medical billing is here to stay, though the business may change as new technologies come to fruition and as new insurance and Medicare regulations move the industry in the same direction as banking and finance. So, if you are getting into this business, stay abreast of changes and look to a bright future!

3 Medical claims assistance services

Do you believe in helping the little guy? Does your hair stand on end when you hear about unfair hardships and corporate injustice? Do you enjoy verbal sparring with a lofty opponent? Do you like to nitpick and find mistakes? Do you feel drawn to helping others fight "the system"?

If your answer is "Yes" to these questions, then perhaps the medical claims assistance professional (CAP) is the right career for you. As mentioned earlier, claims professionals work for ordinary people (not doctors) as consumers of medical services. Their primary role is to help people organize, file, and negotiate health insurance claims of all kinds. Like tax assistants or personal business consultants, their job is to ensure that the consumer gets the maximum benefits and the best possible services from both medical providers, and the insurance companies who underwrite the health insurance policies in question.

This chapter explores the business of a claims professional, explains the necessary background and preparation for this career and explores the many ways you can conduct and market this valuable service.

Anyone who has ever read a health insurance policy or who has waited months for a health reimbursement check knows the frustration and confusion that can overwhelm even the brightest individual when it comes to dealing with doctors and our complex healthcare system. More than 2000 different health insurance carriers in the United States with nearly 10,000

What is a claims assistance professional?

different types of plans, it's easy to see how consumers can feel totally baffled whenever they have to deal with health insurance claims. Today, people frequently change jobs and, consequently, get new health insurance policies, or both spouses work and each has a different health plan or one spouse is retired and on Medicare while the other still works and is covered by an employer health plan. These scenarios depict the complexity of health coverage for millions of people when it comes to filing health insurance claims.

Enter, however, the medical claims assistance professional who knows health insurance rules and policies inside out—who has the exact phone numbers for all the local Medicare and insurance company offices right at the tip of his or her tongue or Rolodex, and who fears not when it comes to arguing with doctors or health insurance claims adjusters. Such people are in effect, a combination of professional consultant, personal advisor and representative, and hardcore negotiator, wearing each of these hats in turn as they help ordinary mortals through the thick and thin of dealing with their health insurance nightmares.

The medical claims assistance profession seems to have actually come into its maturity just in the past few years in fact, when a national association was formed in 1991 to formalize the profession and give it some respect and clout. Called the National Association of Claims Assistance Professionals, Inc. (NACAP), its articulate National Director Norma Border told me, "We currently have over 400 members and expect to grow to 500 shortly. Our primary function is to keep our members up-to-date on changes in healthcare legislation and provide training opportunities and seminars to hone skills and knowledge. We also provide certification for our members that can add to their credibility and respect in the community, and we can provide customer referrals in some cases too."

The formation of NACAP hints strongly at the growing importance of this profession. Border pointed out, for example, that insurance regulations are constantly changing, and so some part of her job is to stay in touch with events in Washington, D.C. so that the association can keep tabs on congressional hearings dealing with the insurance industry and lobby when necessary in their own interest. In addition, one might surmise that the growth of this profession also reflects a serious social and political policy issue in this country, as much is at stake when it comes to health insurance and money. As I've pointed out, the healthcare business and insurance industry have become a monstrous part of the country's economy, consuming more than $735 billion or more than 12 percent of our gross national product in 1991. With more than 220 million people covered by public or private health insurance, and more than 600 billion insurance claims filed each year, everyone involved—-from the consumer and doctor to the hospitals and insurance carriers—has money to gain or lose in the filing of health insurance claims.

In fact, Border mentioned a very important point for someone who thinks about starting this business, which is covered in more detail shortly, but which demonstrates its political and social nature: in at least 14 states, a claims assistance professional must be licensed or bonded in ways similar to insurance brokers or what are called "public adjusters." This makes sense in some ways, because claims professionals deal with the public and must be knowledgeable and skilled, so as to not mislead people or intentionally dupe them. But such regulations also suggest that the states and insurance companies hold a powerful sway over the average consumer of health insurance. Figure 3-1 lists those states that have such regulations, although Border suggests that you check with your state's insurance commissioner regardless of where you live to make sure you are adhering to any licensing requirements.

Alabama
Alaska
Arizona
Connecticut
Florida
Hawaii
Kentucky
Minnesota
Nebraska
New Hampshire
New Mexico
Oregon
Rhode Island
Vermont

3-1
States requiring medical claims assistance professionals to be licensed.

In any event, it is certain that medical claims assistance professionals are gaining in notoriety. As Mr. Harvey Matoren, owner of Health Claims of Jacksonville, Inc. (Florida) and, ironically, a former insurance company senior executive himself, explained to me, "Nobody is out there to fend for the average [health insurance] subscriber. There are lots of people to protect the interests of the insurance companies, hospitals, physicians, and other healthcare providers, but when it comes to recovering what is due to the average person, most people can't maximize their reimbursements and live under tremendous frustration and stress."

Let's turn our attention now to how the claims professional can help, and what people in this profession do day-by-day.

Who claims professionals' help

In the previous chapter on medical billing services, you learned that all doctors must file Medicare claims on behalf of their patients, and that in some other cases, many doctors voluntarily file commercial insurance claims as well. You may therefore wonder, as I did when I first began researching this business, why would a claims assistance professional be needed if doctors are handling more and more of the "dirty work?"

As discussed in chapter 1, one reason is that the number of people with health insurance has skyrocketed in the past decade, and so millions of claims are still filed by individuals themselves. In 1991, there were more than 1.3 billion physician contacts in the United States, which TABLE 3-1 breaks down by age and sex. (Note: women see doctors more frequently than men in most age categories, except over age 65 when men surpass women!)

Table 3-1
Number of physician contacts per year per person

	All places	Telephone	Office	Hospital	Other
All persons	**5.4**	**0.6**	**3.2**	**0.7**	**0.8**
Under 5 years	6.7	1.0	4.1	0.7	0.9
5–17 years	3.5	0.4	2.2	0.5	0.4
18–24 years	3.9	0.4	2.1	0.6	0.8
25–44 years	5.1	0.6	3.0	0.7	0.8
45–64 years	6.1	0.8	3.6	0.9	0.9
65–74 years	8.2	0.8	4.8	1.3	1.3
75 years +	9.9	0.9	6.0	1.0	2.0
Male					
All ages	4.7	0.5	2.7	0.7	0.7
Under 18	4.7	0.7	2.9	0.5	0.6
18–44	3.4	0.3	1.8	0.6	0.6
45–64	5.2	0.6	3.1	0.8	0.8
65 years +	9.0	0.9	5.1	1.5	1.5
Female					
All ages	6.1	0.8	3.7	0.7	0.9
Under 18	4.1	0.5	2.6	0.5	0.5
18–44	6.1	0.8	3.6	0.7	1.0
45–64	7.0	0.9	4.1	0.9	1.0
65 years +	8.8	0.8	5.3	1.0	1.6

Source: National Center for Health Statistics, Health Interview Survey, 1989.

Further, even when a physician or a hospital files a claim, there are still frequent breakdowns in communication, such as the amount of the deductible or how to process the residual claim to the person's secondary insurance coverage after the primary insurance carrier has paid. Consequently, the average consumer can often end up erroneously overpaying a doctor's charge or even duplicating a payment already made by the insurance carrier. In some cases, the insurance company has not made an accurate payment, so the subscriber may pay more than he or she is liable.

Claims professionals help many types of people. Here are a few of the major categories of cases that make this business quite needed. The following cases were adapted from the many reports I received in interviewing people in this business.

Many doctors simply refuse to file non-Medicare claims, and so millions of patients end up filing themselves—after they've paid their doctor or dentist—using traditional paper forms and receipts. When they sit down to do this though, many people are simply put off by the technicality of the work and would prefer to have someone do it for them. Particularly if they have an extended illness and end up with many bills over time, these people suddenly realize that they are out-of-pocket several hundreds or thousands of dollars, and so they look to a claims professional to get them out of the jam.

The lazy self-filer

Roberta Stevenson can't stand paperwork. Give her a contract or any document that uses words of more than two syllables and her mind turns right off. It's not that Roberta isn't bright; she simply can't follow the legalese, terminology, and sentence structure typically used in these documents. Roberta would simply prefer to hand over any material longer than a paragraph to an advisor, such as a claims assistant.

The flustered victim of legalese

John and Jane Adams and their two teenage kids practically never have any leisure time. The Adamses, who both work, come home from the office early in the evening, and immediately get involved in dozens of other projects, from shuttling the kids to ballet rehearsals and baseball games, to fixing the kitchen sink and planting the spring garden. The result of their busy lifestyle is that whenever a member of the family visits a doctor, Mr. and Mrs. Adams have no time left in their lives to fill in claims forms and file them. Nor do they have a moment to make phone calls back and forth to their doctor's office and insurance company to clarify any problems of an unpaid claim. For many people like this, paying a small fee to have a professional handle this work makes life more enjoyable.

The busy family

Al Smith works for a local manufacturer and has a family health insurance policy through his employer. His wife Sally also works, and her health insurance plan, which acts as her secondary coverage, will pick up any copayments she owes after her husband's family plan pays out the primary benefits. However, some recent medical bills have totally confused the family as to which insurance company will pay what, and why neither will pay some amount anyway. They are now excellent candidates for a claims assistance professional.

The mixed insurance family

Arnold Pimler believes in health insurance. Over the years, he has collected or purchased five policies. When he finally became ill and had an extended

The multiple insurance person

hospitalization, he left it to a claims professional to figure out who paid what to whom.

The retired lifers

Jack and Bobbie Mormin recently retired to a Sun Belt state to enjoy some peace and quiet, and a bit of golf. While they do not have any major medical ailments, they prefer to spend not a drop of their time thinking about their health insurance policies. So they hire a claims service to handle whatever comes their way each year for a small fee.

The child of an aging parent

Maggie O'Brien's 78-year-old mother recently had surgery and required several thousands of dollars of follow-up treatment and physical therapy. Little did the mother know that her Medicare and MediGap insurance policies did not cover all the procedures. Now Maggie is stuck with trying to figure out how to maximize their reimbursement and minimize their payments. Unfortunately, Maggie works at a demanding job, and has little time to make phone calls to the insurance company or Medicare. She loves her mother, but does not really want this problem dumped in her lap, so she hires a claims professional.

The crisis family

Tragically, 52-year-old Alan Roberts has a terminal illness, and his family is spending every waking minute trying to comfort their loved one through the ordeal. Meanwhile, the medical bills keep mounting and some health claims to Roberts' insurance company are being denied or rejected for unexplained reasons. This family realizes that there are more important things in life at the moment, and so they hear through word of mouth about a claims assistance professional in their area who can handle these claims.

The caught-in-the -middle situation

Mike Loring recently went to his doctor twice in one week for a bad cold, and while he was there, he also received a chest x-ray and blood test from the local laboratory. He paid all four charges (two office visits and two tests) in cash because the physician and laboratory preferred to have the money immediately and insisted that Mike deal with his own insurance plan. When Mike filed the claims ($300), however, his insurance company said that the diagnostic codes were missing from his receipts, and that the procedures didn't match. Mike made a few phone calls, but eventually he became fed up with the runaround, and simply wanted his 80 percent of $300 back. He called a local claims professional, and signed up immediately to have the claims pursued on his behalf.

The Medicare squeeze

Norman Fields, a 72-year-old retired teacher, recently fell off a ladder while painting his house one summer day. He suffered a broken arm and numerous other minor injuries that required a brief hospitalization followed by repeated treatments. Unfortunately, his slew of claims was only partially paid by Medicare, with many claims being downcoded from what the doctor had billed. The problem: he was now receiving bills from his doctor for amounts of money that he thought were greater than the allowable amounts. When Norman contacted a claims assistant, he learned that the doctor was erroneously billing him for amounts he was not allowed to charge.

Ruth Kress was diagnosed with a rare blood disease in the early part of the year. Fortunately, her best friend recommended a wonderful doctor who was using an unusual treatment for this blood disease that was actually an accepted treatment for another disease. Ruth was miraculously cured, but now her insurance company was denying her $25,000 in claims, calling the treatments experimental. Ruth used a medical claims assistance professional to negotiate the case and was able to get many of the claims paid.

The denied claim

Glenda Peterson incurred $30,000 in medical bills over the past year because of serious illness, all of which were completely rejected by her insurance company. In her frustration, she hired a claims assistance company to work on her behalf. When the company took over, they learned that simple errors had been made and that resubmitting the claims with new diagnostic codes was enough to get the claims paid. Unfortunately, no one at the insurance company bothered to tell Glenda that all she had to do was to reprocess them with the errors corrected.

The insurance runaround

Randy Bern hates to argue. Although she knows that her insurance company made a mistake on her recently submitted claim for $860, she must convince the person with whom she spoke about the error. It was a supervisor, who growled and grubbed, and insisted that "Bern doesn't understand company policy." Fortunately, Bern felt burned, and she contacted a claims professional who wasn't afraid to put the supervisor into her proper place.

The intimidated victim

All the preceding scenarios are indicative of the types of situations and circumstances that people get into when dealing with the health insurance system. And in each case, an experienced, knowledgeable, efficient medical claims assistance professional can provide valuable services. Foremost, is getting the reimbursement money from the insurance company for fees the client may have already paid to a doctor, or which the client owes the doctor who graciously awaits the reimbursement. But more than this financial role, claims assistance professionals also provide the following important services:

Saving your clients more than just money

Eliminate stress   They remove a tremendous amount of stress most people experience when dealing with intimidating bureaucratic organizations. From the lunch-hour calls where the insurance clerk puts you on hold for 20 minutes, to the frantic trips to the doctor's office to get them to sign your claim form, most people feel like they are unwitting victims in a Kafka-esque nightmare over which they have no control. And worse, the stress can be unhealthy for some people, particularly the elderly. As Mary Ellen Fitzgibbons, a claims assistance professional in Chicago told me, "I have one client who says she feels like she's going to have a heart attack whenever she speaks with her insurance company. She gets so emotionally upset, she just can't do it by herself."

Save people money   Many people mistakenly pay providers before Medicare or the insurance company reimburses the provider, and so the burden is on the patient to recover prematurely paid monies, which can take weeks. Even when the physician or hospital provides assistance to the insured person, it is self-interested service and is often limited in scope to claims for services only they have provided. For example, some hospitals offer clinics to senior citizens to teach them how to handle their own claims, but such people are often too old or too sick to handle the balance of the required work on their own.

Save people time   The average consumer knows little about navigating the channels of the insurance industry and can often spend hours and hours on a situation that a claims professional could handle in 30 minutes. And time is money. Many people would rather pay someone $20 or $50 if it saves them a few hundred dollars and their valuable time.

Save people embarrassment   When a foul-up occurs, many doctors' offices will turn a bill over to a collection agency. Suddenly, the consumer finds himself getting dunning notices, and perhaps even has a report made to his credit record. I had this happen to my family recently. My wife had six charges, all for $80, for blood tests from a laboratory she was sent to by her allergy clinic. We thought we had paid all the bills, but a certain bill never came in the mail, and one day we started getting dunning notices from a collection agency for $80. We called the clinic, and they told us everything was paid. We got more dunning notices, however, as well as discovering one of the bills was erroneously recorded to another doctor in the allergy clinic and that the laboratory had also misdated the invoice, calling it a *post-test result* that somehow predated the *pre-test* result, thereby confusing me into thinking that the bill was a duplicate charge for one I had already paid. In the end, I had no way of knowing that all this confusion was happening behind the scenes, and that I owed $80, but my credit received a black mark. I would have gladly handed over this case to a claims professional!

Help people in times of crisis   Claims professionals preserve family priorities and help people in times of need and crisis. Many families today find themselves in crisis with aging parents. For them, spending a few dollars is less important than being with their family and being sure they can devote their time where it is most needed. Irene Card of Medical Insurance Claims, Inc. in New Jersey also notes that many times people in divorce utilize a claims professional to avoid seeing a spouse or dealing with the sticky financial arrangements divorce often engenders.

Maximize investment in health insurance   The majority of people don't know what to expect when it comes to health insurance reimbursements. Consequently, they have no protection against mistakes, errors, delays, and even intentional malfeasance on the part of some insurance companies. In this business, few people doubt that insurance companies intentionally delay claims payments or give people the runaround when they don't want to pay a claim. Obviously, it is hard to prove, but every claims person I spoke with had quite a few horror stories about people who had lost claims because of a minuscule error or a simple mistake. Harvey Matoren of Health Claims of Jacksonville, Inc. had one client who had $60,000 of bills rejected by her insurance company. When he looked into it, he discovered that the claims had been submitted under the wrong component of her insurance policy, but no one at this company bothered to tell the woman to send the claims in the name of the other component— Major Medical—under which they would be accepted and paid. Harvey easily got 90 percent ($54,000) back for the client. As ludicrous as this sounds, Harvey and many others I spoke to indicated that it happens all the time.

Advising about health insurance matters   Claims professionals also provide certain advice about health insurance. Many professionals counsel clients on which health insurance policies to purchase, especially when it comes to Medicare supplement policies (MediGap). This is considered insurance brokering in some states and not all claims professionals are allowed to do this. Many provide informal advice, however, about the quality of a company's service and their claims payment history so that their clients can make more informed decisions than they otherwise would be able to.

Provide a service to physicians and hospitals   Medical claims professionals indirectly provide a service to physicians and hospitals, although most of the latter don't quite understand this. When patients owe money to their physicians, the faster the insured parties get reimbursed, the faster they, too, can pay off the physicians. Unfortunately, many doctors and hospital billing departments don't recognize this.

In researching this chapter, for example, I called a few hospitals in the Los Angeles area and pretended to be a patient. I asked if they could refer me to someone to help me fill out my insurance claims. No billing person knew what I was talking about! The claims professionals I interviewed were not surprised. They indicated that many doctors and hospitals don't acknowledge them or refer people to them because they think it is beyond the scope of their duties to help people obtain insurance reimbursements.

The medical world is changing though, and no doubt claims assistance professionals will be playing a more active role in the scheme of healthcare.

The life of a claims professional

The day-to-day life of the people I spoke with in the claims business were invariably hectic and busy. Most claims professionals operate full-time, on-going businesses, with 300 or more active customers, that is, people who contacted them at least periodically over the course of a year or less to take care of their medical business. It was not surprising, therefore, to hear of 10-hour days, largely spent doing the following:

Typical duties	Time spent (hours)
Taking phone calls or in-person meetings from current customers	3
Making phone calls to insurance carriers and doctors	2
Filling out claims forms and appeals	1.5
Reading professional materials and insurance policies	1.5
Marketing (phone calls or in-person meetings with potential new clients)	1
Opening mail	1

As you can see, much of the business is occupied by phone calls or in-person contact with both clients and insurance companies. Because a claims professional handles all routine claims, they constantly receive materials in the mail or in person. For routine claims, the procedure is twofold.

1. The claims professional obtains a copy of the receipt that the client has from the doctor's visit. Sometimes this is a photocopy of the person's general ledger card or sometimes it is a copy of the superbill from the doctor indicating the diagnosis and the fees charged.
2. The claims person fills out a paper claim form from the client's insurance carrier or perhaps a HCFA 1500 form, pops it in the mail, and voilà, the claim is taken care of. (Ironically, the claims professionals I spoke to told me that most insurance carriers still insist on receiving their own version of a paper claim, not the HCFA 1500).

If the professional didn't get a copy of the carrier's claim form from the client, he or she must call the specific insurance carrier and have one sent. So much for standardized claims forms! For nonroutine claims, where a payment is not made or the client knows there is a problem, the professional might need to make several phone calls to the doctor's office to ask about a fee or a procedure, then to Medicare, then to the secondary insurance carrier to find out about what happened to the payment, then to the client, and so on until it is straightened out.

A few claims professionals had even busier schedules because they traveled to the homes of their clients in order to provide a more personalized, private service. Nancy and Tom Koehler, owners of In Home Medical Claims in Poway, California, make it their policy to conduct business at the premises of their clients. As Tom told me, "People feel better by having us come to them. They trust us more and feel they are getting a service." See the sidebar on the Koehlers for more details on how this couple operates their successful business.

Nancy and Tom Koehler   When Nancy Koehler, a social worker with a variety of work experiences, met a woman in 1986 who was doing medical claims assistance, she was curious about the profession but didn't do anything about it. A year later, when her friend showed up one morning, excited about her upcoming retirement, but worried about the capabilities of the person to whom she was thinking of selling her business, Nancy suddenly realized that an opportunity was knocking at her door. Her friend agreed to cancel the other sale, and Nancy found herself with a new venture in life.

Business was slow at first, but Nancy loved the job and the feeling of helping others. Her enthusiasm was so unbounding, in fact, that her husband Tom, a former navy fighter pilot of 20 years, came home one day and decided to quit his job as a project manager for a defense department manufacturer of navigation systems. Never imagining that one day they would find themselves working together, Tom and Nancy now recognize they have the exact complement of skills that makes a business work. With her medical background, Nancy brings in many contacts and a solid understanding of Medicare and the claims business, which Tom has now learned, too. But with his project management background, Tom takes charge of the business planning and handles what he calls P&L responsibility for the business. He uses a Casio digital diary to keep track of his daily appointments and an IBM 386 DX using various programs such as Timeslips (Timeslips Corp.) to keep track of his clients and do monthly invoicing.

After five years in business, Nancy and Tom now have about 200 clients for whom they regularly handle claims assistance and other personal matters, such as balancing checkbooks, paying bills, and year-end medical expense reports for tax purposes. Living in a nice southern Californian retirement area, they were fortunate enough to get a few clients in a large apartment complex, who then referred them to others. Nancy also does a lot of speaking engagements and has become somewhat of a noted expert on Medicare in the area.

Tom admits, "What makes our business great is the demographics here. But we also did our homework. We took several workshops from the Small Business Administration (SBA) on marketing and business planning, and Nancy also went to SCORE for some advice and managed to get a former Blue Cross executive from Michigan who had retired here as her mentor. Our operation is sophisticated but simple. We limit the number of clients we cover so we can maintain quality service and trust, which is one of the most important aspects of this business."

Business profile in home medical claims

Overall, many professionals compared their day-to-day life to a tax preparer who knows the rules and regulations inside out and can quickly assess a situation and know what to do and with whom to deal. The job often sounded to me more like a detective's life though, in the sense that working with claims is like putting together an unsolved puzzle. A claims professional must be dedicated to seeing the big picture, and then putting the pieces together so it all fits.

Finally, the claims profession was unanimously described as a real people-oriented business, in which the claims professional is like a public defender who protects the poor innocent victims of our nightmarish health system against the penurious corporate giants of the insurance industry. Everyone I spoke with loved their work, especially the thrill of winning a claim for their clients. As Rikki Horn, founder of Medical Claims Management in Newbury Park, California, proudly announced, "I like providing a real service. People come to me and they are vulnerable. You need to care about the people you work for. When your client gets a check for $1200, you feel as if you did it for yourself."

Knowledge & skills needed

Like medical billing services, a claims professional deals in-depth with the complex rules, vocabulary, and forms of the insurance industry and medical offices. Also, like medical billing, a claims person must spend time and energy setting up the business and getting clients. Many of the same skills and knowledge apply to this business as for medical billing services, including a:

❑ Moderate to high level of knowledge of the health insurance business, especially claims procedures, medical coding, and Medicare/commercial insurance policies and regulations.
❑ Moderate to high level of knowledge and skills in business, including marketing and sales.
❑ Low to moderate level of knowledge with computers and business software.

Just as with medical billing services, the more experience you have in any of these areas, particularly in the medical industry, the easier your job will be if you are just starting out as a claims professional. If you worked as part of a physician's billing staff within the health insurance industry, or at a corporation in their personnel department, you will probably have an easier time getting your business off the ground.

All of these skills are learnable, however. The novice will just need more time or a slightly different entry path into the business, such as working first in a medical office or with an established claims service to build up your background. After reading the following sections and exploring these areas in detail, you might want to do the activity suggested in the previous chapter in which you informally plot your learning curve across the three areas previously mentioned: insurance industry knowledge, business skills, and computer literacy. See chapter 2 for more information about this planning activity.

First and foremost, a claims professional must have a complete understanding of the health insurance business—who the players are; how doctors, hospitals, and insurance companies interact; and how claims are processed. Without a sound grounding in these areas, one simply cannot be a "professional." As Tom Koehler of In Home Medical Claims characterizes it, "This profession requires integrative skills; you have to look at claims EOB (Explanation of Benefits), the physician's bill, and all the insurance policies a client has, and then put it all together to come out with one conclusion: did the person get paid the right amount." As a result, you need to know the:

❑ Different types of health insurance policies and companies for primary insurance.
❑ Relationships among primary insurance and additional client policies.
❑ Medicare policies and regulations.
❑ Complex terminology of the billing and insurance industries.
❑ Terminology and basis of medical diagnostic and procedural coding.

Rather than repeat information on a few of these issues, please read through chapter 2 on the health insurance industry, on how paper and electronic claims are filed, and the explanation of the diagnostic codes (ICD-9) and procedural codes (CPT–4).

I also suggest you take a few moments to review your own health insurance policy or ask your employer if you can read the full policy on file in your personnel office. I'm sure you can imagine the type of obtuse and convoluted language typically used in health insurance policies. This exercise will give you a taste of what you might need to read daily as a claims professional.

In addition, you should be familiar with how insurance companies pay, such as the guidelines for UC&R, Schedule of Benefits, Maximum Allowances, and Capitation. The sidebar on Payment Speak can help.

According to the *Health Insurance Carrier Directory*, a doctor's guide to insurance carriers, published by Practice Management Information Corporation, there are four primary methods different insurance companies use to pay physicians:

Payment speak

1. UC&R (usual, customary, and reasonable). In this method, the insurance carrier essentially chooses the lowest of three categories:
   ❑ Usual fee—the "usual" fee is the amount the physician charges for a service. The irony is that insurance companies determine this charge because they keep records for providers over each year and average out

the median (50th percentile) charge, which they then call the *usual charge*.

❑ Customary fee—this fee is also determined by insurance carrier profiles and is based on the 90th percentile of all fees charged by all providers within the same specialty area in the same geographic location for a specific service.

❑ Reasonable fee—the reasonable fee is the lesser of the billed fee, the usual fee, the customary fee, or another fee that might be justified under special circumstances.

Using these three categories, the insurance carrier picks the lowest fee. If Doctor A submits a fee for $220 as his usual but $225 is the customary, she will receive only 80 percent of $220. If Doctor B submits a fee of $250 as her usual fee, but it is higher than the customary fee of $225, she could receive 80 percent of $225. As you can see, Doctor B gets more, and the system seems to actually encourage doctors to charge higher fees on a regular basis to ensure that their usual fees exceed the customary range.

2. Schedule of benefits method. In this method, the insurance company maintains a table of benefits that represent its total obligation to pay for a specific procedure. If the physician charges more, the patient might need to pay the copayment (20 percent) amount as well as the difference between the billed amount and what the insurance company has determined to be their maximum.

3. Maximum fee schedule. In this method, the insurance company maintains a maximum payment amount and the provider agrees to accept that payment as his or her total reimbursement.

4. Capitation method. Capitation refers to a prepaid plan wherein the insurance carrier pays the provider under contract a specified amount, usually on a monthly basis, for each patient in the plan. This is the system used in many Health Maintenance Organizations.

Understanding these four methods of payment are useful to a claims professional in order to assess if a physician and insurance carrier are correctly billing a procedure and if the patient is somehow paying too much. From what claims professionals told me, many doctors either erroneously or intentionally bill patients for amounts greater than what the usual and customary or schedule of benefits methods allow. Here is where the claims professional protects the little guy!

Understanding medical coding is almost as important for a claims professional as it is for a medical billing service. A claims professional must have an excellent command of these codes (though you shouldn't memorize them, because there are thousands) because many claims are rejected or downcoded (i.e., reimbursed at a lower amount) because of incorrect coding, missing modifiers, and wrong location codes. This means that patients (your clients) could be reimbursed nothing, a lower amount, or end up paying the doctor more than is necessary. You might recall from the previous chapter that insurance companies, which have a vested interest in minimizing their payouts, are not bending over backwards to ensure a patient is properly paid. In short, if you don't know your coding, you cannot protect the interests of your clients.

In addition, staying abreast of Medicare rules and regulations is vital, because many of the people who use claims professionals are the elderly. They need assistance with every aspect of Medicare, from basic coverages to supplemental insurance. Medicare has very specific exclusions about payments for certain procedures, as well as limitations on payments for a variety of reasons such as time or location. For example, some procedures can only be conducted in a doctor's office: so if the location coding on the claim form was wrong, the claim could accidentally be denied.

There are also important rules about when Medicare is not the primary insurance even though the person is age 65 (referred to as MSP—Medicare as Secondary Payer), such as when someone is still working and has an employer plan, the spouse is still working and the family is covered, or if the medical service was related to a work injury or automobile accident.

You must also know the Medicare changes that occur each year in the amount of the deductible for Parts A and B, as well as the dollar limitations placed on some services and hospitalizations. Last, you must understand the realm of Medicare supplementary insurance (MediGap), which is currently undergoing changes in standardizing the plans.

Simple errors occur constantly, and if you are unable to detect the reasons, you cannot do your job. Mary Ellen Fitzgibbons told me about one incident where a hospital made several serious errors in billing Medicare for services rendered to a woman who eventually died. The secondary insurance company wouldn't pay the difference, and so the hospital held the family liable for the deceased woman's bill of $2000. "The average person would pay the collection notices without question," she said, "but in many cases, there's been a misunderstanding or error made."

Nancy and Tom Koehler of In Home Medical Claims also related several stories to me how many errors are made. "We've had all kinds of simple mistakes. One hospital in this area billed a client for outpatient services, and when we called to ask if they had billed Medicare first, it turned out they hadn't. Another client received a bill for the copayment amount on a Medicare Part B outpatient service, and because he had neglected to tell the hospital that he had supplemental (secondary) insurance, he thought he had to pay. We simply told the hospital to forward the bill to the secondary insurance, and it was taken care of. In another case, the doctor billed both our client and the secondary insurance company, and so we made sure the doctor didn't get paid twice. We also have a client who retired from a company in Tennessee that was self-insured, and for some reason, the hospital didn't want to send the bill to them. So we helped the client get it taken care of. He paid the 20 percent copayment and then we made sure the company received the bill and paid it. The client was happy and it saved him a lot of time and stress."

A claims professional also needs to be able to read and understand the EOB (Explanation of Benefits) sent from commercial insurance carriers to beneficiaries, and the EOMB (Explanation of Medicare Benefits) that people receive from either the Medicare insurance intermediary handling Part A inpatient or Part B outpatient hospitalization charges, or from the representative Medicare insurance carrier, which handles Part B claims for physician services. Figures 3-2, 3-3, and 3-4 are copies of EOMB notices.

Finally, a claims professional must also know what to do when a claim is denied. One indication that claims professionals are now being recognized is that, while in the past it was very difficult for claims professionals to get information on behalf of their clients for appeal, it is now much more commonly accepted that some people hire a claims service to handle this work. In fact, Medicare now allows claims professionals to fill out the appeal Form 0938-0033 (see FIG. 3-5) and sign it as a representative of the insured person. Most commercial insurance companies don't use appeals forms, and so knowing who to contact can be critical. As Tom Koehler told me, "It is often knowing exactly the right person to call that can make a difference. I had one client, and when her insurance company denied the claim, I just got on the phone to my person, and asked why was this claim denied? It didn't make sense. When I explained the circumstances, she took care of it right away and got it paid."

As you can see, there is an extensive array of insurance industry knowledge and inside information a claims professional must know. If you approach the field as if it were a puzzle, you'll be challenged rather than frustrated and confused. One piece at a time does it!

Developing your business savvy

Earlier in the chapter, I mentioned that the claims professionals I spoke with indicated they had 200 to 300 clients or more. As you might imagine, it takes time to build up such a clientele, and so knowing how to market and sell your services is a critical skill if you want to stay in business. Many of the same marketing ideas and concepts discussed in chapter 2 apply here, except that medical claims assistance professionals deal with the public at-large as their potential customers, not with a small market of doctors. Therefore, your marketing and sales needs will be quite different. You are targeting tens of thousands of people.

Marketing   Unlike medical billing services, your market is broad, unfocused, and does not usually know about your service. Doctors at least know about medical billing and have probably heard about medical billing

U.S. DEPARTMENT OF HEALTH AND HUMAN SERVICES/HEALTH CARE FINANCING ADMINISTRATION   1921691602

MEDICARE BENEFIT NOTICE

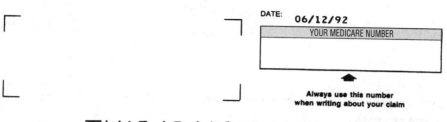

DATE: **06/12/92**

YOUR MEDICARE NUMBER

▲
Always use this number
when writing about your claim

THIS IS NOT A BILL

This notice shows what benefits were used by you and the covered services not paid by Medicare for the period shown in item 1. See other side of this form for additional information which may apply to your claim.

1 SERVICES FURNISHED BY	DATE(S)	BENEFITS USED
HOSPITAL	05/06/92 THRU 05/12/92	6 INPATIENT HOSPITAL DAYS

2 PAYMENT STATUS

MEDICARE PAID ALL COVERED SERVICES EXCEPT:
    $652.00 FOR THE INPATIENT DEDUCTIBLE.

YOU HAVE 60 DAYS REMAINING TOWARD YOUR LIMIT OF 60 HOSPITAL RESERVE DAYS.

IF NO-FAULT INSURANCE, LIABILITY INSURANCE, WORKERS' COMPENSATION,
VETERANS ADMINISTRATION, OR, IN SOME CASES, A GROUP HEALTH PLAN
FOR EMPLOYEES ALSO COVERS THESE SERVICES, A REFUND MAY BE DUE THE
MEDICARE PROGRAM. PLEASE CONTACT US IF YOU ARE COVERED BY ANY OF
THESE SOURCES.

If you have any questions about this record, call or write

▶ BLUE CROSS OF CALIFORNIA - MEDICARE
P. O. BOX 70000
VAN NUYS   CA   91470
TELEPHONE NUMBER   (818)-593-2006

FORM HCFA-1533 (9-83)

3-2   *Example of Medicare EOMB, Part A Hospital.*

Blue Cross
of California

P. O. Box 70000
Van Nuys, California 91470

PLEASE READ OTHER SIDE OF THIS NOTICE FOR IMPORTANT INFORMATION

THIS IS NOT A BILL

DATE: FEBRUARY 28, 1992

YOUR MEDICARE NUMBER
HEALTH INSURANCE CLAIM NUMBER

ALWAYS USE THIS NUMBER WHEN
WRITING ABOUT YOUR CLAIM.

OUR RECORDS SHOW
YOU RECEIVED
SERVICES FROM
1920440852

PROVIDER NAME, ADDRESS AND STATE
HOSPITAL

DATE OF FIRST SERVICE
JAN. 09 1992

LAST SERVICE
JAN. 09 1992

TYPE OF SERVICE	COVERED CHARGES	REMARKS
EMERGENCY ROOM	173.00	
RADIOLOGY	53.00	
PHARMACY	15.50	
OTHER	71.50	

A.	313.00	TOTAL COVERED CHARGES	313.00	¹ $ 100.00 OF YOUR 100.00 DEDUCTIBLE IS NOW MET FOR 1992
B.	$ .00	COUNTED TOWARD YOUR PART B CASH DEDUCTIBLE		ALL AMOUNTS PAYABLE BY YOU SHOULD BE PAID DIRECTLY TO THE HOSPITAL. DO NOT SEND PAYMENT TO BLUE CROSS OF CALIFORNIA.
C.	$ .00	PART B BLOOD DEDUCTIBLE CHARGE		
D.	$ 62.60	COINSURANCE, 20% OF (A, MINUS SUM OF B. + C.)		
E.	$ 62.60	TOTAL DEDUCTIBLE AND COINSURANCE PAYABLE BY YOU	62.60	². .00 AMOUNT YOU PAID PROVIDER
F.	BALANCE	ITEM A MINUS ITEM E	250.40	³. 62.60 AMOUNT OWED PROVIDER
G.				⁴. .00 REFUND (ENCLOSED)
H.				
I.		BALANCE OF COVERED CHARGES	250.40	MEDICARE PAID FOR THESE SERVICES

556 8/82

PLEASE READ OTHER SIDE OF THIS NOTICE FOR IMPORTANT INFORMATION.

3-3 *Example of Medicare EOMB, Part B Hospital. This explanation of Medicare Benefits notice is used to show how Medicare Part B benefits were paid. In this case, the beneficiary had to pay 20% coinsurance.*

This is not a bill

Explanation of Your Medicare Part B Benefits

Summary of this notice dated June 29, 1992		
Total charges:	$	38.00
Total Medicare approved:	$	23.71
We paid your provider:	$	18.97

Your Medicare Number is:

Details about this notice (See the back for more information.)

You received these services from your provider:

MED CORP, Mailing Address:

Services and Service Codes Claim Control Number 92170-4011	Dates	Charge	Medicare Approved	Notes
Office/Outpatient Visit, Est (99212)	June 4, 1992	$ 38.00	$ 23.71	a

Notes:

a The approved amount for this procedure is based on the Medicare fee schedule.

Here's an explanation of this notice:

Of the total charges, Medicare approved	$ 23.71	The provider agreed to accept this amount. See #4 on the back.
Less Medicare copayment amount	− 4.74	We pay 80% of the approved amount; you pay 20%.
Approved amount less copay	$ 18.97	**You have met the deductible for 1992.**
Medicare owes	$ 18.97	
We are paying the provider	$ 18.97	

COUNSELING OFFICE

IMPORTANT: If you have questions about this notice, call Medicare at (213) 748-2311 (toll free - So CA only 1-800-675-2266) or see us at 1149 So Broadway, Los Angeles, CA 90015. You will need this notice if you contact us.

To appeal our decision, you must WRITE to us before DEC. 29, 1992 at Transamerica Occidental Life Insurance Co., P.O. Box 30540, Los Angeles, CA 90030. See 2 on the back.
(000-0012579)

3-4 *Example of Medicare EOMB, Part B Provider. This explanation of Medicare Benefits shows how a Part B Provider benefit is paid. This physician set a charge of $38, but Medicare's approved charge is only $23.71, of which they only pay 80% ($18.97) directly to the physician. The beneficiary must pay the remaining 20%.*

DEPARTMENT OF HEALTH AND HUMAN SERVICES
HEALTH CARE FINANCING ADMINISTRATION

Form Approved
OMB No. 0938-0033

REQUEST FOR REVIEW OF PART B MEDICARE CLAIM
Medical Insurance Benefits - Social Security Act

NOTICE—Anyone who misrepresents or falsifies essential information requested by this form may upon conviction be subject to fine and imprisonment under Federal Law.

1 Carrier's Name and Address

2 Name of Patient

3 Health Insurance Claim Number

4 I do not agree with the determination you made on my claim as described on my Explanation of Medicare

Benefits dated:

5 MY REASONS ARE: (Attach a copy of the Explanation of Medicare Benefits, or describe the service, date of service, and physician's name—NOTE.—If the date on the Notice of Benefits mentioned in item 3 is more than six months ago, include your reason for not making this request earlier.)

6 Describe Illness or Injury:

7 ☐ I have additional evidence to submit. (Attach such evidence to this form.)

☐ I do not have additional evidence.

COMPLETE ALL OF THE INFORMATION REQUESTED. SIGN AND RETURN THE FIRST COPY AND ANY ATTACHMENTS TO THE CARRIER NAMED ABOVE. IF YOU NEED HELP, TAKE THIS AND YOUR NOTICE FROM THE CARRIER TO A SOCIAL SECURITY OFFICE, OR TO THE CARRIER. KEEP THE DUPLICATE COPY OF THIS FORM FOR YOUR RECORDS.

8 SIGNATURE OF **EITHER** THE CLAIMENT **OR** HIS REPRESENTATIVE

Representative	Claimant
Address	Address
City, State, and ZIP Code	City, State, and ZIP Code

Telephone Number	Date	Telephone Number	Date

Form HCFA-1964 (8-85)

(over)

CARRIER'S COPY

3-5 *Medicare claims appeal form. This form is used to appeal denial of benefits to a beneficiary for a claim. Claims assistance professionals are now allowed to sign the form as the beneficiary's representative.*

services, so they represent a much easier target for a person getting into the medical billing business.

A claims professional must have a good sense of how to market a service to the general public, however. Because this market is so vast, it is not worthwhile to consider cold calling as a primary method of developing a customer base. In the medical billing business, cold calling (or at least "warmed up" cold calling) is generally useful, because your goal is to meet face-to-face with a doctor or a decision-maker in the doctor's office to close a deal that could bring you thousands of claims each month. In this business, however, cold calling is not productive. Your best bet is to learn how to get people to come to you. You need to know *marketing mix*, the proportion of four major marketing methods: advertising, public relations, direct mail, and sales promotions.

For example, you could advertise in the newspaper, on a mid-day talk show on the local radio, or even on the back of cash register receipts, in which case you must learn about advertising rates and designing effective print or spoken advertisements. You will need to calculate your budgets and what the payoff might be in comparison to what you spend in advertising. Consider local newspapers and other less expensive or free sources for your advertising. You might also want to design unique brochures to leave at bus stops, stores, parking lots, or any number of methods that are used when you need to reach thousands of people. Your copywriting and graphic design capabilities need to be developed.

Every claims professional I spoke with indicated that public relations was one of their best forms of marketing. Writing articles or getting them written about you and your business is an extremely cost-effective method of advertising. It can get your name in front of thousands, even millions of people who may need your service. The sidebar on Harvey Matoren, whose company Health Claims of Jacksonville, Inc. has been written about in numerous newspapers, including the prestigious Kiplinger's Personal Finance Magazine.

How would you like to have your company written up, at no expense to you, and paraded in front of millions of people who are your potential customers? Sound too good to be true? It's not, and that's exactly what happened over time as Harvey Matoren and his wife Carol found their company Health Claims of Jacksonville, Inc. written about in several local newspapers and then in the prestigious Kiplinger's Personal Finance Magazine.

Business profile: Publicizing your business

Started in 1989 from home, Harvey and Carol left excellent positions in the insurance industry in Florida to found their own business as claims assistance professionals. Harvey had been a senior vice president with Blue Cross and Blue Shield, and president of their HMO subsidiary; Carol was a senior health industry analyst and a registered nurse. But they had dreams for their own business, and they felt drawn toward helping the average person navigate through what they knew firsthand to be a rough world in the insurance business. As Harvey told me, "We are in our late 40's and we looked at this as an opportunity to grow a business that has lots of potential and that we feel is much needed in our country. We know how difficult it is to get through the system."

Thanks to hard work, good previous experience and knowledge, and lots of publicity, Harvey and Carol now have a suite in an office complex, and two employees. Their goal is to grow a bigger business as well, with offices in other locations, and training workshops for interested new business startups. Harvey added, "My feeling is that we have hardly scratched the surface of clients for this business. Anyone and everyone may need this type of service, from Medicare recipients to couples who just don't have time."

While Harvey wasn't sure how many clients he has received from the publicity, there's no doubt that having these articles appear has contributed to his prestige and credibility in the public's eye. After all, what better advertisement could be made than a page of laudatory comments about your business, especially one that does the talking for you in a market where most people don't know what you do.

Harvey can be reached at (904) 733-2525, or by writing to him at 3926 San Jose Park Drive, Jacksonville, FL 32217, if you want to contact him for more information or to write an article on his behalf.

The third area of a promotional mix—direct mail—is, of course, a major undertaking and probably worth studying if you are inexperienced at it. It costs money and time to print thousands of cards, find a good mailing list, and get your mail out properly. Learning from others or simply hiring a direct-mail consultant could prove useful. A few useful resources on direct mail are *The Complete Direct Mail List Handbook*, by Ed Burnett (Prentice-Hall) and *Direct Mail Copy that Sells* by Herschell Gordon Lewis (Prentice-Hall).

The last aspect of your marketing mix—promotions—can be quite valuable. Because people don't know what you do, you could offer a one-time assistance on a claim or a reduction in your fee to get people to check out your service. Promotions can be important when you need people to sign on initially, because they often will come back if they like your service.

Last, one additional aspect of any marketing campaign—no matter what the business—is networking and getting word-of-mouth referrals. Nearly every claims person I spoke to said that getting people who know your service to recommend you to prospective clients is the most surefire way to find new clients. Whether it's your relatives, doctors you know, or current clients, you want to encourage people to talk about your service to others and spread the word. You can support this by letting people know, diplomatically, that you welcome referrals, and you might even offer a discount to new people who come to you through a referral, as well as a special thank-you discount to the person who made the referral.

To learn more about marketing, get a copy of one of the best books in this area, *Getting Business to Come to You* by Paul and Sarah Edwards (Jeremy P. Tarcher). I also recommend *Selling Your Services* by Robert W. Bly (Holt) but you can find literally dozens of other titles with many, many tips and ideas in each. This is the sort of topic where you should build up a bookshelf of a half dozen or more books and consult them regularly for new ideas, writing tips, and brainstorming tools.

Sales   One major point to make about sales: if you are a claims professional, you are dealing with the general public and that means you must remember that, although people are very different, the customer is always right. Whatever you do, you must think of your long-term reputation and image. One dissatisfied customer tells, on the average, nine people about how unhappy they are with your service. Clearly, it is worthwhile to ensure you please your clients.

Many people might not fully understand what you do and getting a client can be time-consuming. Make sure you have good marketing literature (brochures, articles about your service, and so on) to mail out or in your office for people to read so they can get a sense of how you help without taking too much of your time. Good communication skills are also a must. The entire insurance business is confusing to many people, so be patient when you go through your sales pitch with a prospective client.

As mentioned earlier in the book, the claims professional does not deal with electronic claims so you do not need to purchase specialized medical billing and electronic claims software. All the claims professionals I interviewed conducted most of their business by simply using common paper filing and planning systems.

Using your PC

As with any business, however, you should ensure you have the equipment and skills necessary to run general business software. These programs can ensure you keep up with, if not ahead, of your competition. Because you might deal with hundreds of people and claims in a given month, you can benefit by using software that tracks their status and reminds you which claims need continual follow-up until they are paid. You can also use such software to track your prospect leads and your mailings, to record your appointments and daily schedule, and to plan your finances. Tom Koehler of In Home Medical Claims uses an IBM 386 with an integrated software package, Spinnaker's BetterWorking Eight-in-One, which he uses for word processing and spreadsheets. He also uses an easy database manager, Spinnaker's OnePerson Office, to keep track of of his many operations.

You, too, should know about the newer versions of many database management and specialized "contact management" software, both of which allow you to track your clients and claims. While the software field is volatile, some programs that received good reviews as of this writing include:

- File Express 5.1 (Expressware Corp.)
- PC-File (ButtonWare)
- FileMaker Pro (Claris)
- Alpha FOUR (Tiger Software)
- Approach (Approach Software)
- Act! (Contact Software)
- PackRat (Polaris)
- SmartOffice (E-Z Data)

Be sure to get a program that matches your hardware capability, as some of the programs are GUI (graphical user interface—pronounced *gooey*) designs that work with Windows-type environments, while others are MS-DOS character-based environments. Chapter 5 contains more information on software.

If you are unfamiliar with such programs, you should not fear their highly technical-sounding names; as they are really only software versions of filing cabinets and Rolodex indexes, although they are much more powerful and help you organize more information quickly. Database and contact management software are moving toward being the same product; both serve what is often called a *personal information management* function. These programs contain electronic recordkeeping systems in which you either get pre-formatted screens or ones that you design to track your contacts. Each screen contains fill-in "fields" such as name, address, phone number, fax number, date of last meeting, action plan, and so on. Each screen (or perhaps two tied together) is called a record, and is similar to an index card or file you might keep on a person or company you wanted to track. A group of records composes a database, so you can rifle through a database very quickly on your computer and find the information you want. Even better, you can have multiple databases, such as one for all your insurance companies, and another for your clients, one for your prospects, one for your daily appointments, and so on. The power of the database is that you can link records in an interrelated fashion (called a relational database) so you can jump from one database to another .

Database management programs effectively allow you to keep tabs on all your clients, which claims you've filed for them, how often you see them, how much time you spent on their project, and what results you achieved. Most let you produce weekly schedule listings, customizable calendars, and laser Rolodex cards. Some database and time-management programs offer automatic dialing of phone numbers you store in your database records, and send a fax directly from the program, as long as you have a modem or fax/modem connected to your computer.

Other programs, such as Timeslips (Timeslips Corp.), currently a best-seller, allow you to track your time if you bill on a time basis. You can also use it if you charge on a flat-fee basis so that, by keeping count of your time, you can compare how many hours you put into a project and see if you are really charging too little or too much.

Database and contact management programs are quite powerful but they generally require some time to learn. However, they can assist you enormously and make you more efficient, so time spent up-front pays off in the end. You will need to find the right program, depending on your prior computer sophistication and tolerance for learning new programs. Of the people I interviewed, only two used software (both Timeslips) and that was because they billed clients on a per hour basis and needed to track how much time they spent on each project.

In the short run, at this time, it does not appear that claims professionals were suffering from a lack of high technology to run their business. Their work is nearly all achieved one claim at a time using paper correspondence and phone calls. However, the decision to computerize is up to you, and I am certain that the person who uses either a general database management program or a contact management program, as well as a time-keeping/invoicing program like Timeslips, will greatly improve their efficiency and through-put rate. In theory, you could handle more clients each day and to be better organized, ensuring that no claims fall through the cracks.

Finally, let me also mention that Harvey Matoren of Health Claims of Jacksonville, Inc. offers a specialized software program for the profession. Developed for his own business, the software tracks clients, claims, insurance companies, providers, and has the capability to generate management reports to run your business more effectively. The program is essentially a relational database, but is quite user-friendly. You can obtain details about the cost and availability from Harvey by calling (904) 733-2525. Irene Card of Medical Insurance Claims, Inc. also sells a software program called the M.I.C.-Express Software, that was designed for her office, which bills on a percentage basis. The program is a comprehensive package that allows medical claims processing companies to track client records, including client listings (active, inactive, deleted), up to nine insurance companies per client, claims histories by client, year-to-date deductibles per client, claims status reports, monthly invoicing, and many other functions. Her software sells for $1950, but when you take a workshop on the business offered by Card, she discounts the software. Irene Card can be reached at (201) 492-2828 in Kinnelon, New Jersey.

Income & earning potential

Projecting your income potential in the claims business is difficult. First, every claims professional I spoke to mentioned that it took at least half a year to a year to build up the business to a level that could even be classified as income. Second, how people charge for their service is varied, with four different methods of pricing. As a result, the best way to discuss income potential is to evaluate the four basic pricing strategies and extrapolate from there.

Flat-fee pricing

Using the flat-fee pricing method, the claims service simply charges a single annual fee to a client for however many claims that person has during the year. One business, Health Claims of Jacksonville, Inc., for example, charges $190 per year for a single person, $325 per year for a couple, and $425 per year for a family of four, plus a one-time registration fee of $35 to set up the account. For these prices, they work on as many current claims the client has. They do charge on a percent of recovery basis for claims that occurred in the past in order to bring a client up to date.

The advantage of this method is you obtain your money up-front (or in a few installments). The disadvantage is you could end up with some clients who have far more claims than the average person and for whom you could spend dozens of hours working while getting a very low payback. In general claims professionals who do this told me they felt it all averaged out, because many people who pay the one-time fee have only a few claims per year.

To illustrate earning potential, TABLE 3-2 shows what your income might look like over one year with the following assumptions: you are just starting out, and over the course of the year, you get 144 clients joining your service at the hypothetical rate of five singles, four couples, and three families per month. Each pay you $200, $350, and $450 respectively for their annual fees plus a $35 registration fee.

As you can see, this scenario can lead to more than $50,000 gross income in a year, but it is based on an optimistic estimate. Remember this is only a projection and your monthly growth in paying customers could be much lower depending on how successful your marketing is and the size of the your client base. You could end up with only 50 or 75 clients in the first year rather than 144. Consequently, your earnings could be much less. The projection also does not account for a single dollar of expenses, such as marketing, phone, overhead, gas, which could consume up to 40 percent of your income. Be sure to also calculate your overhead and direct expenses. If you work from home for a while, you can probably keep your overhead low, spending only a few thousand dollars for brochures, business cards, stationery, and computer supplies, without paying for office space or secretarial help.

Table 3-2
Income projections for a claims service charging on an annual fee basis

Month	1st	2nd	3rd	4th	5th	6th	7th	8th	9th	10th	11th	12th	Total
# of single clients @ $200 per year	5	5	5	5	5	5	5	5	5	5	5	5	60
Income	$1000	$1000	$1000	$1000	$1000	$1000	$1000	$1000	$1000	$1000	$1000	$1000	$12,000
# of couples @ $350 per year	4	4	4	4	4	4	4	4	4	4	4	4	48
Income	$1400	$1400	$1400	$1400	$1400	$1400	$1400	$1400	$1400	$1400	$1400	$1400	$16,800
# of families @ $450 per year	3	3	3	3	3	3	3	3	3	3	3	3	36
Income	$1350	$1350	$1350	$1350	$1350	$1350	$1350	$1350	$1350	$1350	$1350	$1350	$16,200
Total # of clients	12	12	12	12	12	12	12	12	12	12	12	12	144
Plus $35 registra. fee for each client or family	$420	$420	$420	$420	$420	$420	$420	$420	$420	$420	$420	$420	$5040
Total monthly income	$4170	$4170	$4170	$4170	$4170	$4170	$4170	$4170	$4170	$4170	$4170	$4170	$50,040

Hourly pricing   Several of the companies I interviewed tried the flat-fee structure, and decided it wasn't earning enough for their needs so they switched to an hourly fee basis. As one owner said, "I think an hourly fee is more fair to the client, and they know what they are getting." On the other hand, one company felt that charging an hourly fee makes the public compare you to an attorney or a tax accountant, and they feel you don't deserve to make as much as those professionals.

Nevertheless, in many locales, an hourly fee probably makes sense. It might be difficult to get people to pay a flat fee up-front, because they are not sure whether they want to use you for an entire year. People are often more willing to shell out a small amount until they know you can handle their needs.

As you might guess, there is no uniformity among the hourly fee charged. It ultimately depends on your location, your clientele, and perhaps your competition. The lowest rate I found was $24 per hour, with $40 being an average rate, and $80 being the highest. Note that even if you charge an hourly rate, you should still always bill in at least 10 or 15 minute increments, just like lawyers or accountants. This is fair to you because you might spend 15 minutes on a few phone calls and still want to get paid. It is also fair to the client who wouldn't want to pay you for two hours work when you only put in 1.5 hours.

TABLE 3-3 illustrates one income projection based on billing at $40 per hour and starting out very slowly. In this conservative scenario, you bill only 20 hours in your entire first month of operation, then build up your monthly billing hours every consecutive month by an additional 5 or 10 hours.

As you can see, even under conservative circumstances, if you build your business slowly over 8 to 10 months, you can still arrive at a reasonable $30,000+ income per year. If you begin your business more quickly, you can easily outpace this projection. Don't forget that handling one claim might not take an hour's work, so in this scenario of 795 billable hours over the course of a year, you might need several hundred clients to bill at this monthly work rate (even more to bill at a higher work rate).

The percentage method   Few companies use the percentage method, but it is certainly talked about and was implemented by at least one claims professional I interviewed, Irene Card's Medical Insurance Claims, Inc. Using the percentage method, you effectively take a percentage of any claim you work on for your client. Card's company charges a registration fee of $75 for a single individual, $125 for a couple, and $25 for each child. On top of that, they take 10 percent of any reimbursement they obtain greater than $300, and 15 percent of any reimbursement they obtain less than $300. In short, for every single claim they touch, they make some income.

Estimating your annual income under this method is, by far, the hardest. Without any experience in the field, you would have no way of knowing how many claims you might handle or how much they are worth. Even with

Table 3-3
Income projection for a claims service using an hourly fee rate

Month	1st	2nd	3rd	4th	5th	6th	7th	8th	9th	10th	11th	12th	Total
# of billable hours per month @ $40/hour	20	25	30	40	50	60	70	80	90	100	110	120	795 hours
Income	$800	$1000	$1200	$1600	$2000	$2400	$2800	$3200	$3600	$4000	$4400	$4800	$31,800

experience, you still cannot count on the type and number of claims you might handle over the course of a year. You also need to track your claims in great detail, probably using a computer.

On the flip side, the percentage method probably has the greatest earnings potential. Assuming the average claim is $300–$400, you get $30–$40 per claim. Your earnings would be similar to the hourly method shown in TABLE 3-4, and if you add on an annual registration fee as Card does, you enhance your income further. Because some claims are much greater than $400, you can earn more on a few claims, and thereby, earn more in the neighborhood of $40,000 to $60,000 per year.

The mixed method

The last pricing structure is to mix and match the methods according to your risk tolerance, clientele, locale, and expected needs. You might, for example, charge a lower annual fee for up to 10 claims per person, and then an hourly rate for additional claims. Or you might charge a flat fee for new claims and an hourly rate or percentage for old claims that a client brings in when they first sign up expecting you to take care of.

However, the mixed method makes predicting income very difficult, and it can also confuse clients, especially the elderly. Nevertheless, the mixed method can be a useful way to open your business and make people feel that you are offering a special promotion. For example, you could offer a low annual fee for the first year to cover a person's first 10 claims, followed by an additional fee or hourly rate or percentage commission for all claims thereafter. In the second year of each subscriber's term with your service, you might simplify the rate and offer a simple hourly fee or annual charge.

Estimating your expenses

The one advantage of the claims business, your start-up costs are generally very low. Most of the claims professionals I spoke with began by working out of their homes, although some moved to a small office in an effort to enhance their credibility and to increase their storage space after a year.

Your investment in office equipment (computer, printer, phones) and supplies is fairly low, $2000 to $5000 on average, and you could even get by with less if you already have a computer, a home office with furniture, and a few other pieces of general business equipment. Your expenses might amount to:

Office equipment (computer, printer, software)	$1500–$3500
Business cards, letterhead, envelopes	$ 200–$ 500
Brochure	$ 500–$1000
Office furniture	$ 600–$1000
Photocopier	$ 400–$1000
Phone (including installation)	$ 300–$ 500
TOTAL	$3500–$7500

Now that you've reviewed the first part of this chapter about the claims profession in general, you might be at a point where you would like to decide if this is a business for you. The following checklist will, hopefully, help with your decision or prompt you to think about the conclusions you might have already drawn. Take a moment now to do this 15-question checklist before reading the remainder of the chapter.

Deciding if this business is for you

✔ Am I organized, logical, punctual, attentive, and patient? _____

✔ Can I track many projects at once without getting confused, lost, or forgetful? _____

✔ Do I have some business background or medical background that would serve me in this business? _____

✔ Do I enjoy working with the public? _____

✔ Do I enjoy office work, filling in paper forms, filing, and managing information? _____

✔ Do I enjoy or am I willing to spend much of the day on the phone _____?

✔ Do I enjoy being a detective and working with numbers and technical details? _____

✔ Do I understand or am I willing to learn about health insurance procedures and claims? _____

✔ Do I find it easy to read a legal document, such as an insurance policy, and understand what it says? _____

✔ Can I tolerate the bureaucratic snafus and snarls that invariably happen in this business? Do I persist with the nitty-gritty, such as calling Medicare eight times if I have to? _____

✔ Am I articulate and able to convince other people to listen to my point of view? _____

✔ Do I feel comfortable disagreeing and negotiating with intimidating people in positions of authority at insurance companies or Medicare? _____

✔ Do I enjoy marketing, networking, and putting my face out in the public in order to drum up business? _____

✔ Do I like working with elderly people who might be a large percentage of my clientele? _____

✔ Are people drawn to me because I give them a feeling that I am trustworthy and confident? _____

If you answered the majority of these questions affirmatively or if you have any doubts but want to proceed, the next section will provide you with some brief guidelines on how to get started in this business. The section is organized according to the sequence of steps you might want to take: setting up your office; resources for training and learning; tips for pricing your service; marketing your business; and overcoming common start-up problems.

Most claims professionals begin their business in their home, and only over time and with a growing practice do they move into an outside office. A

Setting up shop

home office obviously saves on overhead expenses, nonetheless a professional home office where clients can meet you and spend time reviewing their health claims and discussing their needs is very important.

You must carefully evaluate your home office environment. Do you have a separate location away from the rest of your house? Is it soundproof so you can be undisturbed by children, pets, and neighborhood noises? Can you make a separate entryway so that clients will not disturb your family? Will people need to climb stairs to get to it (not a good idea if many of your clients are elderly)? Do you have a professional looking desk and comfortable chairs for yourself and your clients? Do you have enough space in this area for at least three people to sit comfortably (since many couples may visit you together)?

Consider all these issues in the design of your office space, or hire a space planner or an interior designer to help you make the best use of the space you have. Look into modern office designs frequently described in computer and home business magazines, and check out ergonomic furniture at office stores. Furniture products from companies like Herman Miller and Steelcase have received good reviews for comfort and health. Plan ahead so your filing systems, in-boxes, and wall charts all work together.

Second, as pointed out earlier, you do not need to computerize, particularly when you first start and probably have only a few clients for whom you can manage with traditional paper files. However, you will greatly enhance your image and your productivity if you have a computer and the right software.

If you intend to purchase a computer, or if you are upgrading your current hardware, consider the long-term consequences of your purchase. While you can probably buy an inexpensive 286 machine, you might want to purchase a 386 or 486, which provides faster speeds and more computing power with the most current database programs, project managers, and word processing/desktop publishing software.

If you intend to offer your services at a client's home, you might consider getting a laptop computer you can take along with you to take notes and examine records. This is a worthwhile investment if many of your clients expect you to come to them.

Software Find a database manager or contact management program that fits your computer experience and budget. Many programs are available ranging from less than $100 for programs like File Express or PC-File to $250 and up for PackRat (Polaris) or $395 for SmartOffice (E-Z Data). You may want to start with an integrated program that includes word processing, a spreadsheet, and a database like Microsoft Works, WordPerfect Works, or Borland's Quattro. You get a single design interface for all programs, which makes them easier to learn.

As for other office equipment, I recommend the following:

Printer   An ink jet or laser printer provides clean, crisp documents that can enhance your professional image. They also come in handy if you are designing and printing your own brochures, letters of introduction, and other marketing materials. But since they cost an additional $400 to $1000 more than the dot matrix printers, you might wait until you have generated some cash flow before buying one.

Label printer   Since you will most likely do much correspondence via mail, an investment into a dedicated label printer, a special narrow gauge printer that handles a long line of stick-on mailing labels, is a smart move.

Phone system   As indicated earlier, much of your business will be done by phone, so spending your money on this inexpensive technology makes sense. Invest in a business phone distinct from your family phone, and possibly a two-line phone so that you can take more than one business call at a time, in lieu of Call Waiting. If you really find yourself spending hours on the line, you might also want to get a headphone set, to alleviate the strain on your neck and arms.

Be sure to have a high-quality answering machine or voice mail, so you never risk losing messages. If you make many long-distance calls to insurance companies, you might want to bill your clients for the extra charges. Consequently, you may want to pay the extra fee to your phone company to track your phone calls and tag them according to your clients. You could also use a software program such as WindowPhone (AG Communication Systems) or Hot Line 2 (Smith MicrosoftWare) to track your phone calls when you use your modem to make the call.

Car phone   With the price of car phones coming down, you might seriously want to invest in a lightweight portable cellular or transportable car phone ($150–$1000), particularly if you travel to clients' homes. You can use the phone to take other calls, do business while you drive, or let clients know you are on the way.

Modem   You will probably not need a modem, unless you plan to use communications software. Norma Border of NACAP indicates that, in the near future, claims assistance professionals might be able to access their clients' records through a network or clearinghouse connected with the Medicare carriers.

Photocopier   A personal copier would be a valuable investment for those copies of items you will constantly be mailing out to insurance companies and doctors' offices. Good record of clients' claim forms, receipts, and correspondence is critical to this job, so get the best personal copy machine you can afford!

Fax   You will not have much use for a fax machine, but it is strange that new technology engenders new services and products. It is conceivable that some of your clients might want to fax you their claims information, so consider a fax machine a possible purchase in the future.

Resources & training

The first place to turn for information and assistance in the claims profession is the National Association of Claims Assistance Professionals (NACAP). For a mere $95 per year membership, you will receive a newsletter, research support on your claims filings, continuing education, access to a network of other members with whom you can share ideas and information, and referrals for new customers in your area. Contact Norma Border, National Director of NACAP at 4724 Florence Avenue, Downers Grove, IL 60515, (708) 963-3500 or FAX (708) 803-6334. Figure 3-6 illustrates a few of the items they will send you. Border also indicated that NACAP will offer regional training seminars through its Claims Academy in various nationwide locations beginning in January 1993. Check with them to find out whether they have one in your area. The average cost of a three-day program is under $500, with one-day courses for under $200. If there is no training seminar near you, try getting the name of a member willing to speak with you about the job. This could be difficult as they might consider you as their competitor.

3-6
Brochures from the National Association of Claims Assistance Professionals.

Second, you must contact your state's insurance commissioner to find out about the appropriate rules and requirements for doing claims work. You might need to take an exam. If so, the commission likely has a manual to help prepare you for the exam, such as the Florida Adjuster's Study Manual, which contains general information about health insurance, types of policies, and Medicare information and so on. (If you live in a state that does not require an exam, you might get a friend who lives in a state that does, and ask him or her to request the study manual for that state for you. You might find some useful information, even if you don't need to take the exam.

Third, the next place to go to is your local Medicare office for a copy of their *Medicare Handbook*. This guide is invaluable in helping you to understand Medicare's complex policies, annual changes in coverages, and limitations to coverages. The book is published each year, so be sure to get a current copy. You can also browse the Government Printing Office (GPO) stores located in 21 cities in the country or call the order desk at the Superintendent of Documents in D.C. at (202) 783-3238. The GPO publishes additional information on Medicare and information from various congressional hearings and laws regarding the insurance industry and topics of note to people in the medical professions. Your public library may also have a copy of the GPO Monthly Catalog and GPO Sales Publications Reference File. Other resources for training and education include:

Courses   You can find courses on medical billing and health insurance policies in many community colleges and extension schools. Such courses can help you to learn medical coding and various kinds of insurance regulations and policies. *Entrepreneur Magazine* also offers a home course called the Medical Claims Processing Business Guide (800) 421-2300, but several people have informed me that this material was quite sketchy and incomplete for the price they charge.

As mentioned earlier in the chapter, many local chapters of the Small Business Administration (SBA) also offer courses on starting a new enterprise, business planning, and marketing. The Service Corps of Retired Executives (SCORE) may prove valuable, as it did for Nancy Koehler, who ended up with a former executive from Blue Cross who had retired to her locale in southern California.

Irene Card also offers a two-day workshop in many locations in the country for $3000. She can be reached at (201) 492-2828 in Kinnelon, New Jersey. Harvey Matoren offers a variety of workshops for people interested in the business as well. For information, contact him at (904) 733-2525.

Books   For information on medical coding books, call the GPO for a copy of the ICD-9 manual, or go to a medical book store in your area. You can also call Practice Management Information Corporation (PMIC) for many relevant titles (see chapter 2 for a list). Their number is 1-(800)-MEDSHOP ext. 432; Mr. Joe Kopacz can help you with your book needs. Don't forget, he offers a 10 percent discount to readers of this book. Another book that was recommended by Norma Border is *Principles of Life and Health Insurance*, a college-level book published by Life Office Management Association

(LOMA), a private association for the national insurance industry, located in Atlanta, Georgia. You can order this book from Professional Book Distributors, Inc. at (800) 848-0773. LOMA can be reached at (404) 951-1770.

For improving your knowledge of marketing, consulting, sales, or running your own business, simply drop by a bookstore in your area for an unlimited assortment of titles. There are literally hundreds of books you can select from, and so even browsing for a few hours among them will teach you quite a few things. You should definitely read three books from Paul and Sarah Edwards—*Working From Home*, *Making It on Your Own*, and *Getting Business to Come to You* (all published by Jeremy P. Tarcher). These cover nearly every major topic you need, from how to set up your home office, to doing your own marketing and sales. *Selling Your Services*, *How to Promote Your Own Business* by Robert W. Bly (Holt), and *Growing Your Home-Based Business: A Complete Guide to Proven Sales & Marketing Strategies* by Kim T. Gordon (Prentice-Hall) are also helpful books.

If you find yourself with little time to read, I recommend subscribing to a few business magazines and reputable business newspapers. This way you can read shorter articles and still manage to get good information about new software and new business ideas. You might also want to subscribe to *Medical Economics*, a magazine for the medical profession that covers matters of financial interest to doctors and healthcare providers. Call (201) 358-7200.

Computer networks   Both CompuServe and Prodigy have networking bulletin boards where you can communicate with others who do this business or know something about medical issues and claims. On CompuServe, access the Working From Home Forum, and on Prodigy, you can communicate with others via the MONEY TALK bulletin board, topic: YOUR OWN BUSINESS. You can spend hours on these bulletin boards, although talking in person with people in your area may prove more useful. You can reach CompuServe at (800) 848-8199 and Prodigy at (914) 962-0310, or go to a retail computer or software store to obtain information about subscribing to these services.

Pricing your service

You can choose from among four methods to price your services, but you need to consider several factors before determining which method makes the most amount of sense (and cents) for you. Your choice will clearly be influenced by the following:

Your clientele   If you expect to serve a large elderly population, some may balk at paying a flat fee if they do not know you or trust your service. They may be more willing to pay an hourly fee. On the other hand, those with many claims may prefer a flat rate, since they will think they are saving money. If you expect to have families and younger couples, you may find they prefer a fixed rate, since they may not like paying a high-priced hourly fee.

Your competition   There may be competition in your area, so do find out how much they charge and by which method. While another agency which charges a lower price may not prevent you from charging what you think you are worth, it may be difficult to go much higher than a competitor since people who don't know what a claims professional does, will be adverse to paying a premium price for the service. You should also give some thought to how likely it is that you will have a competitor in the next few years. If you start at a high fee, and a competitor opens shop a few months after you and charges a lower fee, you need to protect your territory.

Your locale   Some locations will tolerate a $300 per year annual fee or $60 hourly rate, while other locations where the cost of living is much less, will force you to charge a much lower annual or lower hourly fee. If you intend to charge an hourly fee, it would help to know the going rate for similar kinds of services in your area that charge hourly fees, such as accountants.

Your reputation and experience   Obviously, you will have a difficult time charging $60 per hour if you have little experience in this field, but if you have years of previous background in the insurance industry, many people would probably be quite willing to pay you that fee since they feel you could get the job done quickly. If you have little experience, you also do not want to be in position of defending your billing if a customer wonders why it took you three hours to do something that an experienced person could have accomplished in one hour.

Your cash flow needs   Some people may wish to start out using Other People's Money (OPM) to finance their venture. If so, the annual membership fee method for pricing your service would allow you to bring in large amounts of money more quickly. You need to remember, however, that once you receive that money from a client, you will need to spend the time working on their claims without further payment for your time. As the months go by, you must remain as courteous and helpful to that client as you are to new ones.

Your other policies   Are you going to charge for phone calls, postage, or mileage? In determining your pricing structure, don't forget to allocate enough to cover your direct expenses per client. If you intend to charge $25 per hour, you may want to see if you can get $28 or $30 to be sure you cover your expenses.

Your projected number of clients and claims   You may feel that your area has much potential and, because of your contacts and reputation, you will be able to bring in many clients quickly. If so, you might want to charge on a percentage basis, since this method is by far the most lucrative.

Your pricing is your value   You have probably heard that when you charge too little, many people don't think you're offering a service of value, and so you need to be careful that you don't underprice your service.

In sum, your best plan of action is to spend some time with a spreadsheet (paper or electronic) and calculate a number of different scenarios. Compare and contrast your income opportunity using these various methods. Be as specific as possible: have your plan estimate income for each week of your first year, showing your growth in clients times either billable hours, annual fees, or percentage (the hardest to estimate). Then examine which plan maximizes your income while offering you the most logical and viable pricing scheme given your location, competition, clientele, reputation/experience, and other factors that have an impact on your business. While you may find that you can earn the most with an annual fee, you may nevertheless need to operate on an hourly basis if a sizable portion of your potential clients would balk at paying you $200 to $400 all at once. (NOTE : if you offer them the ability to pay an annual fee on a monthly basis, which might be more acceptable to them, you will need to invoice clients every month. This adds to your overhead and time. You certainly should have a computer if you do monthly invoicing.)

Whichever method you choose, it seems reasonable to charge a registration fee in the first year for each client. It takes time to set up their account, call their insurance companies to obtain claims forms, set up files for them (paper or electronic), and take care of initial preparatory work. While this might be as low as $9.95, many claims businesses charge $30 to $50 for this fee. Again, it all depends on what the market will bear.

In addition, consider if you are going to offer other services, such as those performed by Nancy & Tom Koehler of In Home Medical Claims, who help people pay their monthly bills, keep records, and occasionally make appointments with attorneys and accountants for their elderly clients during tax season. If so, you need to either add a surcharge to your annual fee, or choose to bill hourly. Your goal is to keep your pricing simple and clear so that your clients can understand what they are paying for.

Last, let me mention a sober point that was made to me by one of the claims professionals I interviewed. Whichever method you use, you need to account for losing customers if a portion of your clientele is elderly. People do die, and you could lose 5 to 10 percent or more of your clients each year.

Marketing tips

The biggest challenge facing a medical claims assistance professional is marketing. There are many types of clients you can capture, but most people do not know about the profession or even that they are sometimes losing money on their own claims. Your start-up efforts must be directed, therefore, at informing the public about both the profession in general and your new business.

Second, if you intend to operate your claims service full-time, remember that this is a business in which the size of your customer base is critical. Unlike an accountant or attorney who might have some clients from whom they can earn tremendous amounts of money, since their cases are very complex, you need many clients so that you seldom have downtime! Your goal is growth: you need to increase your client base and never let up. Most claims professionals have 200 or more clients, and Irene Card's business serves over 2000 clients coast to coast. If you get too many clients to handle, then either hire an employee to do filing, typing, and invoicing or a partner to share in the marketing and claims filing aspects of the business.

Nearly everyone I interviewed indicated that the claims business is slow in the start-up phase. You will need to be prepared for a few months of intensive marketing. The following guidelines address what you can do to respond to your challenges.

Get the demographic data on your community or those areas where you plan to conduct your business. Know the population by age group and sex, residential location, and what income level. After all, you are a service business catering to the general public, so knowledge of your clientele is vital. It appears to help considerably to live in an area with a heavy concentration of elderly people, mixed with busy families and working singles.

Know your market

Word of mouth is by far the most important marketing method in this business. People are putting their financial faith in your service, so you need customers who can trust you with their personal medical information and financial situation. Just as people usually choose their accountant, tax preparer, or attorney based on recommendations from others, you want to have clients who already know something about you and the quality of your work.

Use word-of-mouth power

Begin by making a contact tree of everyone you know: friends, relatives, former colleagues, employers, neighbors, and so on. Send each of them a flier or brochure with a personal note to make sure they know you are now in this business. Ask them to sign up with you, and to keep you in mind when they speak with others. If every client generated 10 leads for you, you could go from zero to 100 clients in just a few months. The sidebar on Fitzgibbons & Associates illustrates the power of word-of-mouth communications.

Mary Ellen Fitzgibbons of Fitzgibbons & Associates runs her claims practice about 20 hours a week, without doing a shred of marketing. Her clients come to her through word of mouth. Some of her clients are elderly people who have seen Mary Ellen save them thousands of dollars, and refer their friends to her. Other clients come from friends, and even an attorney, who heard of her and subcontracted to her for a problematic case he was handling. As Mary Ellen says, "I am not just a claims submitter, I am a health claims

Getting clients through word of mouth

management service. Clients send me their paperwork, and I clean up all the problems they have had."

Mary Ellen got into the business from a varied background that included working in the personnel department of a major food manufacturer, a nursing degree, a few years experience in a hospital, and insurance administration for a consulting company where she monitored insurance claims to protect its retired employees. She says, "This job demands toughness and negotiation skills. Sometimes people at the insurance companies tell you, 'Oh this is not possible,' so you need to ask to speak to the manager or someone higher up in the organization. Otherwise you can't get the job done. Trust is also really essential. You want people to know how you do the job, so that they trust you and don't think you're a maverick." Mary Ellen bills usually at a high hourly rate, and is doing well while not spending a dime on marketing!

Use flyers and brochures

With your need to disseminate information, don't be surprised by the recommendation that you print 5000, to 20,000 one-sided, one-page flyers. You can put them in stores, on cars in parking lots, or even go door-to-door in high-density neighborhoods. Keep the flyers simple, clear, and to the point. Focus on the benefits you can provide. Include wording that shows how anyone can gain from your services, not just the elderly or people with health problems. To heighten the effect of the flyer, get an artist to do a small illustration that dramatizes the issue, such as showing a concerned-looking couple reviewing their doctor's bill, or a perplexed-looking person with a stack of bills next to him. Quote some testimonials from people indicating how much money, stress, and time you saved them.

Regarding brochures, you may first wish to print 500 to 1000 trial brochures since these will be more expensive. Choose a high quality paper stock and print in two colors if you can. You may wish to hire a designer to work on the brochure with you, or use your laser printer and desktop publishing program to design one yourself. This brochure should be an 8½ × 11 sheet of paper, single or double-folded so that you end up with four or six surfaces on which to present your message. The folds add drama and meaning to the brochure, since people need to turn the page to find out more. Figure 3-7 shows a few brochures from Health Claims of Jacksonville, Inc. and In Home Medical Claims. You might make one page of your brochure into a business reply return card that the reader could mail back to you for more information, as does the brochure from Health Claims of Jacksonville, Inc. The right hand fold is a perforated tear off card. Use your brochures wisely since they are expensive. Take them with you to meetings, public speaking engagements, or put them into stores (like pharmacies) which agree to let you exhibit them.

Offer a Promotional

Above all, when you start out, consider offering a promotional to induce people to join your service. Everyone likes to feel that they are getting a good bargain, so try offering 10–15 percent off the first year's fees if you charge on

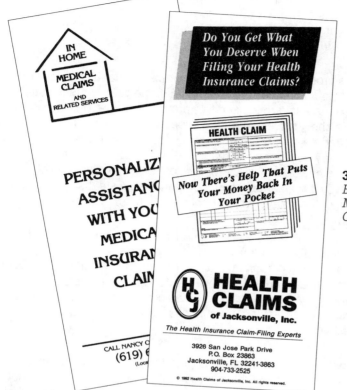

3-7
Brochures from In Home Medical Claims and Health Claims of Jacksonville, Inc.

the annual basis, or one-hour of free claims consulting if you charge on an hourly basis. The key is to get people to call or see you, to give you an opportunity to explain how much you can help them and close the sale. Also, you may want to offer a free consultation, and include your business telephone number. You may want to offer a special promotion, such as one free claim filing to the first 200 customers. Many people will have more than one claim to process, so although you will be doing one for free, you can generate some business from the same people. Once they sign on with you, the chances are that they will become repeat business over the years, assuming you perform adequately. In a service business, particularly when people don't think they need your service, a promotional is often the single most powerful draw to get people to make up their mind.

Make one of your goals the following: each week or month, inform thousands of potential clients about your business. You should try to get publicity in local newspapers, community bulletin boards, cable television, local radio shows—wherever you can find it. You are performing a very curious service and many reporters and show hosts would love to have you relate some of your most interesting successes to the public. After all, the public always

Publicize

enjoys a moralistic victory where the little guy defeats the corporate giant and proves that persistence pays off. Once you get one story, you can use that publicity in your press kit to get more stories, and keep building until you have developed a widespread reputation.

Use selective advertising

Most of the claims professionals I spoke with indicated that advertising did not help them very much. Some who advertised in the yellow pages, found that people often don't know to look up this profession in the yellow pages. As for newspapers, the ads were often too expensive for the results they got. Spending a few hundred dollars for an advertisement that only brings you one or two customers may be money wasted. An advertisement in a small local paper or community newsletter might make more sense for this type of business, particularly if the name of your company suggests that you too are local, or reputable, or are able to work at people's homes.

Use direct mail

It also appeared that direct mail was not a particularly useful technique in this business. Nevertheless, you may wish to experiment with a mailing list of targeted individuals in a certain area of your town, or of a certain age range or income bracket. Another option is "card decks," groups of small direct response cards you receive in the mail. In many communities, you can find publishers of these card decks or coupon books whose prices may allow you to afford a few test ads.

Networking

While many people feel that networking is glad-handing or being immodest about themselves, it is really a highly appropriate and successful way to get business. Any meeting you attend, let people know what you do. You will be surprised at how many people will respond with a horror story about a relative or friend who just experienced difficulty with a claim. Remember, errors and mistakes on claims happen all the time! Be sure to bring your business cards to such meetings.

Try to locate especially other people in the health professions: nurses, home care agencies, nursing registries, hospital and retirement home personnel, and so on. Each of these contacts may be able to refer business directly to you or at least refer to other people who can help you find customers. Some hospitals have programs, for example, to help people with claims, but such programs will only do so much for people. If you can befriend the staff at a local hospital, you may find yourself with plenty of referrals.

The other value of networking is that you might meet accountants, lawyers, and people in executive positions with corporations in your area who understand that their clients or their company might also not be getting the best treatment from an insurance carrier. You might find that you can get yourself hired to work on claims for their clients or employees on a contract basis to be sure that both the firm and the individuals are getting the proper reimbursements on their medical policies.

As part of your informational campaign, find opportunities to speak to groups, associations, or boards with senior citizens, about the health insurance industry, Medicare, and errors on medical claims. Develop and use any previous expertise you have to make an interesting, informative talk that people will enjoy and benefit from. Be sure that anytime you speak for a group, you hand out your brochures or leave them for people to take.

Public speaking

While a medical claims business is a great entrepreneurial opportunity for many people who have the right mix of personal experience, medical or business knowledge, and a love for this type of work, take the advice of all those already in the business: "It takes time to build the business." In short, you will encounter start-up problems, from getting clients, to developing the right contacts at insurance companies to help process the claims, to figuring out your pricing schedule.

Overcoming start-up problems

This is one reason why starting this business part-time could be a very valuable option for some people. Without leaving the security of another paycheck, you can learn the ropes of the business and move cautiously to build up your clientele through word of mouth and networking. Remember though, this business depends on availability during the day to see clients and to make phone calls, so avoid having your other part-time work interfere with your ability to follow such a schedule. Here are a few additional guidelines concerning common start-up problems.

First, determine why you might not have enough clients, or fewer than you expected. Are you spending enough time marketing (60 percent or more in the beginning of a new business). When you tell people what you do, are they aware of your business? Are you generating leads but not closing the deal? Do you have competition from another business?

Not enough clients

Each one of these calls for a different response. If you are only spending a few hours marketing per week, you clearly need to get out and generate more leads. Get your publicity campaign in gear; print up more flyers and distribute them in new locations. Give some talks to a few groups and get feedback. If after some amount of publicity in your area, you find people are still not aware of your business, you need to continue educating the public about your service. Boost your publicity campaign and do more networking. If people are calling but don't sign on with you, then examine your communication style and sales pitch to see if you are saying something which alienates or turns people off. Also, check your pricing structure. Perhaps people think you are charging too much; so you might offer a promotion or lower your fees. If you have a competitor who is doing well, you will need to change something in your pricing or service (or how people perceive them) that will allow you to capture your share of the market.

Although you might feel you cannot change your pricing, you might be able to offer more services, such as in-home assistance on paying bills, organizing

Poor cashflow

things, and errands. Your niche for organization could prove useful to your clients. More services mean more money for you.

In addition, consider running a medical billing service that uses many of the same background skills as a claims professional. Irene Card of Medical Insurance Claims, Inc. in New Jersey offers two services on both sides of the fence, maximizing her expertise and her cashflow.

Few referrals People often don't know whether or not a business wants referrals or they don't stop to think about it. It is perfectly acceptable to let people know that you would appreciate any referrals they can make for you, without badgering them or shaming them if they are not able to do so. Most services provide a "reward" for referrals such as a discount on next year's fees or a free one-time consultation. You can even have a flyer or business card printed up that says "We appreciate your referring us to your friends" and mention what you will offer in return for the courtesy.

Unless you have an exceptionally strong background that matches the requirements of this business, you will need to build your medical claims assistance service client-by-client. Few businesses get off the ground without hard work, overtime, and tight financial times. But as every claims professional told me, you need not worry about the future of this profession. Unfortunately, it appears that we will always have a need for claims professionals, even if the U.S. has a national healthcare system. Our country's medical preferences seem to support fee-for-service insurance policies and a wealth of insurance options—both of which mean we will continue to have a confused, even chaotic claims system where mistakes are commonly made and the average consumer needs help.

4 Medical transcription services

On the surface, a medical transcription service seems very easy to explain. A transcriptionist types up dictated reports and documents for healthcare professionals of all kinds (including doctors, nurses, counselors, physical therapists, psychologists, etc.) which are then stored in hospital patient files and medical record departments. However, while this definition captures the essence of the job, it only scratches the surface in portraying the importance and value that medical transcriptionists play in our healthcare system. Medical transcription is actually a vital occupation that is highly underrated and quite difficult to perform; it is also a career in high demand. In fact, some American hospitals send their transcription work overseas, because there is a serious shortage of qualified medical transcriptionists here, and to take advantage of the time difference in order to get work done quickly.

In this chapter, I'll cover the complex skills that are needed to become a medical transcriptionist, the day-to-day work issues faced by people in the profession, and the best methods by which you can enter the business. You'll learn the advantages and disadvantages of the job and how to plan your career so you can maximize your enjoyment and financial potential.

What a medical transcriptionist is

Each day, healthcare providers dictate tens of thousands of reports that range from a few paragraphs to a dozen pages. Such dictations are done for every operation performed, every hospitalization admission or discharge (of which there are over 30 million each year), every physical exam or radiological study, and for dozens of other procedures. Included in the dictation are the details of what happened, how the patient looked, what was examined, and the healthcare provider's conclusion of the case.

These dictations are useless, however, unless they are transcribed into documents that can be read by any physician, and filed or microfilmed for future reference. It is estimated that transcriptionists transcribe billions of lines of dictations each year. As an example, TABLE 4-1 shows an interesting breakdown in the numbers and types of operations performed in the United States in a typical year.

Transcriptions are actually medical-legal documents and are important for many reasons. They are:

❑ Part of the medical history for a patient who might later need continued treatment from another physician.
❑ An important source of information for any physician to whom the patient has been referred for additional treatment.
❑ Frequently required for the payment of a medical claim. Medicare and commercial insurance companies typically want to verify a procedure or dispute a fee.
❑ Used to aid in medical research in tracking diseases and in furthering our understanding of symptoms and illnesses.
❑ Required by lawyers and insurance companies whenever litigation occurs between two parties following an accident, a work injury, or a crime.
❑ Required by insurance companies underwriting doctors and hospitals as evidence in medical malpractice cases.
❑ Required in many states for Medicaid and other state-funded programs.

The role of medical transcriptionists throughout the country is therefore quite pivotal to our entire healthcare system. Without high-quality transcription, reports can be inaccurate, leading to poor decisions by an attending physician or an unfair settlement in an insurance dispute. Transcriptionists are a major link between healthcare providers of hospitals, and insurance companies, effectively protecting everyone involved from mistakes, lost money, and even the loss of life.

In the past, transcriptionists have been perceived as glorified typists, but today, their leading organization, the American Association for Medical Transcription (AAMT), is spreading the word that the medical transcription profession demands respect, greater recognition, and, most of all, higher wages. AAMT lobbies around the country, encouraging members of the medical community to understand better and reward more appropriately the high level of knowledge and professionalism of a trained transcriptionist.

According to Claudia Tessier, CAE, CMT, RRA, executive director of AAMT, "No longer content to be viewed as clerical robots, more and more MTs (medical transcriptionists) are moving into their rightful place as medical language specialists—professionals with unique qualifications to translate

Table 4-1
Procedures provided to patients discharged from short-stay hospitals by sex and age (1988) (numbers in thousands)

Procedure	Total	Sex Male	Female	Under 15	15–44	Age 45–64	over 65
All procedures	*40,506*	*15,916*	*24,590*	*1960*	*16,186*	*9052*	*13,308*
Operations on the nervous system	952	479	472	210	314	214	214
on the endocrine system	96	26	70	—	40	31	23
on the eye	350	174	176	16	74	76	184
on the ear	137	73	64	81	27	18	11
on the nose, mouth, and pharynx	585	327	258	140	254	112	79
on the respiratory system	975	555	420	66	177	296	436
on the cardiovascular system	3881	2317	1564	154	429	1438	1860
on the hemic and lymphatic systems	361	187	174	20	80	109	151
on the digestive system	5271	2194	3077	212	1487	1386	2185
on the urinary system	1664	946	718	41	390	426	807
on the male genital organs	594	594		46	40	127	380
on the female genital organs	2440		2440	10	1711	495	223
obstetrical procedures	6792		6792	19	6763	10	—
on the musculo-skeletal system	3132	1624	1508	161	1273	733	965
on the integumentary system	1387	580	807	85	527	355	419

Table 4-1 Continued.

Procedure	Total	Sex Male	Female	Age Under 15	15–44	45–64	over 65
miscellaneous diagnostic & therapeutic procedures	11,890	5842	6048	694	2600	3225	5371

Note: Details may not add to total due to rounding
Source: National Center for Health Statistics, Advancedata, 1989

physician dictation about patient condition and care to the printed word, whether that print is viewed on paper or on the computer screen."

AAMT appears to have been at least partially successful in its role, and it constantly continues its efforts to inform others. Through its own publication, the *Journal of the American Association for Medical Transcription (JAAMT)*, which is now in its 12th volume, the association informs its current members about new technologies, new ways to get training and improve skills, and new ideas for making hospitals and physicians treat them better. In 1985, President Ronald Reagan even declared a National Medical Transcriptionist Week (see FIG. 4-1). The sidebar on AAMT explains more about the organization.

The American Association for Medical Transcription

The American Association for Medical Transcription is a young organization, but it already has more than 9600 members. Those numbers are actually small and reflect the paucity of MTs in the country.

Among its primary goals, AAMT aims to encourage a high standard of training and qualification for its members, which increases the respect and value for the profession as a whole. AAMT developed a Model Curriculum for Medical Transcription™ that suggests a specific sequence of core courses they believe students should follow at colleges and through academic medical transcription programs. To make this program meaningful, AAMT has also developed a set of standards by which educators can evaluate programs and students can assess the development of real-world skills. Called COMPRO®, which stands for COMpetency PROfile, the standards are guidelines for what a transcriptionist needs to know in four areas: English language usage, technology, medical knowledge, and discrimination & integration (which covers the student's ability to recognize and evaluate inconsistencies and discrepancies in a report).

To help people already on the job who suffer from the pressure and expectations of hospital supervisors, the AAMT has also developed a Model Job Description, which encourages hospital records administrators and

National Medical Transcriptionist Week, 1985

By the President of the United States of America

A Proclamation

Record-keeping is a vital function in our society, and one of the most important records for every American is the medical record. That record, including reports prepared and edited by a medical transcriptionist from physician dictation, is the permanent history of a patient's medical care.

A century ago, physicians knew many of their patients from birth, knew all their ailments, and provided all their medical care. Today, with medical specialization and greater mobility among people, many skilled physicians may treat the average American during a lifetime. Using transcribed medical reports, each physician can easily and quickly review a patient's medical history even if the physician has never seen that patient before. Because of the work done by trained medical transcriptionists, patients can be assured that the history of their medical care is portrayed accurately and legibly. Medical transcriptionists have therefore become a vital link between the physician and the patient.

It is appropriate for our Nation to recognize the contributions of medical transcriptionists. We should encourage hospitals, allied health education programs, and community colleges to provide appropriate courses of instruction recognizing the high standards that must be met by medical transcriptionists and the vital function they perform.

In recognition of the need for medical transcriptionists in today's society, the Congress, by Public Law 98-609, has designated the week beginning May 20, 1985, as "National Medical Transcriptionist Week" and authorized and requested the President to issue a proclamation in observance of this event.

NOW, THEREFORE, I, RONALD REAGAN, President of the United States of America, do hereby designate the week of May 20 through May 26, 1985, as National Medical Transcriptionist Week, and I urge all Americans to participate in appropriate ceremonies in observance of this event.

IN WITNESS WHEREOF, I have hereunto set my hand this twenty-first day of May, in the year of our Lord nineteen hundred and eighty-five, and of the Independence of the United States of America the two hundred and ninth.

Ronald Reagan

AAMT.

4-1 *With the 1985 proclamation of National Medical Transcriptionist Week, Ronald Reagan acknowledges the importance of the profession.*

physicians to understand the underlying truths behind quality transcription, such as paying more attention to a low error rate than to the number of keystrokes per minute. As transcriptionists like to retort when people judge them by words per minute, "Do you pay for the keystroke that puts a space between two words?" They also are quite verbal in pointing out that many errors are dictation errors, technical mistakes with equipment that malfunctions, and even physician mistakes, which transcriptionists must recognize and either decide to correct or point out.

The AAMT is quite serious about its destiny and the role it plays to ensure that medical transcriptionists around the country can benefit from its existence. They offer a full range of services, including:

❑ A voluntary certification program for medical transcriptionists.
❑ The *Journal of the American Association for Medical Transcription* (JAAMT), a bimonthly publication.
❑ Videos with training workbooks.
❑ Audiocassettes with practice dictations for training.
❑ Word books and reference materials.
❑ A style guide for medical transcription.

AAMT sponsors an annual meeting to which members, students, and other interested parties are invited. They are usually held in August, with the 1993 conference scheduled for Dallas, August 6–9 at the Hyatt Regency Hotel, and the 1994 conference set for San Diego. For further details, contact Pat Forbis, Director of Member Services, at AAMT by calling (800) 982-2182 or writing her at P.O. Box 576187, Modesto, CA. 95357.

Above all, AAMT has made many transcriptionists, whether they are home-based or employees of hospitals, clinics, private physicians, or services, recognize that they bring an extremely high level of competency to their profession. You needn't stop long to think how difficult it is and how much training you must have to understand the typical report of a cardiologist who has performed an operation, the medicolegal report of a doctor involved in a worker's compensation case in which the patient was paralyzed, or the autopsy report of a coroner. For instance, get someone right now to read the following passage to you, while you close your eyes, and imagine yourself hearing this dictated by a Pakistani doctor who is eating lunch as he talks:

"Procedure in detail: With the patient in the dorsal supine position, a thorough prep and drape of the face and neck was done. The vibrissae were shaved, the nose infiltrated with 0.75% Marcaine with 1:100,000 adrenaline and the airways were packed with cotton moistened with 4% cocaine.

Initial incision in the patient's left nasal sill. The entire face was draped with a sterile plastic sheet with gauze over the eyes to protect the eyelashes. A sterile 4×4 was placed over the exposed parts to protect my gloves from touching the skin.

The initial incision was made in the patient's left nasal sill and carried anteriorly along the columella for 4–5 mm. A Joseph elevator was used to dissect tissue away from the nasal spine going laterally past the alar facial grooves bilaterally. A Cottle periosteal elevator was then used to make certain all soft tissues were dissected away from the site. A 3-mm roll of

Marlex mesh saturated with Ancef was placed in the pocket, making certain that the marked center of the implant was over the maxillary spine . . ."

Well, that should suffice for now (and that wasn't even the good part!). If you could imagine yourself listening to such dictations on tape, then you perhaps can visualize what it would be like to be a medical transcriptionist. Note, though, that if you felt a bit turned off by that poetic passage, you shouldn't necessarily form a conclusion now. There are many types of dictations, just as there are many types of physicians. Figure 4-2 is a sample transcribed operative report. While some transcriptionists handle many different doctors, and thus do a variety of work, others specialize and work only in areas they enjoy listening to and feel most comfortable with.

```
        XXXXXXXXXXXX AMBULATORY SURGERY CENTER
         XXXXXXXXXXXXXXXXXXXXXXXXX #XXX
             XXXXXXXXXXXXXXX CA 9XXXX

PATIENT NAME:   XXXXXXXXXXXXXXX         MEDICAL RECORD #XXXX

DATE OF SURGERY: XX-XX-9X               SURGEON:   XXXXXXXXXXXXXXXX, M.D.

ANESTHESIOLOGIST:   XXXXXXXXXX, M.D.

                        OPERATIVE REPORT

PREOPERATIVE DIAGNOSIS:        Stenosing tenosynovitis, right thumb.

POSTOPERATIVE DIAGNOSIS:       Same.

PROCEDURE:                     Release of flexor tendon sheath, right thumb.

PROCEDURE IN DETAIL:           Under 2% Nesacaine, a local infiltration
                               anesthesia, augmented by intravenous
sedation, the right upper extremity was prepped and draped in the usual
fashion.  The operation was done under tourniquet control and using 3.5
power loupe magnification.  A V-shaped incision was made at the volar base
of the right thumb.  Dissection was carried down to the underlying flexor
tendon sheath.  Bilateral digital nerves were carefully identified and
preserved.  The A1 pulley appeared stenotic and thickened.  The patient had
reproducible clicking on active flexion.  The A1 pulley was then incised
longitudinally and this allowed free and unencumbered excursion of the
flexor tendon.  The wound was irrigated and closed with nylon sutures.


Dictated:      XX/cms
Date Dictated: XX-XX-9X
Transcribed:   XX-XX-9X

          _____
          XXXXXXXXXXXXXXXX, M.D.
```

4-2 *Transcription of an operative report.* Joan Walston, Words Times 3 Medical Transcribers.

In short, medical transcriptionists perform an important communications function and must, therefore, have the skills and experience commensurate with the tasks. They must know one, two, or all of the following subject areas depending on their work specialty: anatomy, physiology, biology, chemistry, pharmacology, psychology, neurology, cardiology, pediatrics, as well as surgical procedures and medical technology. They must also know how to format reports so that headings stand out and readers can find information clearly. They must know correct English grammar, punctuation, and patterns of capitalization and abbreviation. And finally, they must be able to type fast enough to make it worth their own time, if not their employer's (usually 50–60 words per minute or higher). We'll look at these requirements in more detail shortly.

Let's turn our attention now to the nitty-gritty truth behind medical transcription—what does an MT do while on the job, and how do they cope with the level of pressure they must face.

How a transcriptionist works

Many transcriptionists are employed by hospitals, clinics, or private physicians' offices, where they frequently work in tight quarters transcribing a tremendous variety of dictations from the many doctors who practice in the facility. Other transcriptionists are employed for service bureaus that subcontract to hospitals and private physicians for work. Last, the independent or home-based transcriptionist can be either self-employed or employed by a service or healthcare facility, but by working from home, this person has more flexibility and ability to choose his or her own schedule and clients.

Large hospitals typically have a staff of transcriptionists, ranging from three to ten people and sometimes more. These transcriptionists are frequently supervised by and associated with the medical record department. Working from tapes or from digital dictation systems, they use a transcribing unit with a foot control pedal that allows them to stop and start the dictation, along with an earpiece or headphone. For legal reasons and the processing of insurance claims, these transcriptionists often have very tight turnaround times for the dictations that must be transcribed, printed, and returned to the physician within a few hours or, at most, 24 hours. The transcriptionist who does hospital work also typically handles very complex dictations loaded with surgical terminology and nomenclature for the high-technology machines used in many hospital-based procedures.

Dictation technology has slightly changed the way transcription is done in many hospitals, thanks to digital equipment that uses magnetic discs to record voice. As Gary Opalewski, District Manager for Lanier Voice Products explained to me, "In the early 1980s, digital dictation equipment came around, and hospitals saw tremendous increases in productivity, from not having people wasting time over simple things like rewinding tapes, erasing, or even walking around to get the tapes. While these systems cost more, they save money overall. In these systems, physicians call the digital machine, and without using tapes, they dictate over the phone. One benefit of these systems is that they allowed transcriptionists to work from home, since they could call and access the dictating system with an ID number. The hospital staff may do the priority work, but the independent person does second priority work from home. He or she can even modem back the transcription where it can be printed at the hospital."

Continuing this description of change, Opalewski added that many hospitals are under pressure to cut costs and save on salaries or benefits, and are using more offsite transcription services. Many of these are larger companies which employ transcriptionists on site but many of them also employ independent contractors working from home. Opalewski seemed to suggest that this might portend an end of in-house hospital transcription positions, but his projections are probably ahead of the times, according to Pat Forbis, CMT, AAMT's Director of Member Services.

In any event, the life of a hospital transcriptionist is usually hectic, pressure-filled, and quite challenging. Transcribing many types of reports requires exceptional experience and knowledge, and so many hospitals don't hire new recruits. The advantage of the hospital boiler-room situation, though, is that it provides transcriptionists with a collegial atmosphere—live people to whom they can turn for help and support. Many transcriptionists swear by the dictum that you can often get into a spot where you just don't understand the physician, but by checking with another transcriptionist who can offer a "fresh ear," the two of you can finally figure out what was said.

The life of the home-based or the independent transcriptionist is often much more enjoyable, and perhaps a bit less pressured. These transcriptionists have more time to spend with their families while having more flexible hours that allow them to work in the early morning, evening, or while a child is napping. Home-based transcriptionists also report that they are usually more productive because they can get to work without wasting time commuting. However, some say that they sometimes miss the company of colleagues and that maintaining self-discipline to work can be a challenge.

Above all, the main advantage many independent self-employed transcriptionists cited was having their own business and doing well at it. They are able to choose their clients and schedules. Some home-based services work only for a few local physicians, as does Linda Noel of Linda's Billing Service (see chapter 2), while others do regular work or overflow jobs for hospitals, as well as handling physicians in private practice.

The sidebars on Vicki Fite of Southwest Medical Transcriptions in San Diego and on Joan Walston of Words Times 3 in Santa Monica, California, are indicative of two successful transcription businesses. Although Vicki works from home and Joan has moved from home to an office, both love their work and feel proud of their entrepreneurial accomplishments.

Vicki Fite, Southwest Medical Transcription, San Diego, CA.
From the time she left high school through her early adulthood, Vicki worked in some aspect of the medical field. She was a medical claims examiner, a

Business profile

secretary to a hospital administrator, and an on-site hospital transcriptionist. After 12 years of working for others, Vicki decided that the only way to make more money was to go into the field on her own.

Starting with one transcriber and one typewriter, she moonlighted doing transcription for one year while keeping her full-time job. Faced with a mortgage and a family to support, she played it safe while she built up a clientele that allowed her to establish her own niche—hospital transcription. "I decided to focus on hospitals as my specialty," Vicki explained. "While there is better money in working for private physicians because you can type more lines more quickly, hospital work is more diverse and more demanding." She pointed out, however, that for her the hardest issue was that hospitals often have poor-quality tapes, with noise in the background like babies crying or nurses yelling while the doctor is dictating. Another issue is that in many hospitals, the physicians are from other countries, and so their English is hard to understand.

Nevertheless, Vicki worked long, hard days (and nights) and now employs nearly 10 other home-based transcriptionists. She quickly added, "I never have enough people, in fact. I would hire three people right now if I could find qualified ones." Vicki says she deals with hospital deadlines by using express mail a lot. Despite this nontraditional setup, Vicki mentioned quite modestly that she constantly gets calls to take on more work, but she has to turn some of them down.

Vicki points out that working from home is not as easy as people think, at least not in medical transcription. "It's very hard to do this business. It doesn't matter if you're home-based; you're still a business with deadlines and pressures to do quality work."

Business profile

Joan Walston, Words Times 3 Medical Transcribers, Santa Monica, CA. When I first called Joan to interview her about her business, she told me she was so busy that I needed to schedule an appointment with her . . . two weeks later! I was actually not put off by this, but rather was so impressed that I felt I had to interview this successful entrepreneur. I was right!

Joan Walston is probably one of the lucky ones in medical transcription. When she started 20 years ago, the requirements for entry into the business were much less rigorous. Joan was an English major and had a minor in art history. Because she felt that she had excellent language skills, she decided to try medical transcription. She started by doing overflow work for hospitals. Today, she handles work for several physicians in a local hospital, as well as a number of private doctors. Over the years, Joan says she has developed enough expertise to cover nearly any area of medicine, except neurosurgery and cardiovascular surgery.

To pass on her philosophy, Joan hires out (when she can find and train one) a good liberal arts graduate. She says, "I like to look for literacy and people with good language skills who are conversant with WordPerfect 5.1. I can teach them to do transcription my way. I don't feel that learning vocabulary is hard, but it's knowing proper English and fixing grammatical mistakes that really counts." Joan added that she finds some doctors very articulate but many others depend on her to correct their dictations.

Half of Joan's clients phone in their dictations to her machine, a Lanier, which takes the dictation over the phone lines. She picks up tapes for the other half of her clients. When we spoke, Joan was thinking of upgrading to a 386 or 486 PC, but she swears by WordPerfect (as did nearly everyone I spoke with).

Although she began out of her home, Joan explained that, after four years, she jumped at the chance to have an office, and as we spoke, she was about to take a new office right across from one of the hospitals in Santa Monica.

Joan was kind enough to send me a few of her best literary endeavors, one of which you will find in FIG. 4-2. It's not Hemingway, but Joan can sure type up a transcription!

Knowledge & skills needed

Unlike medical billing services or even medical claims assistance, the preparation for becoming a transcriptionist is extensive and sometimes arduous. This is not said to suggest that only the most gifted individuals need apply, but simply to help you understand that if you are planning a career in medical transcription, you should consider your training as a long-term endeavor and not become discouraged or disappointed with the path in front of you. You might need to devote 18 to 24 months to study, and then another few years in an apprenticeship position. In the long run, you can then build your own business or choose the hospital or service bureau with which you want to work.

The starting point for a career in medical transcription is not difficult for anyone with a high school diploma. If you have a fairly good command of English, know the difference between good and bad spelling, and can type 45 words a minute on a computer, you are ready to begin a more specific program for learning medical transcription. The following are areas of knowledge you will need to develop:

❑ Medical terminology (word origins, spellings, meanings) and transcription styles.
❑ Medical sciences, including anatomy, physiology, pathology, pharmacology, disease processes, and a few others in which you might specialize—radiology, neuroscience, cardiology, or psychology/psychiatry.
❑ English grammar and punctuation and spelling.
❑ Skills with PC computers and general word processing software.

The section later in the chapter on Resources and Training explains in more detail the types of programs you can find to take such courses, but note for now that many community and junior colleges offer medical transcription training. You will also find a few home-study programs such as one offered by a company called At-Home Professions, which I'll explain more about shortly.

Medical terminology & transcription styles

As most people know, medical terminology is not the average daily speech of mortals. While the government can make insurance companies and lawyers prepare documents in English rather than legalese, medical reports cannot be reduced to some common language below the language of medicine. It is a field that, by its very nature, uses specific terms for the millions of body parts, diseases, processes, diagnoses, chemicals, and technical terms that fall in its path. How does one learn this terminology?

One major aid to mastering such language comes from studying *etymology*, the origins of words. Most medical words are based on Greek or Latin root words plus a prefix or suffix, and knowing a few hundred of these can go a long way as most words are simply combinations of a root plus a prefix or suffix. Think, for example, of neurology, neuritis, neuropathy, neurosurgery, neurologist, and all the words that use the root *neur-*, meaning nerve, and you have won half the battle at understanding the meaning of these words. Many root words you will easily recognize from related words used in English, and similarly you will easily get to know the prefixes and suffixes used to indicate various procedures or diseases, such as the suffixes *-itis* (inflammation of), *-oma* (tumor), *-ology* (study of), and *-ectomy* (removal of).

Other language issues you will need to learn are how to recognize and identify homophones (words that sound the same) and antonyms (opposites), and how to punctuate, abbreviate, and capitalize medical terms. For example, you need to be able to distinguish clearly between *The patient's hypertension* and *the patient's hypotension*, because the first means high blood pressure and the second means low blood pressure.

Picking out which phrase a physician said can be difficult. A physician may speak quickly or with an accent, and you can't know which term was used unless you know the context. You need to know where to put periods when you type a series of blood tests, or where to put a comma when you list a group of statements. You also need to know to type Bells palsy (capitalize the B and don't use an apostrophe on eponyms) and to capitalize and underline any statements relating to allergies (THE PATIENT IS ALLERGIC TO IODINE) because it could save someone's life. There is a multitude of conventions and terminology to learn, so much that this book could not do justice to even teaching you a few. Last, you learn about the basic types of medical transcription reports, as shown in FIG. 4-3.

- History & physical (H&P)
- Consultation
- Operative
- Discharge summaries
- Pathology
- Radiology
- Electroencephalograms (EEG)
- Electrocardiograms (EKG or ECG)
- Autopsy
- Labor & delivery
- Death summaries
- Rehabilitation notes
- Emergency room notes (ER)
- Psychological
- Social services

4-3
Frequently transcribed standard medical reports.

While your prior background and language facility might allow you to do all this in one semester or a four-month course of study, AAMT recommends two semesters of medical terminology and three to four semesters of practical experience in transcription, including one semester in a practicum.

Second, a medical transcriptionist must have a solid understanding of the major medical sciences: anatomy, physiology, pathology, pharmacology, and so on. This means having an overview course in each area just as a premed student or nurse might. While your goal is not to learn enough to identify and analyze a disease, you must have the equivalent of an aural-graphic knowledge of this "foreign" language, meaning that you need to identify and understand the significance of the word when you hear it and be able to transcribe it.

Medical science training

A transcriptionist cannot work in a vacuum, typing up reports as if the words were nonsense terms that simply need to be spelled right. The mark of high-quality medical transcription is documents that make sense. While transcriptionists are not technically responsible for fixing errors dictated by a doctor, they should be able to pay attention to the meaning of a transcription and monitor it for sense and context. If a doctor starts a transcription discussing a procedure performed on the right side of the body and then accidentally uses terminology related to the left side, the transcriptionist needs to recognize that an inconsistency has occurred and draw the supervisor's or physician's attention to the issue.

Transcriptions still use English to connect the hard words. In other words, you still need to know how to write proper English, how to punctuate correctly, and how to maintain a consistent style. As Joan Walston and others I interviewed were all eager to say, physicians are usually not the best grammarians, often slipping into the passive voice and misplaced modifiers (e.g., "The patient was examined by me on the table," instead of, "I examined the patient on the table."), or rambling on when one sentence would have

English language skills

done it. While many transcriptionists, particularly in hospital settings, are told to transcribe verbatim without making any changes whatsoever, many home-based transcriptionists reported that doctors looked to them to fix up their documents to be grammatically accurate. While they were not invited to change any medical terminology or phrasing (which would be completely unethical), they had the flexibility to help make the doctor's report read intelligently, with well articulated sentences and proper punctuation. Without this, many transcriptions would simply be a long running series of clauses, with few sentence breaks or indications of meaning.

Claudia Tessier, executive director of AAMT, wrote in an article for the Journal of American Health Information Management Association (JAHMIA) reprinted in JAAMT, "This is not to say that medical transcriptionists should tamper with dictation. Clearly, the transcriptionist must accurately represent the dictator's description of patient condition and treatment. Both the physician's style and meaning must stay intact. But it is the rare dictation that can be transcribed verbatim . . . The spoken word is different than the printed word, and it takes a qualified transcriptionist to make the transition appropriately."

Computer literacy

Today, nearly all medical transcription is done on computers using high-quality word processing software, with WordPerfect being the program of choice for most people. In addition, there are many specialized spelling checkers available, such as *Stedman's Medical Dictionary Spelling Reference* (with 68,000 words) or Sylvan *Software's Complete Medical Dictionary* (with 90,000 words), or Spellex Development, Inc.'s *Spellex Pharmaceutical Dictionary* (with 15,000 pharmaceutical terms).

A transcriptionist must know how to use a personal computer, as well as the operating system DOS and basic word-processing software. These skills can usually be picked up in a few weeks, however, if you have no experience with a PC.

The personality skill

Last, one issue you cannot simply learn but must be aware of if you seek to become a medical transcriptionist is the type of personality factors that make for success in this field. You needn't think too long and hard to realize that first, you must be the type of person who is extremely detail-oriented, organized, and compulsive about doing a good job and handing in quality work. A medical transcriptionist needs to be as precise as a neurosurgeon, as detail-oriented as an interior designer, and as attentive in listening skills as an orchestra conductor. While some level of error probably goes unnoticed and might even be within a level of statistical tolerance, the transcriptionist's charter is to avoid mistakes and to be ever vigilant in monitoring the work. In short, you must be a person of high standards.

Second, it is also important to recognize that this career is best done by a person who has self-management skills because you largely work alone, even if you report to a supervisor in a hospital or service bureau. You must be willing to listen to tapes or digital dictations for hours on end, without much other contact with people except for occasional breaks and discussions. Your time is spent in silence, listening to the dictations and watching yourself work. Can you see yourself in place of this woman in FIG. 4-4?

4-4
The working environment of a home-based medical transcriptionist.

Third, you must enjoy the challenge of figuring out a puzzle. Often, you'll find that a dictation is not clear or you are just not able to recognize the words used. Nevertheless, you must be patient, curious, and open to finding out exactly what was said on the dictation without becoming frustrated and willing to abandon your task.

Fourth, you must be able to maintain a high degree of ethics because of the extremely privileged and confidential information you are working on. You must respect both the rights of the patient and the work of the healthcare provider, firmly committed to an inner vow not to reveal what you type or hear. In fact, the matter of confidentiality is extremely important in this profession. There are federal and state laws that protect patient privacy. AAMT also has a Code of Ethics, shown in FIG. 4-5, addressing the matter of confidentiality.

AMERICAN ASSOCIATION OF MEDICAL TRANSCRIPTION

CODE OF ETHICS

1. Be aware that it is by our standards of conduct and professionalism that the entire Association is evaluated, for the conduct of one individual can be the vertex upon which the future of the Association may depend.

2. Conduct ourselves in the practice of our profession so as to bring dignity and honor to ourselves, the profession of medical transcription, and the American Association for Medical Transcription.

3. Place the goals and purposes of the Association above greed, personal gain, and interpersonal relationships by discouraging dissension and by working for the good of the majority.

4. Refuse to participate in or conceal unethical procedures or practices in relationships with other associations or individuals.

5. Recognize the source of authority and powers delegated to us as individuals and observe the limitations and confinements of said authority and powers.

6. Discharge honorably the responsibility of any Association positions to which we are elected or appointed.

7. Preserve the confidential nature of professional judgments and determinations made by the official committees of the Association.

8. Represent truthfully and accurately all professional committees in any official transaction whether that transaction be within the Association or in the form of representation of ourselves as members of the Association.

9. Protect the privacy and confidentiality of the individual medical record to avoid disclosure of personally identifiable medical and social information and professional medical judgments.

10. Strive to increase the body of systematic knowledge and individual competence of the medical transcription professional through continued self-improvement and the constructive exchange of knowledge and concepts with others in our profession.

4-5   *AAMT Code of Ethics for medical transcriptionists.*

Fifth, you must also be at least a little distant from your work, as you are often transcribing tapes about real people who are ill or who die. While none of the transcriptionists I interviewed said they suffered from depression or sadness when transcribing reports, I am sure there is an emotional challenge spending your days transcribing reports about seriously ill or dying people.

Last, while many think that the best personality for this job is an "introverted" person, I believe that it actually helps to be at least a bit outgoing and interested in having an active lifestyle. Two of the primary detrimental aspects of the job are burnout and stress-related physical illnesses, such as carpal tunnel syndrome, thoracic outlet syndrome, radial entrapment in the arms, eye and ear strain, lower back problems, and a host of other ailments that stem from keyboarding and sitting. However, the type of person who has hobbies (including physical exercise), who regularly seeks things to do outside of work, and who does not hesitate to establish a regular schedule of outdoor activities for amusement and life enhancement, will avoid many of the common problems of people in the business. As Vicki Fite confirmed for me, "It's a very isolated job; even if you are in a hospital, you're not with other people. You need a hobby to balance the stress and lack of people contact."

The profession of medical transcriptionist offers an excellent opportunity to make a good living while maintaining stability in a demanding field. I am sure you have never heard of medical transcriptionists who were laid off in the past few years! (Or if they were, they probably went out and started their own business.)

Income & earning potential

How much a transcriptionist actually earns varies considerably around the country. In hospitals, the starting pay ranges between $8 to $15 an hour with an average salary for an experienced transcriptionist at $30,000 a year or slightly better. For independent transcriptionists, the earning potential can be much greater, amounting to $40,000 or more if the transcriptionist is highly qualified and works full-time.

There are several ways home-based transcriptionists can price their services, ranging from hourly rates to charging by the page, line, or character. The average hourly rate is about $20–$24 per hour, though in some areas it is only $15 per hour. Some people prefer to break down their charge to reflect their output, charging either $5–$6 per page or $0.12 to $0.18 per line.

Your location is the determining factor. Transcriptionists in major cities can charge closer to the top limits of those figures than people living in small cities or rural areas. Also people define lines or pages a bit differently, and so comparisons are not necessarily accurate. Charge the highest amount you possibly can, so that whether you charge a flat fee or on a per-page/line basis, you can maximize your hourly earnings.

If you can type six pages per hour and charge $5 per page, you can earn $30 per hour, as did Lynne Rutherford of Med$_x$ Transcribers in Los Angeles. She brings in $3000 per month part-time. On the other hand, if you charge by the hour, you need to standardize how much is expected of you so that both you and the physician do not have any misunderstandings about your output. While you might feel comfortable charging $20 per hour, if the doctor expects you to turn in 10 pages for that amount, you will find yourself without a client.

Lynne Rutherford, Med$_x$ Transcribers, Los Angeles   Lynne Rutherford, like Joan Walston, is perhaps another of the fortunate ones for whom getting into medical transcription was a lucky break. Lynne began her career working in a law firm, where she learned legal transcription and a bit of medical transcription as well since her firm handled personal injury cases. One day while visiting her own doctor for an appointment just a few years ago, she mentioned what she did for a living and he asked her to do some transcription for him. She accepted and started her new business.

Today, Lynne works her transcription business largely at night, after she gets home from a full-time day job as transcriptionist for a chiropractor. She didn't know as much as she should have when she started, but has always been a self-starter. She taught herself nearly everything she knows about computers, legal work, and medical transcription. She feels confident now that over the years she has built up her skills to a level that allows her to handle many types of transcription work. However, she highly recommends that other people take the traditional route, and get training. She says, "I wish I had the training because it gives you the confidence to go into a doctor's office and convince them that you have experience to do a good job."

Lynne continues to do a lot of personal injury work for doctors who provide testimony about a patient's condition. She says that when she transcribes the notes of a conference for example, she must do it verbatim, including the ah's, um's, and hmm's, because it reflects how the person speaks.

Lynne likes her transcription work because it allows her to increase her income to help with expenses for her three children. "I can work at night at home, and I don't need to hire a babysitter. I'm well paid, too. For example, one month I earned an extra $3000 from one large client." The biggest bonus for her is that the profession is quite mobile, allowing her to move anywhere. Her goal now is to move to Montana, where she wants to raise her children amidst green mountain meadows and bison. Not a bad choice of a lifestyle for many of us!

Whichever way you charge, assuming you bill either $15, $20, or $25 per hour, TABLE 4-3 shows a projected income based on various scenarios of billable hours per week. As you can see, there is a widespread difference between $15,000 for the part-time worker who bills at only $15 per hour, and $56,250 for the full-time person billing at $25 for 45 hours per week. The table indicates that two-thirds of these hypothetical scenarios are between $20,000 and $40,000—reasonable income ranges for either a single person just starting out or an experienced person with a family to support—with only four numbers in this grid higher or lower. If you are ambitious and seek more income, you have to work very hard and bill many hours, or work very fast and bill many lines if you want to earn in the $50,000 plus range.

Table 4-2
Gross annual income projection
using hourly pricing (50 weeks per year)

Fee	Billable hours per week × 50 weeks per year			
(hourly)	20	30	40	45
$15	$15,000	$22,500	$30,000	$33,750
$20	$20,000	$30,000	$40,000	$45,050
$25	$25,000	$37,500	$50,000	$56,250

The lower end of these salaries is perhaps a bit disappointing, as they are to transcriptionists everywhere. In fact, an AAMT survey shows that many transcriptionists with 10 years of experience are still earning only $20,000 to $30,000, while court reporters—a comparable profession—report average earnings of $45,000 for the same amount of experience. However, given that times are rapidly changing for transcriptionists and that the profession is increasing in demand, one can be optimistic that future years will reap much better salaries for hardworking, good medical transcriptionists.

By now, you probably have a good indication of the rigorous preparation medical transcriptionists must have and the lifestyle they lead. The following checklist will hopefully help with your decision or prompt you to think about the conclusions you may have already drawn. Take a moment now to complete this 15-question checklist before reading the remainder of the chapter:

Deciding if this business is for you

- ✔ Do I enjoy medical terminology and descriptions of cases?
- ✔ Do I enjoy working behind the scenes, without contact with the public?
- ✔ Do I like words, details, and working on documents?
- ✔ Do I like working on my own?
- ✔ Do I enjoy listening to doctors?
- ✔ Do I like figuring out puzzles and trying to identify missing pieces?
- ✔ Do I enjoy constantly learning and encountering words I don't know?
- ✔ Do I have a good ear for sounds, language, and voices, and a good eye for spelling, punctuation, and grammar?
- ✔ Am I willing to listen to something over and over again until I get it right?
- ✔ Do I have good concentration skills and the ability to block out things that interfere with my ability to work?
- ✔ Am I accurate, organized, and fastidious?
- ✔ Do I like writing, typing, and working with computers?
- ✔ Can I read or write about serious illnesses without becoming upset or sensitive?
- ✔ Am I trustworthy and able not to disclose medical information about people whose names I know?
- ✔ Do I mind working in a profession that is sometimes given short shrift?

If you have answered the majority of these questions affirmatively, or if you have some doubts but want to proceed, the next section provides you with some brief guidelines on how to get started. This material is organized differently from the preceding chapters, since it is unlikely you will start your business immediately. Therefore, I've included information on locating resources for training and development; information on equipping and furnishing your office for medical transcription (or the study of it), and how to build your career once you've finished a transcription program.

Resources & training
Associations

If you are interested in medical transcription, I recommend that you first contact AAMT to obtain more information about their organization. They will be happy to mail you a packet of materials or to discuss resources and training issues. You can reach AAMT at P.O.Box 576187, Modesto, CA. 95357 or call either (800) 982-2182 or (209) 551-0883. Most states also have a local association of medical transcriptionists to which AAMT can refer you. These groups may have meetings which you can attend or can refer you to a medical transcriptionist in your area.

Academic programs

The primary source of training to become a medical transcriptionist is a junior- or community-college-level or vocational/technical program. These programs usually last two to four semesters, and usually adhere to a specific sequence of courses, sometimes following AAMT's Model Curriculum or another set of guidelines.

While it is true that academic credentials don't always count, it can help in establishing your career to have a professionally recognized degree behind you. This means, however, that you must be able and willing to sit through a classroom environment with a broad mix of people whose pace may be faster or slower than yours. The advantages to attending a credentialed program are twofold: you may get a more comprehensive education and you may achieve a higher level of credibility in finding a part-time job if you try to work and attend school simultaneously. Many employers eagerly seek out people who show enough interest in a career to spend money studying it.

At-home study courses

On the other hand, many people may feel beyond the age where full- or part-time school is appropriate for them, or they may simply not enjoy the classroom environment and prefer to learn on their own in a shorter period of time. For such people, home-study programs may be the answer.

One example of a home-study program, is a course from At-Home Professions, in Garden Grove, California. The company began originally as a developer of home-study courses for court transcriptionists, called notereaders. They later realized that a related medical transcription course could also help many people who wanted to learn at home. The medical transcription course was developed under the guidance of Dr. Caroline Yeager, a UCLA physician who had helped establish the Teaching

Department at the UCLA School of Medicine, Martin Luther King Hospital. Caroline explained to me that, in addition to being a radiologist, she had a background in instructional design. Her interest in this area spurred her to write the course with At-Home Professions. In outlining the course, she pointed out that it follows "objective-based training" principles. You are not graded, but instead you move through the course by demonstrating that you have mastered one topic which is the foundation for the next topic. This course won a prestigious award from the Professional Society of Instructional Designers.

Figures 4-6 and 4-7 illustrate some of the materials from the course. The program consists of five modules; each module contains many lessons on written explanations, activities, and tapes. According to company spokesperson Cole Thompson, At-Home Professions estimates that someone who studies on the average 20 hours per week can complete all five modules in about six months, although a few people do it faster. "It's a completely self-paced program, in which the students do the lessons at a pace they feel comfortable. There are specific milestones in each module, and there are activities and assignments that students do which are self-correcting, followed by an activity that they mail." Cole also added that in this program, students have regular one-on-one conversations with their instructors using At-Home's toll-free number, so that there is not just a mail-order-type program contact between faculty and students.

4-6
At-Home Professions home study reading and exercise course materials.
At-Home Professions.

4-7
At-Home Professions home study audiotape materials. At-Home Professions.

The course includes many hours of practice tapes, which include voices of foreign doctors and voices of doctors who lunch while dictating. The five modules teach all necessary medical transcription skills: specialty reports, hospital terminology, operative reports, and essentials of anatomy and physiology. Cole indicated that students are exposed to all of the common specialties of medicine, such as orthopedics, chiropractic, internal medicine, and radiology.

You can reach At-Home Professions at (800) 359-3455, or write to 12383 Lewis Street, Suite 103, Garden Grove, CA. 92640. Each module costs $450 or $2250 for the entire program. Ask about workshops in your area, since At-Home Professions travels around the country with informational workshops to interested parties at no charge.

Another home-study course that has received excellent ratings is the Systems Unit Method (SUM) Program for Medical Transcription Training, available from Health Professions Institute in Modesto, CA. This program is also composed of modules; the first is an introduction to over a dozen medical topics with 12 hours of authentic dictation tapes. This is followed by five specialty modules which prepare students for more advanced work in hospital settings, including: cardiology, gastrointestinal (GI), orthopedics, pathology, and radiology. As the SUM program literature explains:

"To organize and sequence the vast amount of material to be studied, a method was selected to combine multiple medical disciplines into one integrated approach based on body systems. Each unit in the program concentrates on one body system or medical specialty."

Again, this program is self-paced like the At-Home Professions course, so it is difficult to say exactly how long you will need to complete it, but the Health Professions Institute indicates that the 12 hours of dictation samples in the Beginning Medical Transcription course require at least 240 hours of time to complete and an additional 80–160 hours are needed for the textbook readings and exercises. The advanced courses require 60 to 80 hours per unit to complete plus an additional five hours per week of textbook study.

A spokesperson from the company indicated that their program is used not only by students in home-study situations, but also by hospitals, college courses, and transcription services, that provide ongoing training to their employees. The Basic Medical Transcription course costs $840, while the advanced courses are $280 each; Radiology which costs $210. The cost of several textbooks suggested or required by each course is additional. There is no degree awarded with completion of this program, since the Institute is not a school but rather a research and development facility which provides educational materials to individuals, schools, and hospitals. According to SUM personnel, "independent study students who have properly completed the program should not encounter difficulty finding employment."

Contact Health Professsions Institute at P.O. Box 801, Modesta, CA 95353, or Call (209) 551-2112 for more information.

The institute also publishes reference and word books for medical transcriptionists, and a quarterly magazine, **PERSPECTIVES** on the medical transcription profession; you can call for a complimentary issue.

If you prefer to have a degree, The SUM program is also offered as a home-study course through the California College for Health Sciences, a licensed degree-granting, private postsecondary institution in that state. They offer the same program as part of an Associate of Applied Science degree, which may entitle you to be eligible for tuition assistance or reimbursement from some employers. You can contact the school at 222 West 24th Street, National City, CA 91950.

Finding the best program for you

Whichever method you prefer, academic or at-home study, degree or not, you should find out as much as you can about how the program works, how long it takes, how much it costs, who the instructors are, and what kind of instruction you will actually receive. In particular, ask if the program covers hospital transcription, physician transcription, or both, since hospital transcription tends to be more rigorous, with more technical vocabulary and more surgical procedures, and if it covers all of the major types of special reports. Ask how many hours of listening you will receive, and if the audio component of the program includes a variety of accents and voices which increase in the level of difficulty.

Following those questions, find out how the graduates of the program have fared. Ask for a referral list so that you can speak to graduates to learn firsthand what they thought of the program and how they fared when they sought employment. A good program will not hesitate to give you such a referral list as a good-faith measure that their graduates were happy and qualified enough to have landed positions somewhere in the industry.

If you are considering a full-time degree program, find out also if you need to take other general curriculum courses. If you want a degree, this may be a good option for you, but if you simply want to focus on learning medical transcription, you may wish to find a program that gets you there the quickest. Ask also if the program adheres to the AAMT's Model Curriculum or a similar set of criteria for transcription training.

If you investigate home-study courses, ask who designed their program, how long it takes to complete it, and exactly what it covers. Be wary of any program that suggests that you can finish it in six weeks or three months, or some other low number. Any comprehensive program worth paying for will challenge you and take time to learn. It is simply a waste of your money if your program doesn't properly train you.

Online resources

Online networking using your PC and modem is an excellent additional source of information about medical transcription as a profession and about various study programs. You can log onto the Prodigy service and by going into the Money Talk bulletin board, under the topic "Your Own Business," you can ask other Prodigy members to answer questions you may have about any topic—from specific questions on medical transcription to general questions about running a home business. You can reach Prodigy at (914) 962-0310, or go to a retail computer or software store to obtain information about subscribing to this service.

You can also obtain several services through CompuServe. First, there is the Working From Home Forum, an online network where you can communicate with others who share an interest in home-business issues. CompuServe also has a Medical Forum (MEDSIG), which acts as a clearinghouse to exchange information and ideas among many segments of the medical community. You can reach CompuServe at (800) 848-8199 for more information.

Equipment & furnishings

Most medical transcription today is done on computers with specialized word processing software with medical spelling correctors installed.

You should invest in an inexpensive PC. You might consider buying a used machine or a low-end XT or AT style PC, as your needs for memory and computing power are minimal, at least at the beginning of this career. WordPerfect, the most popular program for transcriptionists, works well on XT-style machines and accomplishes nearly all your basic needs. On the other hand, some people find using a mouse a more efficient way to work. If you are already accustomed to a mouse, you would want to get a machine that can support other software or WordPerfect for Windows.

The one item you might include in your equipment package is a hard disk, since using a word processor and spelling corrector is much easier when you can store both programs on your hard disk. A 20-megabyte hard drive will suffice, though you can easily buy a larger one without spending much more money. For a printer, in general a good letter-quality dot matrix printer is acceptable, though more and more people are moving to laser printers.

Office furnishings

Because you will spend much time at your keyboard, be sure to purchase an ergonomic desk that allows your arms and wrists to rest on a pad to avoid muscle spasms, inflammation of the wrist, and nerve entrapment due to swelling of the wrist. Dr. Earl Brewer, M.D, a specialist in arthritis in Houston, TX, and author of *The Arthritis Sourcebook* (Lowell House), cautions that overuse of the wrists and arms by people who use computers heavily is one of the primary causes of long-term injury to the muscles and joints of that area and a contributing factor in arthritic problems. It has also been long known that poor ergonomics (the study of how fit and function interrelate) combined with repetitive motions can lead to cumulative trauma disorders (CTDs), which include such ailments as tennis elbow and carpal tunnel syndrome, a debilitating disease of the wrists. Consequently, it is usually recommended that you have a chair with armrests that allow you to relax your forearms. It is also useful for the chair to have castors so that you can move around to change positions frequently, and that its height be adjustable. Ideally, you want to be slightly higher than your computer so that you do stretch your neck, arms, or wrists to reach your keyboard. You can also purchase a keyboard platform to raise or lower your keyboard to accomplish this. You also want your monitor to be at about a 20-degree angle lower than your line of sight, and positioned between 13 and 18 inches away from your eyes to avoid eyestrain. You might consider an antiglare filter, which absorbs reflected light on your screen that can overload the eyes.

Call BackSaver Products at (800) 251-2225 for more information on their back support products, Microcomputer Accessories at (800) 521-8270 for information on their keyboard accessories, and BackCare Corporation in Chicago at (312) 258-0888 for information on their newsletter, the *BackCare Report*. Watch computer magazines for regular reports on new furniture, lighting equipment, and ergonomic computer designs that can improve your office or study conditions.

Transcription equipment

The many manufacturers of transcription equipment are naturally very competitive in designing leading-edge technology that can accomplish more and more tasks. Whereas in olden days, your basic choice was a small desk unit with a foot pedal control, today, you can select from a host of fascinating products—from Lanier, Dictaphone, Sony, Sanyo, Philips, and so on.

Today, many transcriptionists use sophisticated desktop models to control the speed of the dictation, the volume, the tone, and to track the number and length of dictations on the tape. Midsize systems for busier transcription offices or the home-based person can have four tapes, with people dictating remotely over the phone on two lines while transcriptionists are typing away at the other two. Figures 4-8 and 4-9 show a few of Lanier's models.

4-8
Lanier Model 205 transcribing unit. Photo courtesy of Lanier.

4-9
Lanier Model 600/650 transcribing unit. Lanier.

Many manufacturers have excellent digital recording equipment by which a magnetic hard disk, either in a separate unit or in your computer, stores voice dictations from over the phone lines. A 20-megabyte hard disk can store 1.5 hours of recording and a 40-megabyte hard disk can hold as much as five hours of recording. This way, home-based and service transcriptionists can accept dictations from hospitals whereby doctors call in, dictate from their own location, and then have the transcriptionist type up the document at their own location and return the document via modem back to the hospital where it is printed, or the transcriptionist can deliver the document in person.

Some of the larger transcription services that service big hospitals in major cities, have invested hundreds of thousands of dollars in such modern transcription equipment. According to Gary Opalewski of Lanier, some of these services process more than a million lines of transcription per month, and they even buy the dictation equipment for hospitals to keep them as customers.

As hospitals and service bureaus seek to save money, more home-based transcription will be done, and we will undoubtedly see new equipment and advances at affordable prices for the smaller entrepreneur. An individual medical transcriptionist can expect to spend between $600 to $800 for a good transcriber unit.

Reference and word books

One additional mark of how important medical transcription has become is the growing number of reference books published in the field. There are literally scores of dictionaries, word books, style guides, and medical reference sources. Some are general, but many are reference materials that specialize in one medical field or another, from new technological vocabulary to psychology to pharmacology. Because new names are continually invented for diseases, procedures, diagnoses, instruments, and drugs, these books need constant updating. Pat Forbis of AAMT told me that, whereas they previously published two pages of reference books in 1991, they published four pages within one year. She just finished her first book on psychiatric terminology, *The Psychiatric Word Book and Street Talk Terminology* (F.A. Davis), which included 50,000 terms. Claudia Tessier's book, *The Surgical Word Book*, first published in 1981 with 30,000 surgery-related terms, was published in its second edition in 1991 with 105,000 entries, 2500 of which were specific to surgical forceps.

You can order a few reference materials and word books directly from AAMT, including the *Neonatology Word Book* and the *Style Guide for Medical Transcription* by Claudia Tessier and Sally Pitman. This has become the industry standard for punctuation and grammar. AAMT's four-page list of titles is excellent, and they also offer a yearly index to articles they have published in JAAMT. You can purchase reprints, including articles about the profession, origins of medical words, and humorous transcription incidents. Ask for these lists by calling (800) 982-2182.

You can also order various books and reference materials directly from the American Medical Association. To obtain their catalog, call (800) 621-8335 and ask for customer service. Also call major publishers of medical books such as F.A. Davis Company, 1915 Arch St. Philadelphia, PA. 19103, (800) 523-4049; Health Professions Institute, P.O.Box 801, Modesto, CA. 95353, (209) 551-2112; J.B. Lippincott, East Washington Square, Philadelphia, PA 19105, (800) 638-3030; South-Western Publishing, 4770 Duke Drive, Suite 200, Mason, OH 45040, (800) 242-7972; Springhouse Publishing Company, 1111 Bethlehem Pike, Springhouse, PA 19477, (800) 346-7844; W.B. Saunders Company, 6277 Sea Harbor Drive, Orlando, FL 32887, (800) 545-2522; and Williams & Wilkins, 428 East Preston Street, Baltimore, MD. 21202, (800) 638-0672

Practice Management Information Corporation (PMIC) is another source of word books and reference materials, some of which are their own publications, while others are distributed from other publishers. You can reach PMIC at (800) MEDSHOP extension 432. Joe Kopacz can help you with your questions or order and he gives a discount of 10% to readers of this book. Another company that provides mail order services is Rittenhouse, at (800) 345-6425. Their advertisements indicate that they stock a full line of dictionaries, terminology texts, word books, and medical translation guides. They are located in King of Prussia, PA. and South Lancaster, MA.

For firsthand browsing, many cities with large hospitals have a medical bookstore where you can examine and buy books. College bookstores often stock medical reference materials as well.

Last, you might order the book, *The Independent Medical Transcriptionist*, by Mary Glaccum and Donna Avila-Weil, which contains more than 350 pages of in-depth information on getting training, starting an at-home or independent medical transcription business, getting clients, and much more. For information about the book or to order it, you can write to Avila-Weil at P.O. Box 6017, Kelseyville, California 95451 or you can call the publisher Rayve Productions, Inc. at (800) 852-4890. The price is $29.95.

Building your career

If you finish a program in medical transcription, you will probably want to move right out and start your business. However, it is commonly said that there is a catch-22: you can't get a job until you have two to three years of experience but you can't get experience without a job.

Nevertheless, the strong need for transcriptionists should put even the newest graduates in demand. The most likely place to start is in a medical records department of a hospital where you can obtain continued support and training. Since hospital work is varied, you will also expand your breadth of knowledge and experience. Alternatively, you might find a small service, such as that run by Joan Walston, who seeks out distinctive individuals to train. It is likely that many services will need people as badly as hospitals, and we expect that this decade will open up more professional training programs in this field to handle the growing need to assimilate medical transcription graduates into professional positions.

Many industries are similar in this regard. Like insurance, banking, publishing, and others, you need to put in a few years in which you learn the ropes before you can move out on your own. There is actually some value in this, as obtaining real-world experience and getting paid for it, benefits you in more ways than you think. This is the time to learn about dealing with doctors, with poor dictations, with voices you didn't encounter in school or in your at-home program, and with a myriad of other details of transcription that no one ever taught you. This is also the time to perfect your working style so that when you go off on your own, you are not surprised at your breaks in concentration or little idiosyncrasies that you thought you never had when you were under pressure.

Many people say that with one to two years of experience in a hospital under your belt, you can leave to start your own business or to work for a small service that would provide you with more flexible hours and possible work-at-home benefits. One key, however, to assure that you can control your own destiny. Pick an area in which you can specialize. Learn that vocabulary and develop your awareness and knowledge of the medical issues in the field. With medicine itself becoming an industry of specialists, you would be wise to imitate the doctors themselves. As a matter of fact, it is probably better to specialize in a few related areas, to be sure you do not become attached to too small a clientele. If the one doctor for whom you do most of your work moves or changes practice, you would be left without a source of income.

If you are a freelance medical transcriptionist, you must be careful about working exclusively for one client since the IRS may then determine that you are not really an independent contractor but a statutory employee. If that happens, the financial repercussions for both you and the doctor are not in your favor. Consult your accountant and attorney to review any issues pertinent to your specific situation.

If you ultimately decide to go out on your own, be sure to read the book *The Independent Medical Transcriptionist* by Donna Avila-Weil or the article published in the March-April 1991 issue of *JAAMT*, "Home-Based Medical Transcription." Seven transcriptionists, under the guidance of Terri Wakefield and Claudia Crickmore, illuminate the requirements, benefits, and difficulties of working at home. Call AAMT for a copy of this article.

In addition, if you go off on your own, you will need to set up your business, market your services, and determine your pricing strategy. The following are a few brief guidelines:

Like medical claims assistance, one advantage of this business is that, in general, start-up costs are very low for the home-based person. Your

Estimating start-up expenses

investment in office equipment, supplies, and reference materials will be fairly low, $4000 to $6000 on average. Your expenses might be as follows:

Office equipment (computer, printer)	$1500–$3500
Transcriber (new purchase)	$ 600–$1000
Business cards, letterhead, envelopes	$ 200–$ 500
Brochures	$ 500–$1000
Office furniture	$ 600–$1000
Phone	$ 100–$ 250
Books	$ 200–$ 500
Total	$3700–$7750

Marketing your service

A home-based medical transcriptionist is very much a businessperson. You must, therefore, know how to seek clients and sell your services if you want to remain in business. The first avenue open to a qualified transcriptionist is to obtain overflow work from permanently staffed locations. Nearly every transcriptionist reported that hospitals and services are continually overloaded or have vacationing staff, forcing them to farm out work to independent contractors on a regular basis.

The second avenue to marketing your service is to pursue your field of specialization and create a niche for yourself. When you have such a specialization, you can write a letter of introduction to every doctor in your area who performs that specialty and announce your new business. While direct marketing does not often work well when the client base is the general public, you can tailor your direct marketing letters and cards to a small number of providers who might use your services, and achieve a much higher return on your investment. Lynne Rutherford of Med$_x$ Transcribers in Los Angeles, for example, used her background in both medical and legal transcription to specialize in personal injury (PI) and worker's compensation (WC) cases. She obtained a list of all doctors who do WC from the state board in California, and then sent a letter to each one. She got quite a few responses, and some became clients when she followed up with a personal call and an interview.

Lynne also says that she simply calls many offices to find out about overflow work. While a transcriptionist at an office may not want to admit being behind in getting the work done, Lynne tries to speak to the doctor to find out directly if she could possibly help during busy times.

Last, a useful avenue to any professional is word of mouth. Like accountants, lawyers, and consultants, doctors use recommendations and referrals for finding services they need. This means that the key factor to your best clientile source is your own reputation. After working with a doctor, many transcriptionists say that you needn't hesitate to ask them for referrals. If the physician has a smaller practice, you have already likely become good friends anyway, since you may see him or her while dropping off reports or picking up tapes. It's easy to get referrals if you have been performing well and the physician knows what kind of person you are. Like many professions, starting up your own business can be slow and painful, but a few months of lean times can pay off big in the end.

Your goal is to maximize your hourly billable time because most of your work is done on an hourly basis or on a per-line or per-page basis. At the same time, you are faced with a classic situation of needing to find out how much the market will bear in your locale. For example, Joan Walston of Words Times 3 says that a few years ago, she was charging $21 per hour, and now she can charge $24, but she is just not able to go above that number right now; there is resistance in the market above $24 per hour.

You will need to have a good sense of your competition, your locale, and your productivity before deciding which method to use. If you are a fast typist in an area in which hourly rates are lower, you may prefer to charge by the line or page if you can get it. On the other hand, if your product is high-quality, but you work only in an average timeframe, you might do better by charging by the hour which more fairly compensates you for the extra time and effort you put into making sure that the document is perfect. This will also depend on the standards and expectations doctors have of you. You obviously can't charge $25 for a one-page report just because you say you took one hour to do it. In all likelihood, a physician expects more than one page per hour!

On the other hand, you need to watch out for what one medical transcriptionist called the "bad mental connection." She explained, "What I mean is that your presence in the doctor's office signifies trouble to the physician, as in 'Oh, no, here goes more of my money.' You don't want the doctor to think like that. You want the physician to associate your presence with help, not with money. That's why you also learn to invoice physicians whenever they pay their other employees, so that they don't think that every time you walk in the door while there's a roomful of patients waiting for them, that they have to pull out their checkbook and pay you." Sounds like good advice to me!

Pricing your service

Many independent transcriptionists maintain an informal arrangement with their providers; others operate more formally and ask the physician to sign a contract for their services. Given the efforts you may have extended to sign a new client, it is certainly advisable that you try to work with a contract as often as possible. Contracts can spell out expectations and schedules, and protect you from the whims of changing office personnel in a doctor's office. Remember that turnover is rampant in medical staffing, so a new office manager who suddenly does not like your work or insists on hiring a friend,

Protecting your business

will not benefit your business. Consult a lawyer to design your contract, and make it for a three-month or six-month period of time to start so that both you and the physician can make sure the relationship is working.

Last, while medical transcriptionists are not technically responsible for the correctness of the documents, it is often suggested that you carry errors and omissions insurance. However, since doctors must read every document and sign it, and responsibility for the accuracy of that document is in their hands, the medical transcriptionist is generally not in any danger of being held at fault for mistakes, and the insurance is extremely expensive. Nevertheless, in today's world, you should consult your attorney or accountant to help you make a decision for your business.

While medical transcription demands rigorous training, in-depth technical knowledge, and is often an extremely intense occupation, the rewards can be worth the effort for most people. The current critical shortage of transcriptionists means that a qualified person can easily enter the profession and find steady work at a fairly good salary. Most importantly, it is certainly one profession on the forefront of the home-office movement, allowing thousands of people to establish their own work schedules and run their own businesses from the comfort of their homes.

New technologies, such as voice recognition and computer-based patient records (CPR) in which doctor/patient meetings are notated using extensive coding systems that are punched into handheld or small office computers, may change the face of the profession over the decades. This may lessen the need for transcribing the most routine reports; however, most of that technology is far in the future, and it is likely that there will always be a need for transcriptionists to monitor and review documents and to continue transcribing millions of them each year. In short, this is a profession in which you can be proud to participate!

5 10 steps to starting your business

The goal of this chapter is to leave you with a fun way to think about and to remember a broad range of start-up business guidelines. I have originated a mnemonic scheme to assist you in recalling the sequence of steps to take as you proceed through your future entrepreneurial activities. The mnemonic term you should remember is **DREAM BIG** for $ & ☺, which stands for the following:

Step 1: **D**ouble-check your decision
Step 2: **R**esearch your business
Step 3: **E**stablish goals and a business plan
Step 4: **A**rrange your office
Step 5: **M**otivate yourself
Step 6: **B**e professional
Step 7: **I**nvigorate your marketing
Step 8: **G**row your business
Step 9: $$—Make Money!— $$
Step 10: ☺—Enjoy Yourself!—☺

Notice that this mnemonic device is upbeat and bright; it includes that trite little happy face that was popular years ago that most of us hate, but which has come to represent a certain "Don't worry" philosophy of life that even the most serious of entrepreneurs must have once in a while. The goal of this mnemonic is to remind you at all times of the 10 necessary functions that you must accomplish and keep in mind while undertaking your own business. A good mnemonic sticks in your head for years and years, and thus becomes a permanent way to remember a large load of data that would otherwise confound the mind. Like the mnemonics "Every Good Boy Deserves Fudge" (for the lines of the music staff: EGBDF) and "My Very Excellent Mother Just Sells Nuts Until Passover" (for the planets: Mercury, Venus, Earth, etc.), this mnemonic will hopefully come to be memorable and significant to you.

Let's examine the elements of the mnemonic and explore what you need to remember each step of the way.

Step 1
Double-check
your decision

It's truly amazing how many people want to be in business for themselves. Though there are no official figures, recent estimates from LINK Resources show that about 12 million people are self-employed and work from home in full-time businesses of their own, while another 10.5 million moonlight from home while working another job as well. Small businesses especially are growing, with over 700,000 small business incorporations each year, and additional hundreds of thousands of other sole proprietorships and partnerships. Another statistic of note is that perhaps as much as 70 percent of these small businesses are run by women, with over 300,000 more women trained by the SBA each year.

However, statistics also show that many businesses fail, as many as two out of three (and usually within the first year), for a variety of reasons, including excessive spending, poor management, cashflow problems, inadequate marketing, and bad service/product. The point is: are you sure you are ready and able to launch your venture? While pessimism is not useful, and in fact can destroy the positive attitude that contributes to many successes, I simply suggest that you take time in the initial phase of your exploration to reflect upon your decision and explore its significance to your life in as much depth as you can. Although your choice of this business may arise from your previous background and experience, or from a strongly held belief or desire to work in the medical field, you still need to ask yourself a number of critical questions about your venture. Do you have the personality traits that match the business? Are you willing to learn what you don't know? How hard can you work to make your business a success? How hard will you work? Do you have the character to survive the initial start-up phase?

It can be difficult to sit down and answer these personal questions objectively since we are all a product of our minds. Some people have a larger opinion of their capabilities than is true, and may answer any question in the affirmative as if nothing is a challenge in their life. That can be a good attitude to have sometimes, but overblowing your qualifications can lead to serious business myopia. That explains why so many people fail in new businesses: they just aren't willing to get the right training or to ask the right questions because they think they know all the answers.

But I actually believe that even more people discount their abilities and don't give themselves enough credit for their talents and skills. Many more people can prosper in their own business if they recognize that they truly have the talents, skills, and learning ability to succeed. The problem is, people often tend to glamorize a business and therefore exaggerate the personal strengths and skills needed to be in it. They then fear that they don't have these skills or abilities, or that their intelligence is insufficient to learn it.

The truth is, few people fit into the category of genius (and that kind of intelligence doesn't necessarily guarantee success anyway). Businesses are started by "ordinary people" every day, except those people believe in themselves and have an internal understanding of their strengths and weaknesses. This self-knowledge gives them direction; they know where and how to focus their energy, when to say "I need to learn something new," and when to change direction.

The secret to success is best expressed in the adage from Socrates, "Know thyself." Unfortunately, this adage is too often misinterpreted, as many people make false conclusions such as "I can't learn to do that," or "I don't have the intelligence to master that skill." In reality, a better assessment that might reflect more accurately on yourself would be "I can learn to do that, but I need more time than another person," and "I have the intelligence but I am not interested in mastering that skill."

In other words, you would serve yourself better by exploring those thoughts and feelings that you typically take for granted. Knowing yourself deeply allows you to make more meaningful assessments of your skills, abilities, and interests. Don't just jump to conclusions about your decision to start or not to start a business. Really think through your thoughts, and see if you are minimizing your talents, or perhaps overblowing your immediate knowledge.

Figure 5-1 contains a list of questions for you to consider in double-checking your decision to have a business in the health services. Rather than asking you to answer these questions with a simple yes or no, I've also included a column for your "qualifying thoughts" in which I suggest that you reflect as deeply as you can about why you said yes or no, and what additional factors you may need to consider to support your conclusion. You might consider this column to be your gray area in which you are perhaps a bit more honest in admitting that you don't really know something, or that you actually do believe that you could learn about something in a relatively short period of time if you put your mind to it.

In this way, you might decide, for example, that although you said no to a question that asks about your mastery of accounting and bookkeeping, your qualifying thought might be that you have always enjoyed math. As a result, rather than letting your ignorance of the topic count as a simple "NO," which might deter you from pursuing your business dreams, your most honest

QUESTIONS	Y	N	QUALIFYING THOUGHTS
Personal Questions			
• Have you had an interest in running your own business for a long time?			
• Have you worked in a related business area or had any experience relevent to medical billing, claims filing, or transcription?			
• If you haven't worked in a related field before, are you sure that you want to adandon the experience you already have to learn a completely new field?			
• Do you enjoy technical details, formal systems such as health insurance, and complex terminology?			
• Are you willing to learn new things and to work in a profession that requires continual learning?			
• Is your income potential more important to you than enjoying your work and the people with whom you work?			
• Are you independent minded and a self-starter?			
• Are you persistent, organized, disciplined, trustworthy, creative, and not easily discouraged?			
• Are you confident about yourself and comfortable working with professionals such as doctors, nurses, and medical personnel?			
• Is your family supportive of your interest and effort to start your own business?			
• Are you willing to change your lifestyle so that you can work more hours and more intensely, at least at the beginning of your enterprise?			
• Do you enjoy working alone without feedback or praise from others?			
• Have you considered working with a partner?			

5-1 *Questions to double-check your decision.*

Business Questions			
• Have you had any business training in management, marketing, or sales?			
• Do you know how much money you will need to get started?			
• Have you determined your minimum income needs?			
• Do you know how to do bookkeeping and accounting?			
• Do you enjoy taking classes on business issues or reading about business issues in newspapers and magazines?			
• Do you enjoy working with computers?			
• Are you open to learning to use new software in desktop publishing, accounting, database management, and other areas?			
• Do you enjoy negotiating?			
• Are you willing to do cold calling and selling?			
• Are you willing to seek business advice from others and accept suggestions and criticism?			

5-1 *Continued.*

answer is really closer to a "YES" in that you recognize your potential to learn about it and probably master it without a hitch. In short, you benefit by responding to this type of personal assessment by recognizing your potential energy, rather than your static energy.

Depending on your answers to these questions, you may now be ready to modify your original thinking or even to cancel your plans for one of these businesses. If that is so, you may have just saved yourself a lot of time and headaches, and perhaps money, too. And you needn't feel badly about your decision or feel that you have failed yourself. Not starting a health services business does not reflect a deficit in your abilities; it simply reflects that you are placing your priorities elsewhere. Perhaps you will want to explore other home-based businesses that better match your personal interests and goals, or perhaps you will want to reconsider a decision to work for another company or corporation. With the growth of the health services industry as a whole, you can probably find a wide range of jobs that might satisfy your interest in the field without the aspects of a home-based business that you determined in this questionnaire to be negatives for you.

For example, Daniel Lehmann and Patricial Bertello of DAPA Support Services, a medical billing company mentioned in chapter 2, spent more than a year evaluating businesses to start. They knew that both had a long-time interest in running their own company, but after a year of exploring franchises and many business opportunities, they felt most comfortable choosing a business that matched Pat's previous background in the health field and Dan's background in business. Jay Lerner on the other hand, had been in the furniture business, and when his retail stores folded due to the recession, Jay realized that completely changing fields was for him. Though he had little knowledge of medical coding and billing, he enjoyed the business aspects of medical billing, and also meeting and working with doctors.

Jay Lerner, Quick Claims, Queens, N.Y. Who says you can't move from the furniture business into medical billing? Not Jay Lerner, billing service owner extraordinaire. Running his own businesses since he was 22, Jay Lerner formerly owned a chain of bedding and furniture stores, but was forced to close them down. Not one to mope around, Jay read about medical billing in publications like *Entrepreneur* and *Success* and later encountered Healthcare Management Inc. (HMI) (a business opportunity company from Tulsa, Oklahoma) at a trade show. He decided to sieze the opportunity. As Jay puts it, "I had never touched a computer before and I knew nothing about the medical industry. But I got four clients in five weeks. I had to buy a second computer after being in the business three months, I was doing so well."

Jay feels that many people who start out just become frustrated and give up. But he adds, "This is a simple business, and many people complicate it. The key is to keep it simple. You have to approach doctors the right way. After all, you're dealing with people who have been through nine years of school, and they find they are in practice without being businesspeople. I can make their life easier." He noted one doctor who used only three procedure codes and whose claims, as you might expect, were frequently rejected because of inaccurate coding. Jay had learned so much about coding that he was able to advise the physician how to code better.

Jay's business has expanded and he now employs his wife and sister. He processes electronic claims and provides his clients with daily and monthly reports and demographics specific to their businesses. He also has clients who want him to handle collections. Jay says, "I charge per claim, but if it's an all Medicare doctor or HMOs, I won't charge as much as a private doctor. To collect on dead files, I ask for a percentage of what I can collect."

Jay concludes, "I am having a lot fun at this. I am aiming for three computers and 20 doctors within a few months, where I project I'll average 1200–1400 claims a week."

If you haven't decided to run your own business, you may wish to peruse a few of the resources in FIG. 5-2. If you have decided to continue on your path to opening up a home business in the health services, you are ready to move on to the next step, researching your business.

General Trade Books
The Complete Handbook for the Entrepreneur
Gary Brenner, Joel Ewan, and Henry Chuster
Prentice Hall
1990

Working from Home: Everything You Need to
Know About Living and Working Under the Same Roof
Paul and Sarah Edwards
Jeremy P. Tarcher/Putnam
1990

The Self-Employed Woman: How to Start
Your Own Business and Gain Control
of Your Life
Jeannette Scollard
Simon & Schuster
1989

Finding Your Life Mission
Naomi Walpole
Stillpoint Publishing

5-2
Additional home-based resources.

Running a One-Person Business
Claude Whitmyer, Salli Raspberry, and Michael Philips
Ten Speed Press
1989

Work of Her Own: How Women Create Success
and Fulfillment off the Traditional Career Track
Susan Wittig Albert
Jeremy P. Tarcher/Putnam
1992

Newsletters/Books via Mail Order
ConneXions
Caroline J. Hull, Publisher
(703)791-6264
(A newsletter for home-based mothers who work.)

Homemade Business: A Woman's Step-by-Step Guide
to Earning Money at Home
Donna Partlow
Syntax Services
P.O. Box 82
Barrington, NJ 08007

Step 2
Research your business

Many people do not like the concept of research and prefer to heed their gut feeling, intuition, or perhaps the advice of others. They think research is not action, but busywork that does not influence how they act and cannot help to accomplish what they want to.

Nevertheless, given that most businesses that fail do so during the first year, and that bankruptcy and ignorance are both destructive patterns of behavior, it would seem clearly in your best interest to do at least some amount of research about your business. Why risk your money and your career goals for want of a few hours or days of checking around and snooping out inside information that only appears at the surface if you ask the right questions. Research not only helps you prevent failure, it also allows you to maximize your potential. If you could earn $45,000 in your first year instead of $30,000 because you found a new clinic opening up in a neighboring community and you were the first one to get there, wouldn't that make you happier? The goals of your research should be to: Understand your market's perspective of your business; Find out about the size of the market for your business in your community; Scope out and know your competition, if any; Determine, at least in some preliminary fashion, the best way to target your market and reach that audience; Define yourself in terms of how your business will fit into the industry; Understand the patterns of pricing and fees in the business in your area; and, Learn what types of mistakes people typically make in your business.

These issues are all vital to making sure you have the best advantage when you open your door. The data you get in researching these issues can influence what you name your company, how large a geographic area you should cover and advertise to, how many clients you might be able to get in your first year until you build up a reputation and a referral base, and how long it may take you to break even or have a positive cashflow. As we know, most first-year businesses don't earn much money, but if you intend to stay in the business, you can better plan your activities and goals, and thereby be better prepared than the next guy to outlast your competition with adequate research.

Don't underestimate the power of research! Make some phone calls to doctors' offices and speak with the billing people or to the doctor himself. Call the hospital medical records department and ask to speak to the supervisor for transcriptionists. Call a local hospital and ask if they have anyone they recommend to people to help them fill out claims. Open up the yellow pages in your city and all those cities within 50 miles of yourself, and find out how many companies are listed under medical transcription, billing services, or insurance claims assistance. Call competitors and tell them of your plans. Paul and Sarah Edwards report that this method is actually quite useful.

If you find that competitors are open about their business and willing to talk, that is a good sign that there is business to go around. You might even get some overflow work simply by doing this. If you find that people are a bit close-mouthed, you might conclude that times are rough for them and so you should modify your plans. I found, in researching this book, that everyone I called was very open and willing to speak about their business. Not only did that indicate that they were doing well, but they also all felt that there was plenty of room for more people in each of the three businesses.

Another overlooked avenue for information is your own physicians. Why not use those immediate sources of information about what they know for each of these businesses. You will probably find that they are flattered to be asked, and might even accept an offer to take them to lunch.

Through this footwork and phone calling, you might learn, for example, that you would fare best if you planned on working only part-time because there may be enough competition right now to prevent you from succeeding full-time. In this case, you can scale back your projections until you have more experience and a client base that brings in more business through referrals. You might also learn that you could easily capture a niche market, such as working with anesthesiologists or pediatricians. Perhaps you'll even make a contact willing to introduce you to a client.

Through your research, you might find someone interested in becoming partners with you. Some people recognize that they cannot handle all the work or that they could use a partner who has different skills, such as marketing experience or a nursing background. While this option isn't for everyone, partnerships can be very profitable because you can take advantage of two minds. Many of the people I interviewed were sharing a business with their spouse, for example, but with the proper legal agreements, you might consider working with another person. Alternatively, you might simply use your research to find an apprenticeship position where you can learn about the business. Offer to do some gratis work for a few days or a week.

There are many ways to establish goals and a business plan, from the formalized documents you might need to do for applying for a business loan, to the informal brainstorming some people slap down on a bar napkin the night they lose their job and decide to start their own company.

Step 3 Establish goals & a business plan

Business plans are a map to your destination. They plot the highways and byways of getting from point A to point B and serve as a continual reminder of your course. A business plan usually begins with a statement of what is called your company *mission*, or an explanation of your business. It also stresses what you intend to achieve in the eyes of your customers. The mission statement is best viewed as what you would like customers to think about you, so statements such as "I will make $100,000 within two years," should not be included. An example of a mission statement for a billing service might be:

"To be a service-oriented company that guarantees the satisfaction of its physician clients through consistent attention to detail and timeliness on electronic claims and full-practice management services."

An outline of a typical business plan is shown in FIG. 5-3. Each of these sections serves a purpose in defining and qualifying your goals, expectations, and policies. The more precisely you can identify and target your responses to these questions, the more likely you will be to understand your business and fulfill your objectives. Planning also enables you to weed out faulty thinking, because it forces you to examine your goals accurately. By writing out your ideas and thoughts, you might discover inconsistencies, and gaps.

5-3
Business plan outline.

I. EXECUTIVE SUMMARY
    1. General description of the business plan
    2. Introduction to the company
    3. Mission statement
    4. Brief description of your business goals and
        financial requirements
II. COMPANY ANALYSIS
    1. Strengths and weaknesses analysis
    2. Company history
    3. Product, program, and service offerings
    4. Technology and resources
    5. Major competitors and competitive positioning
    6. Factors determining success
III. INDUSTRY ANALYSIS
    1. Definition and description of industry
    2. Growth rate and key factors
    3. Financial characteristics of the industry
IV. MARKET ANALYSIS
    1. Size of total market
    2. Market segmentation and share
    3. Market barriers
    4. Market demand
    5. Price structures and policies
    6. Marketing mix (advertising, public relations,
        direct selling, & sales promotions)
V. STRATEGIC ANALYSIS
    1. Goals and objectives
    2. Key performance and indicators of success
    3. Tactical plans and completion schedules
    4. Operating assumptions
VI. MANAGEMENT ANALYSIS
    1. Identification of key personnel
    2. Organizational structure
    3. Management and customer service philosophy
VII. FINANCIAL ANALYSIS
    1. Budget projections and pro formas
    2. Financial schedules and statements

If you have a background in the medical field and think you know what you are doing, a business plan can prevent you from falling into a common trap: believing you know your market just because you have been in the business. Working for someone else is, even for many years, not quite the same as working for yourself.

One important aspect of your business plan is your company name. Now is the time to select the moniker by which you want people to know you. Your company name is a critical factor in many businesses. Much has been written about this topic, but let's summarize a few points.

You can choose a name to reflect your location, your service, your goal, or your personal attention. Think, for example, of the businesses named in this book: Health Claims of Jacksonville, Inc.; Linda's Billing Service; In Home Medical Claims; DAPA Support Services; Southwest Medical Transcription; Med$_x$ Transcribers; Compu-Med Claims Systems, and so on. Some people choose names to suggest their medical expertise; others emphasize their personal names and service. Some identify their location (Jacksonville) or the nature of their service (In Home).

Spend time considering your business name, and don't settle too quickly on one. Sound it out with friends and with people similar to your potential clientele. Make sure the name is memorable and portrays your best image. Avoid names that sound like other companies in your area. For more information on developing your business plan, consult the following sources:

Books: *Strategic Planning for the Small Business*, by Craig S. Rice and *The Complete Small Business Loan Kit*, by the Consumer Law Foundation, both published by Bob Adams, Inc.

Software: *Entrepreneur Magazine's* "Developing a Successful Business Plan," Virgin Software, (800) VRG-IN07.

Many states publish various pamphlets and publications, through their department of commerce, that can help you organize and learn about business planning. There are also various bureaus often affiliated with business schools that can assist you in developing your plans.

The SBA has excellent planning and marketing publications. You can call (800) 827-5722 to obtain a list. There is also the SBA Office of Women's Business Ownership which you can reach at (202) 205-6673.

The National Association of Women Business Owners, founded in 1978 and now with more than 7000 members and 50 chapters across the country, can also be of service to women seeking information and mentoring when opening a new business. They can be reached at (312) 922-0465 or by writing to 600 South Federal, #400, Chicago, IL 60605.

Step 4
Arrange your office

Now is the time to organize your home business. Even if you are not a neat, organized person by nature, you can benefit by taking a few days to plan your home office, organize your files, purchase supplies, and set up your computer system.

If you are purchasing high technology equipment—a new telephone system, a fax/modem, or a computer—allow yourself time to become comfortable operating it. Although many software programs have a quick-start lesson, spend sufficient time learning them before you become too busy. Get to know any new software, especially word processors, desktop publishing programs, and database or contact management programs that can facilitate your job and make your work flow more efficient.

One caution in setting up your home office according to Herman Holtz, author of consulting and business guidance books: don't spend excessive amounts of money equipping your business. To avoid this problem, buy only when you've earned the money to make the purchase. Another option is to buy only equipment that improves your productivity and pays for itself in your next job. For example, if you have a need to send out direct mail letters, you can save yourself $500 in typesetting, design, and mailing expenses, by purchasing a laser printer rather than a dot matrix printer. Similarly, splurging on a newer-model high-speed modem that achieves 14,400 bps rather than a 9600-bps modem might pay off in faster transmissions and increase your productivity. Avoid borrowing money to purchase equipment. Don't deplete your cash on hand; you may need it for living expenses while you build your business.

Here's one last tip on setting up your home office. Be sure to do in such a way that you can legally take a business deduction for using part of your living quarters as your office. Whatever space you use, it must be used exclusively for business. Even if you use part of a bedroom, you can deduct it as an expense prorated to the percentage of living space used for business as long as you separate it from living space. If you make any improvements to that space for purposes of your home office, you can also deduct those direct expenses. Be sure to check with your accountant for many specific issues about deducting for your home office. Another good source of information is a 200-page Tax Kit that explains home office tax deductions. It is available from Mark Malone of the American Business Management Association. The kit is $69 and can be ordered by writing to the association at P.O. Box 111, West Hyannis Port, MA, 02672 or by calling (800) 333-4508.

If you buy office equipment such as computers, furniture, and even desk lamps, you can write off up to $10,000 of your expenses against your gross receipts in a year provided your earnings are at least $10,000 in that year. In other words, you can only write off against earnings; you cannot use business expenditures to create a loss against earnings.

Be certain to keep exact records of all your purchases and office supplies. While you might never be audited, you are best prepared to have receipts for everything you have deducted against earnings. Remember that you can write off many standard business expenses, including office supplies, stationery and business cards, business software, shipping/postage charges, professional publications and books, business insurance, and advertising expenses. So keeping accurate records is a must.

Given the preceding consideratons, you should seriously consider a computerized account of your business, using any one of the many easy-to-learn accounting programs available such as Quicken (Intuit), DacEasy Instant Accounting (DacEasy, Inc.), One-Write Plus (Meca Software), M.Y.O.B. (Teleware), or others. Most of these are quite easy to run and will make all your accounting and bookkeeping procedures fast and efficient. These programs allow you to enter transactions once and generate checks to pay bills.

The field of personal performance improvement is a growing field. More people have come to recognize that concepts like creativity, positive thinking, and peak learning are not New Age babble but actual scientific fields that are researched daily by training and development specialists, instructional designers, and even military planners. Many fascinating books have been published in the past five years that extrapolate on much of this research. From Steven Covey's *Seven Habits of Highly Effective People* to Anthony Robbins' *Unlimited Power* to Mihaly Csikszentmihalyi's *Flow: The Psychology of Optimal Experiences*, many people have profited from the recommendations to modify behavioral and attitudinal habits towards work.

Step 5
Motivate yourself

Starting your own enterprise demands that you maximize your work flow and personal habits. You need to stay motivated, learn how to tackle challenges, overcome defeats, and work your very best if you want to succeed. Poor management, one of the leading reasons for business failure, does not necessarily mean the owner did not understand accounting, cash flow, or marketing mix. Poor management can also mean that the owner has a bad attitude, alienates people, or becomes so discouraged that an opportunity to save the business passes right in front of his or her eyes.

To motivate yourself to work and win is to increase your productivity through the use of your computer. Take advantage of the many kinds of software products that allow you to track your clients and leads, maintain accurate business records, handle your invoicing and accounting needs, and compose and design your brochures and client letters. Let's review some important categories of programs which can service home businesses.

Database software including such MS-DOS-based programs as File Express (Expressware Corp.), PC-File (ButtonWare), Nutshell II (Fairhaven Software), or Clarion Personal Developer (Clarion Software); or Windows-based

Database software

programs such as AceFile (Ace Software) and Approach (Approach Software) allow you to design thousands of records—each with many fields of data—to track clients, addresses, phone numbers, companies, prospects, locations, phone logs, project scheduling, financial account status and history, and whatever else you need to keep an eye on. These relational database programs handle much information in linked format and allows you to jump from one group of data records to another to locate related information. Figure 5-4 shows a sample screen from File Express, a database program.

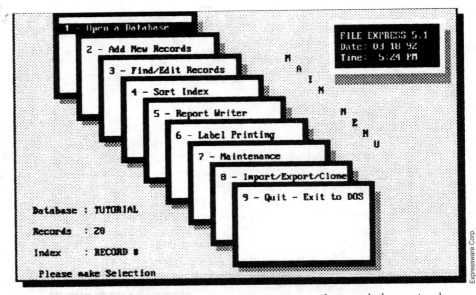

5-4 *File Express is a database management program that can help you track clients and prospects. Its logical menu structure makes it easy to use.*

Contact management programs

Contact management programs such as Act! (Contact Software), FileMaker Pro (Claris Corp.) PFS: Prospect (Spinnaker), PackRat (Polaris Software), SmartOffice (E-Z Data), and Timeslips (Timeslips Corporation) are similar to the database programs above; however, they are easier to use and are tailored to tracking clients, appointments, phone numbers, meetings, actions, and invoices. Several of these programs, like Timeslips and PackRat, also track how much time you spend on projects and can automatically generate an invoice to bill a client according to your rates. They also allow you to dial up phone calls (assuming you have a modem installed), create mailing labels, write short notes, and print out Rolodex cards and your daily or weekly schedules.

A contact management program may not only be sufficient for your needs as a service business, but is also quite powerful and a timesaver. These programs range from $250–$400. Figure 5-5 illustrates the ACT program. The screen exemplifies how the program records each meeting or event you

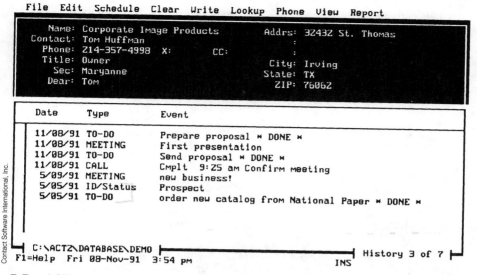

5-5 *ACT! contact management software.*

might have with a client. You can then generate a history file with a simple command. The company also makes a version of ACT for Windows.

Accounting programs

Accounting programs like One-Write Plus (Meca Software, Inc.), M.Y.O.B. for Windows (Teleware), Quicken and QuickBooks (Intuit), DacEasy Instant Accounting (Dac-Easy), ACCPAC: Simply Accounting (Computer Associates) are tailored for small businesses to handle basic cash-basis accounting functions. You can also track bills paid, print checks, and produce customizable reports. Several good accounting programs cost as little as $29–$59.

Integrated programs

Integrated programs offer a little bit of everything that they can use for people who want to learn one program interface which is then applied to several functions such as word-processing, database or contact management, spreadsheet, and graphics functions. These packages include Microsoft Works (Microsoft) PFS WindowWorks (Spinnaker), and Quattro Pro (Borland) among others. Most of these programs retail from $200 to $450. You save a lot of money and learning time with an integrated package.

You'll find a list of phone numbers for the software companies mentioned in this section in FIG 5-6. Call these companies for product literature and demo disks.

A few new services are available that also allow you to try out a demo of the program. One company, Computer Select, puts together a year's worth of reviews from over 170 industry publications on a single CD-ROM disc. You may find this in some retail stores or at libraries. You can also download

5-6
Software Companies.

Claris corp.
(408)987-7000

Contact Software International
(800)365-0606

DacEasy, Inc.
(800)DAC-EASY

Expressware
(800)753-3453

E-Z Data
(800)777-9188

Intuit
(800)624-8742

Meca
(800)388-8000

MicroLogic
(800)888-9078

Polaris
(800)722-5728

Spinnaker (PFS Products)
(800)388-8531

Teleware
(800)322-MYOB

Timeslips Corp
(508)768-6100

demo programs on the major online services. For information, call America
Online at (703) 448-8700, CompuServ at (800) 848-8199, GEnie at (800) 638-
9636, and Ziffnet at (800) 666-0330. Some demos are real programs with the
save or print functions disabled, while other demos are more like a slide show
where you watch flat screens of information, that demonstrate how the
program works and handles data.

Step 6
Be professional

This step encompasses the many bureaucratic things you must take care of
to establish your business legally in your community, as well as such crucial
things as paying taxes and obtaining insurance. It also includes the actions
you can take to enhance your business image in the eyes of your clientele
and the public.

Nearly all home businesses must obtain proper city or county licenses to
operate as businesses. You need to make sure that your neighborhood is
zoned for home-based businesses, even if you don't have clients coming to
your home.

If your company uses a name other than your own, you will also be required
to file a fictious-name statement as well, which means advertising your
business name in a local newspaper for a few days, and then filing some
paperwork with your city or county.

If you sell any type of product (and some types of service) you will need to
register with your state's sale tax board and pay quarterly or monthly sales
tax to the state.

For all these legal issues, it is best to consult a lawyer for information about
your specific situation, and if necessary, to hire one to assist you in preparing
and obtaining your permits. Much of this paperwork is quite simple. The
department of commerce in many states has a division or bureau of economic

development and small business assistance that usually publishes booklets to explain the legal requirements you must fulfill to operate a home business.

Since you are self-employed, you will need to file and pay federal and possibly state estimated quarterly taxes on your income. These are due yearly on April 15, June 15, September 15, and January 15 for income earned in each three-month quarter. One component of this is the "self-employment tax", which pays your share of Social Security and Medicare taxes. Consult your accountant for details about these payments.

Last, consider increasing your home insurance coverages. Because you will have computer equipment and other valuable materials, the extra insurance rider that you can often attach to your home policy for a small additional premium is money well spent in the event of a theft or fire.

Be sure you have the best answering machine, voicemail, or answering service you can afford. Although the medical home businesses in this book don't really need all the options that a digital voice-mail card system offers, you should buy something that gives you flexibility. You might also want a speakerphone so you can talk while working. The message you leave on your answering machine or voice mail is also important. Don't record an informal or unprofessional message. Call your own machine and listen to your message a few days after you've recorded it. You'd be surprised at how fast, or long, or boring it might be. Many machines allow people to press the star (*) key to bypass the message if they are a frequent caller, so be sure to tell people that. Also, to enhance your company image on your message, don't use any music. A busy person doesn't want to hear music when he or she calls you.

It is also useful to have your message indicate that there will be a tone coming, because some answering machines, which use tapes, take a long time to rewind the tape before you hear the tone, and the caller waits not knowing whether or not to begin.

You should look as professional as possible. Men should not wear suits to make calls on doctors' offices. Receptionists usually see you immediately as a pharmaceutical or other salesman and will block your ability to give your sales pitch or elicit information. After all, doctors are prime targets daily for many kinds of sales pitches, from investment counselors to medical equipment salespeople. Instead of wearing a suit, it is better to dress a bit more casually and not to carry a briefcase. You'll have to try this out for yourself.

Each of the chapters in this book has already focused on the marketing concepts pertinent to your business. Every home-based business must squarely face this issue, because without customers, you aren't in business. Many people in home-based businesses particularly suffer when they lose

Step 7
Invigorate your marketing

one or two clients on whom they have relied for a majority of their income. The point is, you need to do at least some form of marketing even when you have enough business at the moment.

Step 7 uses the term *invigorate* quite intentionally. As a home-based business, you don't have the wherewithall to compete with large companies in direct-mail volume or in advertising dollars. Instead, you need to be creative and originate marketing ideas that make your potential client base to take notice of you and hire you. Everyone knows what a big company can do, but they need to know that you can do it better. Figure 5-7 contains a list of many useful books on marketing, publicity, and sales. The following are a few of the most important concepts to keep in mind:

❑ Be classic and creative in the design of your work.
❑ Have people come to you. Focus your marketing efforts on publicity, networking, and special promotions that make people want your service. Save presentations for someone who has already expressed a fairly strong interest in your service.
❑ Obtain personal meetings with your client base. They will see who you are and what you can offer. Be pleasurable and professional. It's hard for anyone to turn down a request for business from a person with whom they've spent some time and have begun to develop a relationship.
❑ Referrals are your very best source of business. Use networking to obtain as many leads as you can.
❑ Don't lose sight of your cold prospects; call them occasionally to see if the situation has changed.
❑ Test your marketing materials. Prepare several different versions of any direct mail cards or letters of introduction so that you can test which one seems to draw the most clientele.
❑ Present your information in a simple way that concentrates on what value the customer will get from the service.
❑ Devote at least 10–20 percent of your time on continuous marketing efforts, regardless of how many clients you have. If for some unforeseen reason, a client leaves you and you must replace that business, you will have a much longer way to go than if you have a few warm prospects waiting in the wings.

Step 8
Grow your
business

When people start their own business, they often don't think they will achieve their target and then are surprised when they suddenly find themselves with too many clients to handle alone. On the other hand, some people have very high expectations and believe they will turn a profit within 30 days of starting out; of course, they don't achieve their sixth-month projection until their 10th month and by that time they can hardly stay in business any longer. The fact is, nothing ever really works the way you planned. Your market could turn out to be flabby for the first few months even though you spent thousands of dollars on your brochures and marketing. Or you might land several good clients before you know it.

Books

How to Promote Your Own Business
Robert W. Bly
Henry Holt
1989

*How to Become a Successful
Consultant in Your Own Field*
Hubert Bermont
Prima Publishing
1991

*Marketing for the Home-Based
Business*
Jeffrey Davidson
Bob Adams, Inc.
1989

*Putting Your Best Foot Forward: How
to Advertise & Promote Your Business*
Steve Diggs
Bob Adams, Inc.
1989

*Better Brochures, Catalogs, and
Mailing Pieces*
Jane Haas
St. Martin's Press
1984

*Selling the Tough Buyer:
A Nonadversarial, Noncompetitive
Approach*
William Huggins
Bob Adams, Inc.
1991

*How to Succeed as an Independent
Consultant*
Herman Holtz
John Wiley & Sons
1988

*Guerilla Marketing: Secrets for Making
Big Profits from Your Small Business*
Jay Conrad Levinson
Houghton Mifflin
1985

Direct Mail Copy That Sells
Herschell Gordon Lewis
Prentice Hall
1984

*Sales Power: The Silva Mind
Method*
Jose Silva
Perigee/Putnum
1985

*The Word for Windows 2.0 Print &
Presentation Kit*
(comes with a disk)
Christine Solomon
Addison Wesley
1992

Tapes

Career Tapes Enterprises
Richardson Shores
P.O. Box 309
Center Harbor, NH 03226
(603)253-7470

5-7 *Resources for invigorating your market*

You must do continuous planning to account for your situation, and to revise your plans for the future. Few two-year or three-year projections are accurate; many one-year projections are also off the mark. If your business is to grow, you need to keep track of the many details that influence your rate of growth, such as cash flow, hours worked, and number of clients, new clients each month, productivity levels, and so on. Accurate recordkeeping and review will inform you when you might need to put in extra hours to get new clients, or when you might need to hire a temporary assistant to help you.

You also need to grow at a pace that is right for you. You may have dropped out of a corporate job because you were tired of 12-hour days and coming home stressed. Now, although you work at home, you might find that your business has gotten you back to feeling stressed and worn out after each week. Once you recognize this, not just in your heart, but also through your computer records, you can take concrete action steps to retarget your goals and make your life more manageable.

Spend one day a month charting your progress. Although you may have started your business because you enjoy the actual work, you still need to be like the president and CEO who stands vigil at the control tower to be sure there are no accidents.

Step 9 $$ Make money $$

How do you know if you are making money? Well, many people look in their checkbook to see if their balance is greater than it was yesterday. Even if it is, does this mean you are making money? Absolutely not. You might have invoices you haven't sent out yet, or collections to make you have not received.

Don't be fooled by your mental or temporary picture of your financial status. Again, use your computer and an accounting package to keep track of your money. Know when you need to get clients to pay, or when you might delay paying a bill yourself to improve your own cash flow.

Consider any hesitations you have about making money and refute them. Although some people say that they are really in business because they like the work, it is downright foolish to earn less than you deserve for your services. Don't underestimate your potential. If you think you can charge an extra $65 registration fee, do so. If you think you can get the physician to pay $500 for you to do the setup of patients in your medical billing software, by all means ask for it. If the physician disputes your fees, tell the good doctor, "Dr. I am just not able to work for free; I appreciate having your business in my billing practice but it will take me two days to enter in all your patients, and just as you get paid for your work, I too have to get paid for mine." You can always back down and settle for a compromise figure. You need to speak from a position of strength although you needn't hesitate to compromise when necessary. But it isn't worth going into a situation with a compromising position!

Step 10
☺ Enjoy yourself! ☺

If you are going into business for yourself, you probably had some goals that included greater control of your life and more self-respect. On this basis, I highly recommend that you periodically take stock of your business and make sure that you enjoy your work.

One important element of your work is your clients. Do you enjoy working with them and are they worth the financial rewards you are gaining? Entrepreneurs often feel desperate to accept business even though some customers bring in more problems than profits. We all know that the medical field has its share of egomaniacal doctors who can also be bad businesspeople. There are also front office staff people who, when faced with tremendous pressure to do more than one job, may take their anger out on you. If you are experiencing personality problems with a client, or what appear to you to be an unusual amount of snafus, you need to do something about the situation by either speaking up or getting out. You do not need to increase your anxiety or financial distress with customers. Don't abandon clients at the drop of a dime if they are troublesome, but look for patterns of behavior that indicate your client is disreputable, egotistical, sexist, or simply not worth your time. Conversely, stressful situations with clients actually can be an opportunity to test out your personal communication skills. Can you make the situation better by trying to find a way to clear the air?

In short, make it your business to run your business according to your pleasure and taste. If you are to succeed, you might as well do it your way! I wish you the best in your venture, whatever it might be.

Appendix

This appendix contains those billing software vendors and business opportunity companies that responded to queries for information.

The Computer Place
Contact: Jeff Ward, Marketing Director
Mesa, Arizona
(800) 333-4747

Software: MediSoft Patient Accounting, MediSoft Advanced, and Medisoft Dental (all proprietary software)

Clearinghouse: ETS
$95 for low-end package/$495 for Medisoft Advanced

Comments: MediSoft is a software-only dealer selling low-cost programs. They also offer short training programs around the country at nominal fees. Several VAR's on the list sell MediSoft packages, but include their own training at much higher prices. Jeff says that MediSoft is one of the best-selling packages for doctors' offices in the country and the company is just beginning to expand into the home-based billing services market. If you know little about medical or dental billing, you will still need to invest in extensive training. MediSoft is a fine alternative when you don't need support. There are some other cost competitive packages on this list too. MediSoft has recently released an extensive training program that includes three books and a video training library (or three books plus a live one-day workshop for two people)—all for $999 at the time of this writing. Contact Jeff Ward for more information.

Cyma
Contact: Brian Kretschman
Tempe, Arizona
(800) 292-2962 ext. 777

Software: Medical Practice Management II proprietary product

Clearinghouse: ETS
$995

Comments: Cyma has been producing software for doctor's offices for more than a decade. The software is nicely designed, but you will likely need training if you have no experience.

Focus Management Solutions (FMS)
Contact: Jennifer Cohen, President
Chicago, Illinois
(800) 995-5515

Software: Medical Practice Management II (Cyma Software product)

Clearinghouse: ETS
$3990

Comments: This company is a reseller providing software plus training and various manuals. Jennifer had started a billing center in 1991 and later realized that she could help others through personalized training.

Health Management Services (HMS)
Contact: Yvonne Gray and Talmidge Amberson, Owners
Atlanta, Georgia
(800) 747-9370

Software: ProClaim (Teleclaims)

Clearinghouse: Teleclaims
$2395 includes medical billing software, two days training in Atlanta plus free lifetime support.

Comments: This new company was started by Yvonne in 1992. A former medical researcher, Yvonne explained that she got into the billing service herself, and is now a VAR for the Teleclaims clearinghouse in Alabama. This software only does electronic claims filing. If you wish to do accounts receivable and practice management you will need to use another software package. She offers personalized training in Atlanta and plans to establish a network of billing services.

Healthcare Management Inc. (HMI)

Contact: Jim Darby, President
Tulsa, Oklahoma
(918) 663-5580

Software: (Med-Net) proprietary software

Clearinghouse: Maintain their own in-house clearinghouse.
$7500 plus a $2500 annual fee beginning in the second year for using their clearinghouse (initial investment includes software, training for two people in Tulsa for three days with lunches.

Comments: HMI operates its own clearinghouse, and charges $0.65 cents per claim, plus $50 per practice and another $2500 per year to cover updates.

Healthcare Management Systems / AKS, Inc.

Contact: Karen Streim, President
Kelseyville, California
(707) 279-8318

Software: OneClaim (Santiago Data Systems)

Clearinghouse: GTE
$4995 includes electronic claims processing software, two days training in San Francisco with hotel accommodations and meals, PC Anywhere software, 15 months telephone support, a newsletter, and registration with GTE Clearinghouse.

Comments: Formerly called AR Professionals, this company is a reseller of OneClaim. A slightly different version of OneClaim can also be purchased directly from Santiago Data Systems.

Health Software Systems

Contact: Merry Schiff, Founder
Burlingame, California
(800) 866-2188

Software: SPS Electronic Claims
$6000 includes software, manuals, two days on-site training at your location (anywhere within the United States). Updates on software and ongoing support costs an additional $750 per year.

Comments: SPS Electronic Claims processes directly to Medicare, major carriers and NEIC in 15 states, as well as to ETS in other states. Merry Schiff has been involved in medical billing for over 30 years. Health Software Systems offers software training, billing fundamentals, and marketing. Her business package is unique in that she delivers training to your location. She will also go with you to assist in making a presentation to a prospective client. Merry says that this policy has been 100 percent effective in helping her clients sign on their first doctor. Her company also offers a full practice management package, SOS Office Manager, for $7500 that includes 3 days onsite training, the first year's $300 sign-up ETS fee, and $50 ETS registration fee for your first doctor. You will thereafter need to pay $750 annually for toll-free support and software.

Hi-Tech Management Systems
Contact: Greg Duvall, CEO and Phil MacDonald, President
Pasadena, California
(800) 832-4008 or (818) 449-2554

Software: Helios (proprietary software)

Clearinghouse: ETS
$9995 includes full-practice management software, three days training in Pasadena, hotel accommodations, meals, and instruction manuals. Also included is one year full technical support, newsletters, insurance industry and Medicare updates, extensive marketing assistance, videotapes, and PC Anywhere software that allows their technical staff to remotely fix problems with your computer.

Comments: Greg Duvall and Phil MacDonald both have extensive backgrounds in medical billing and software. Greg has been in business since the early 1980s. He is a knowledgeable leader in the field and is committed to offering the highest quality service in the business. Hi-Tech tracks changes in Medicare regulations and ECP formats to provide their billing centers with regular software updates.

The company provides both technical and marketing training. They are testing the electronic transmission of EOBs, as well as electronic funds transfer (EFT), which allows patient payments to be automatically deducted from their bank accounts. While their price is higher than most other companies, Hi-Tech offers a solid training and support package.

Medical Management Services (MMS)
Contact: Rhonda Habit, Owner
Gilroy, California
(408) 847-7826

Software: OneClaim (Santiago Data Systems)
$3995 includes software, training, and support

Comments: Rhonda had worked for a doctor nearly two years before she decided to start her own successful billing center which now has nine clients. She became a OneClaim reseller and now applies her experience to helping others get their ventures up and running.

Medical Reimbursement Specialists

Contact: Joyce Tolliver, President
Chino, California
(714) 465-6040

Software: MediSoft Advanced (The Computer Place)
$9995 includes software, a 386 computer with modem, airfare, two days of training sessions in California, hotel, food, plus unlimited support by phone for one year.

Comments: T. Erwin Avent, Vice President, explained that Tolliver has an extensive background in medical reimbursement. She founded her company to offer training and support to a "family" of billing centers that receive her credential certificate upon completing her courses.

Merton Medical Systems (MMS)

Contact: James Halls, President
Fairborn, Ohio
(800) 677-2863

Software: OneClaim (Santiago Data Systems)
$1995 includes software, code books, plus one year support and training guides.

Comments: James Halls' goal is to offer a reasonably priced package of software and modest support, because he doesn't feel a few days training is that helpful. At the time of our interview, he indicated that he is also looking at other software to resell.

National Healthcare Support Corp. (NHSC)

Contact: Bill Saracini, President
Mission, Kansas
(913) 262-3396

Software: (Med-Flex software by ISC) proprietary

Clearinghouse: ETS
$6200 includes medical and dental software, 3 days training for two people, airfare, accommodations, training manuals, PC Anywhere communications software, 90 days technical support and upgrades.

Comments: The founder, Bill Saracini, was a CPA specializing in medical practice management. He advises, "You've got to convince the client that you can personally do something for them. This is a service business, like law or accounting."

Santiago Data Systems

Contact: Tom Banks, President
Irvine, California
(800) 652-3500

Software: OneClaim (electronic billing only) and OneClaim Plus (electronic billing and practice management)

Clearinghouse: GTE
OneClaim—$4995; OneClaim Plus—$9995. Both prices include software, training, airfare, accomodations, hotels, supplies, marketing and technical support, and manuals.

Comments: Several resellers on this list also sell OneClaim. A company spokesperson told me that the versions are different, however some of the resellers told me otherwise.

Specialized Systems, Inc.
Van Nuys, California
(800) 540-SALE

Software: The Medical Manager (From Personalized Programming, in Florida)
$1995 plus additional fees for electronic modules and training

Clearinghouse: ETS

Comments: Specialized Systems is a VAR of The Medical Manager software. A company spokesperson told me that this software is the #1 practice management package in the country, with over 13,000 copies sold. Most of these are in doctors' offices rather than in billing services. The package indicated above for $1995 is specifically intended for billing services. They did not have a demo disk for me to review.

Company President Maxie Guzang agrees that medical billing is a good home-based business if structured properly. He says that getting 10 percent of collections was the going rate if you bill on a percentage basis.

Win Medical Systems
Contact: Gary Boehm, President
Hamilton, Ohio
(800) 825-2524 or (513) 896-5110

Software: WinClaim Proprietary
$490 for WinClaim with electronic billing capability or $990 for Win Medical Professional advanced billing and practice management software. Both packages include manuals and four months of support, plus updates.

Comments: Gary Boehm says he has been a software programmer for many years, has written many programs for others in the business. His goal is to provide low cost software using a clearinghouse in Cincinnati that has no sign up fee and charges only $0.40 per claim at the time of this writing. He also offers a package for a mere $25 dollars, limited to a thousand patients per practice for a couple of practices. This would allow you to try out medical billing for a few months, if you simply want to experiment.

Index

"People are thirsty for specific how-to information that can enable them to earn a living at home," say Paul and Sarah Edwards, authors of *Working from Home* and *Best Home-Based Businesses for the Nineties.*

About the series editors

The Windcrest/McGraw-Hill Entrepreneurial PC series is designed to fill the until-now unmet need for step-by-step guidance for people wanting to make the work-home transition. The Edwards' track the trends that yield opportunities for successful home-based businesses and then find authors to provide the nitty-gritty business-specific information that can spare the home-based entrepreneur months of frustration and costly mistakes.

Paul and Sarah have been working from their home since 1974. It didn't take them long to realize they were participating in what would become a major social and economic trend—the home-based business. That spurred them to want to help others make the transition from office to home and to professionalize the image of home-based business.

Paul and Sarah are contributing editors to *Home Office Computing* magazine and write the monthly column, "Ask Paul and Sarah." They founded and manage the *Working From Home Forum* on CompuServe Information Service, an electronic network with more than 30,000 people around the world who work from home. Paul and Sarah also cohost the hour-long national weekly radio program ``Home Office'' on the Business Radio Network.

About the author

Rick Benzel is a professional writer and editor focusing on business, technology, and health. He has been involved in publishing for more than seventeen years, and has worked in various editorial and marketing positions for Houghton Mifflin, Prentice Hall, and Jeremy P. Tarcher, Inc. before he started his own business. He currently works and writes from his home-based PC in Los Angeles where he lives with his wife, Terry, and his two wonderful daughters, Rebecca and Sarah.